AF478890

AWAKE in the DREAM WORLD

The ART of AUDREY NIFFENEGGER

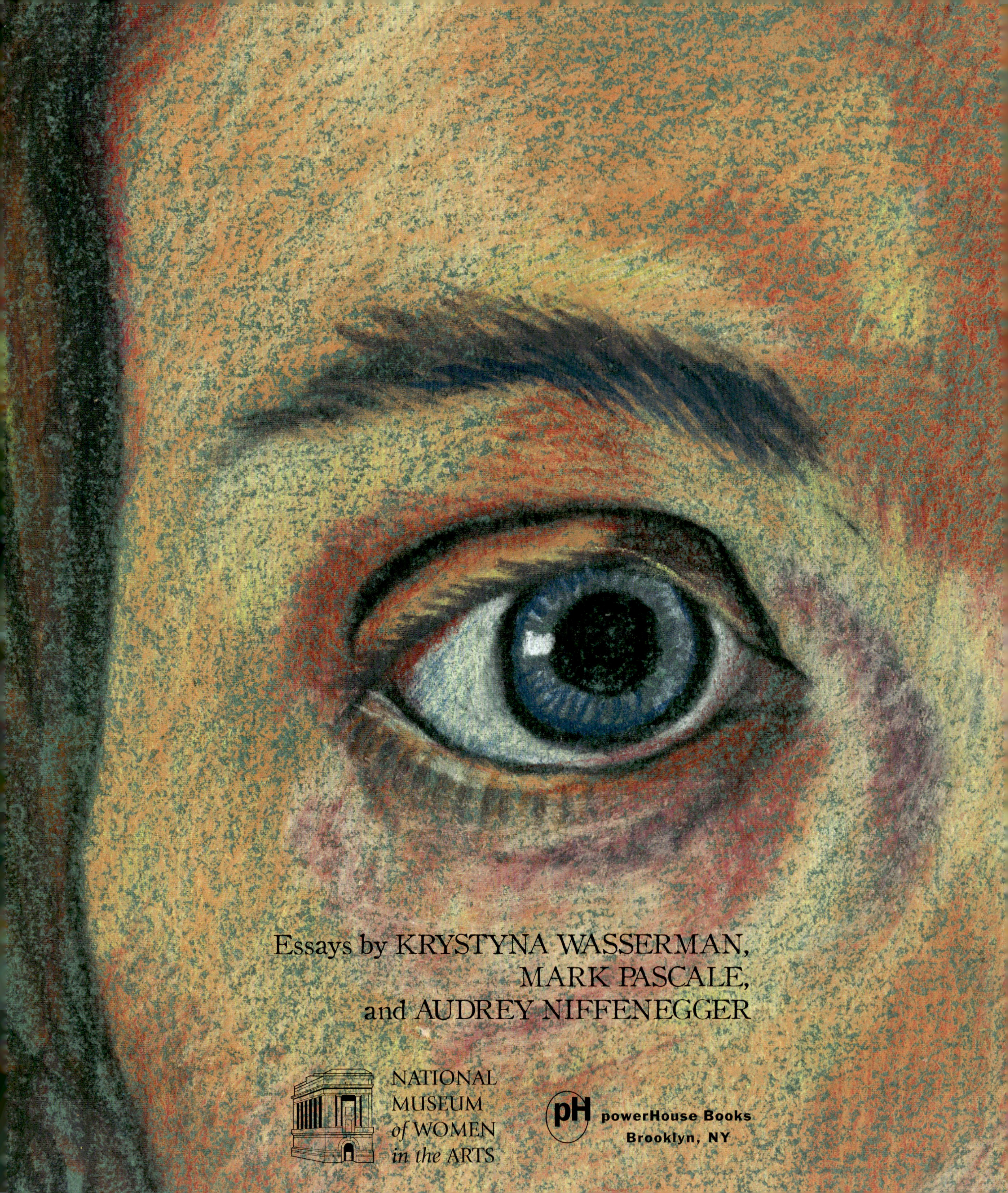

Essays by KRYSTYNA WASSERMAN,
MARK PASCALE,
and AUDREY NIFFENEGGER

NATIONAL
MUSEUM
of WOMEN
in the ARTS

pH powerHouse Books
Brooklyn, NY

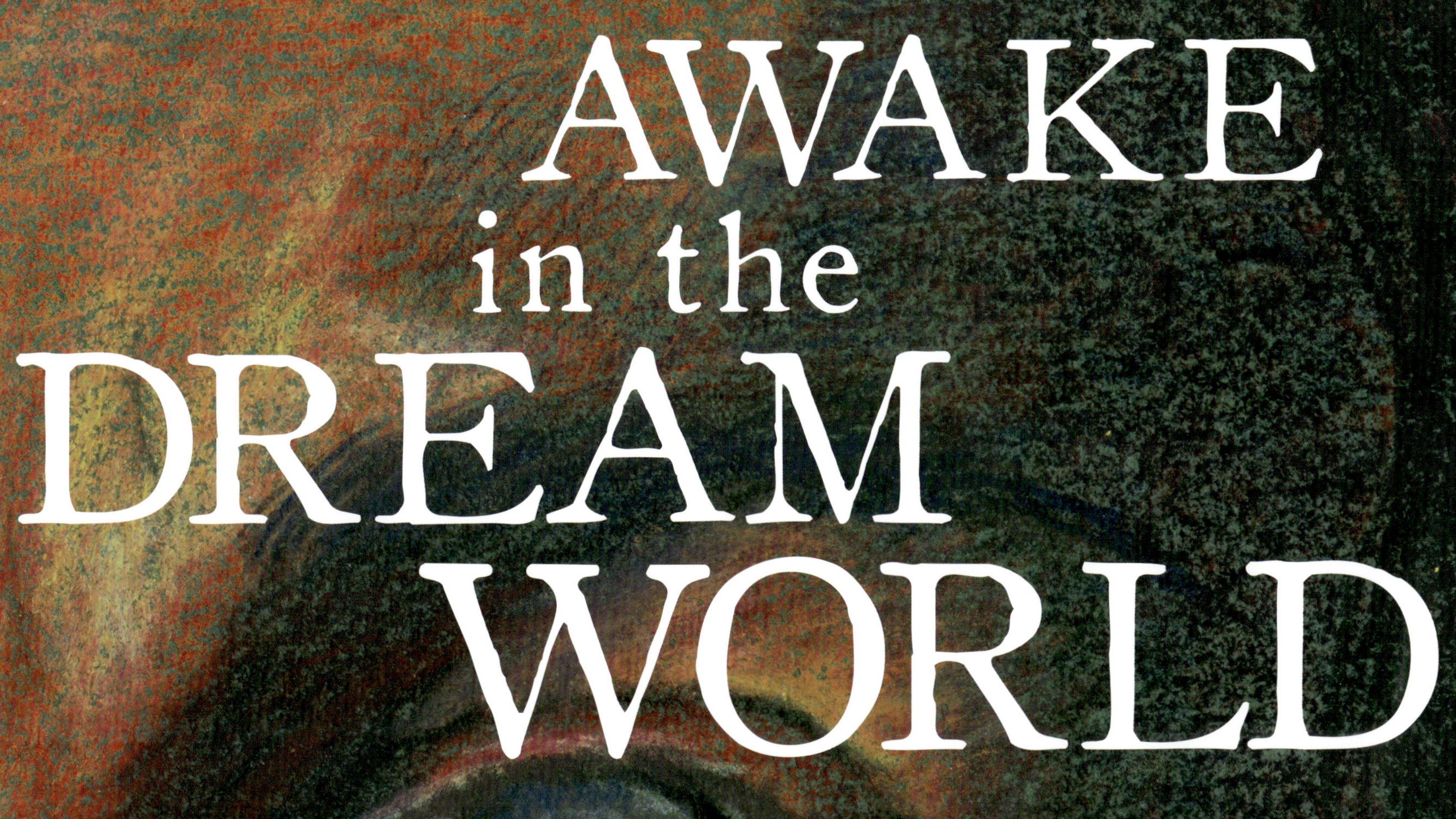

AWAKE in the DREAM WORLD

The ART of AUDREY NIFFENEGGER

Awake in the Dream World
The Art of Audrey Niffenegger

NATIONAL MUSEUM OF WOMEN IN THE ARTS
WASHINGTON, D.C.
JUNE 21–NOVEMBER 10, 2013

The exhibition has been organized by the National Museum of Women in the Arts (NMWA), Washington, D.C.

Major exhibition funding has been given by Margaret M. Johnston, an anonymous donor, and the friends of Audrey Niffenegger.

Published in the United States by powerHouse Books,
a division of powerHouse Cultural Entertainment, Inc.

37 Main Street, Brooklyn, NY 11201-1021
T 212.604.9074 – F 212.366.5247
info@powerhousebooks.com – www.powerhousebooks.com

First edition, 2013

LIBRARY OF CONGRESS CONTROL NUMBER: 2012956262

ISBN: 978-1-57687-639-8

EDITED BY Elizabeth Lynch
DESIGNED BY Krzysztof Poluchowicz
PRODUCED BY powerHouse Books

COVER: *Moths of the New World*, 2005 (see page 79)
BACK COVER: Details from *Moths of the New World*, 2005 (see page 79)
FRONTISPIECE: *Nest* (detail), 2000 (see page 73)
PAGES 34–35: *Mistaken identity.* (detail), from *The Three Incestuous Sisters*, 1985–98 (see page 50)
PAGES 70–71: *Lady with Monkey* (detail), 2005 (see page 82)
PAGES 86–87: *Lovers' Embrace* (detail), from portfolio *Vanitas*, 1989 (see page 90)

Printed and bound in China through Asia Pacific Offset

10 9 8 7 6 5 4 3 2 1

TABLE of CONTENTS

Audrey Niffenegger, author of bestselling novels *The Time Traveler's Wife* and *Her Fearful Symmetry*, was first introduced to us through her artist's books. We were working with the late artist Hollis Sigler on the 1993 exhibition *Breast Cancer Journal: Walking with the Ghosts of My Grandmothers*, when she told us of a fascinating young book artist whose work she had gotten to know in Chicago galleries. On Sigler's recommendation, NMWA Curator of Book Arts Krystyna Wasserman began following Niffenegger's career, and in 1997 we purchased *The Adventuress*.

Sixteen years later, NMWA is proud to present the artist's first major museum exhibition, *Awake in the Dream World: The Art of Audrey Niffenegger*. Her accomplishments as a visual artist may be less familiar to viewers than her fiction, but they are equally marvelous discoveries. Niffenegger is a formidable and versatile artist. Her work deals with the universal subjects of the passage of time, death, and love, and her formal mastery of book and paper art techniques makes her the ideal subject of a NMWA exhibition.

I am so pleased that NMWA has had the opportunity to work with Audrey and her dedicated gallerists and collectors to realize this exhibition and catalogue. My first thanks go to Audrey for her collaboration with the museum, and for writing a beautiful, personal catalogue essay. Working with her was sheer joy. I also offer sincere appreciation to Krystyna Wasserman who conceived of the exhibition and brought it to fruition.

Warmest thanks to Bob Hiebert and Sidney Block, directors of the Printworks Gallery in Chicago. Printworks has represented Niffenegger for more than thirty years, and they have been true friends of the artist as well as immensely helpful in introducing us to collectors for key loans and support. Our gratitude as well to Markus Hoffmann, Audrey's literary agent, for help with many facets of the catalogue planning. I also wish to thank Mark Pascale, of the Art Institute of Chicago and School of the Art Institute, for his insightful essay on Audrey's formative years as an artist. Thanks to Kenneth

ACKNOWL

Gerleve, Audrey's studio assistant, for assistance with the photography, checklist, and many other matters supporting the exhibition and catalogue.

Alongside Krystyna, other NMWA staff members were integral to this project, including Editor Elizabeth Lynch, Registrar Catherine Bade, Chief Preparator Greg Angelone, and Chief Curator Kathryn Wat.

We would like to thank powerHouse Books, especially Craig Cohen, for collaborating with NMWA on the catalogue, and designer Krzysztof Poluchowicz, who translated our vision for Audrey's book into a wondrous reality.

This exhibition would not be possible without the cooperation of many lenders, primarily from the Chicago area where Niffenegger has many enthusiastic and faithful admirers. I wish to particularly acknowledge the generosity of Mary Jean Thomson and Larry and Laura Gerber, for lending numerous works from their collections, as well as Chapman & Cutler LLP, Janet and Sidney Cohen, Elissa Geier, Jerry Ginsburg, Dr. Andrew Griffin, Richard Harris, Joyce Leavitt, Inge Marra, Carol Rosofsky, Pauline Silberman, and Jim Tonsgard.

Major exhibition funding came from artist's book lover and Vice Chair of the Library Fellows Program Margaret M. Johnston and an anonymous donor. I would also like to extend special thanks to the friends of Audrey Niffenegger who helped make this exhibition possible.

Audrey Niffenegger's artwork—ambitious and evocative in its consideration of themes of darkness and light, joy and sadness, whimsy and magic—will have a lasting impact on all who encounter it.

Susan Fisher Sterling
Alice West Director, National Museum of Women in the Arts

EDGMENTS

I would like to thank Krystyna Wasserman for her long interest in my work and for creating this exhibition. It has been a very interesting and thought-provoking experience and I am grateful for this chance to discuss and reconsider my work with Krystyna. Thank you also to NMWA Director Susan Fisher Sterling, Elizabeth Lynch, who edited this catalogue, and everyone at the National Museum of Women in the Arts for their support and help with this exhibition.

Thank you to Mark Pascale for his essay and also for his formative influence on my work as my professor at the School of the Art Institute of Chicago. Thank you to Craig Cohen and Krzysztof Poluchowicz of powerHouse Books. Thanks to Lanny Silverman for his patient and always amusing advice. Thank you Markus Hoffmann for rescuing me when I despaired, and thank you Joe Regal for encouragement and for late-night patience and calm.

Thank you to all my benevolent collectors whose support has been so...supportive all these years. I am more grateful than I can say to be part of the conversations that are your collections. Particular thanks to those who lent work to this exhibition: Mary Jean Thomson, who has been there since the beginning, and to Larry and Laura Gerber, who have been especially enthusiastic. Thank you to Carol Rosofsky, Joyce Leavitt, Chapman & Cutler, Richard Harris, Jerry and Carol Ginsburg, Janet and Sidney Cohen, Elissa Geier, Andrew Griffin, Pauline Silberman, Jim Tonsgard, and Inge Marra.

Thank you to my friends and collectors who helped to support the publication of this catalogue: Paul Gehl and Rob Carlson, Rolf Achilles and Maral Hashem, Fay Clayton and Lowell Sachnoff, Carol and Jerry Ginsburg, Eric Johnson and Mary Whitmer, Mary Jean and Cameron Thomson, Annette Turow, Renee Wallace, Jim and Valerie Tonsgard, Nadine and Tom Hamilton, Laura and Larry Gerber, Inge Marra, Michael and Elaine Bennett, Marjorie Elliott, Barbara Kirschner, Patricia Locke and Deborah Rethemeyer, Jeff Mallin and Marco Pizzo, Carol Rosofsky and Bud Lifton, Teri Tebelman and Janet Silvers, Eleanor and Don Friesen, Mark Friesen and Katerina Moloni, Natalie Van

ACKNOWL

Straaten, Margie Norris and Nadine Navarro, Dr. Pinchas and Talma Ovide, Lee Ann and
Michael Cummings, Richard Harris, and Ronald and Sandra Culp.

Thank you to my dealers, Bob Hiebert and Sidney Block of Printworks Gallery in
Chicago. They have been my friends and partners for the last twenty-seven years,
and it is always a delight to work with them. I especially appreciated Bob's supreme
organizational skills when we began to work on this exhibition; I have trouble locating
work I made yesterday but Bob can find things I made in 1985.

Thank you to April Sheridan, my studio assistant for five years, who helped to make
some of the art in this exhibition; it was a blast. And deep gratitude is due to Kenneth
Gerleve, my current studio assistant, who performed impressive feats of organization,
photography, design, and framing as this exhibition took shape. Thanks also to Todd
Summar for photographing some of the art.

Thank you to my friends and collaborators who have taught me a great deal: Riva
Lehrer, Bert Menco, William Frederick, Lyn Rosen, Amy Madden, Melissa Jay Craig,
Andrea Peterson, Teresa James, and Kari Laine McCluskey of White Wings Press;
Trisha Hammer, Martha Chiplis, and Bob McCamant of Sherwin Beach Press; John
Rush, Lisa Gurr, and Sharon Britten-Dittmer; Pamela Barrie, Mary Kennedy, Teresa
Pankratz and all the Green Windows Girl Printers. Thank you to Marilyn Sward and
Suzanne Cohan-Lange. Thank you to my teachers Joan Flasch, Heinke Pensky-Adam,
Richard Halstead, Philip Chen, James Valerio, Bill Conger, Jim Yood, and Nadine Poole.
Thank you to all my students.

Thank you to my mother, Patricia Tamandl Niffenegger, my father, Lawrence
Niffenegger, and my sisters, Jonelle and Beth Niffenegger.

Thank you, William Wimmer, a truly generous teacher who changed my life. This
exhibition is dedicated to you.

Audrey Niffenegger
October 10, 2012

EDGMENTS

Krystyna Wasserman

*Everything tends to make us believe that there exists a
certain point of the mind at which life and death, the real and
the imagined, past and future, the communicable and the
incommunicable, high and low, cease to be perceived
as contradictions.*
—**André Breton**, from *The Second Surrealist Manifesto* (1929)[1]

SWEPT A
BY MA
THE AR
AUD
NIFFENEG

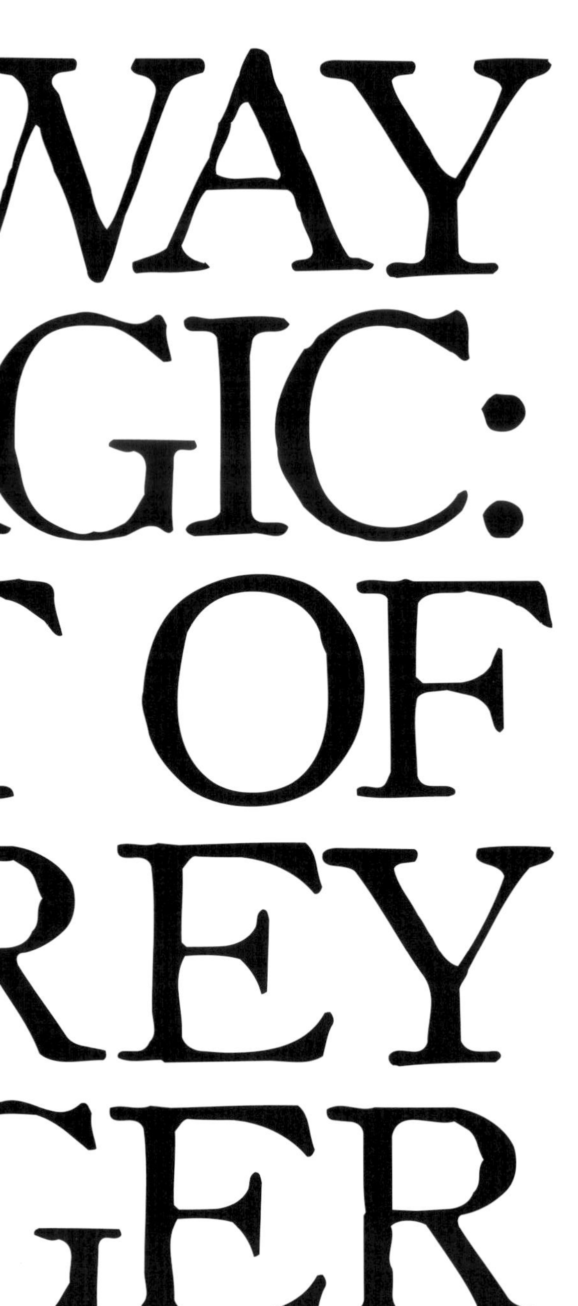

Awake in the Dream World: The Art of Audrey Niffenegger is a mid-career retrospective of the renowned writer and visual artist (b. 1963), who lives in Chicago and London. It includes paintings, drawings, prints, and artist's books in which Niffenegger observes, describes, and reveals a fantastic, strange, and mysterious world, real and imagined. Her narratives give insight into universal experiences such as the need for love, the inevitability of death, and the peculiar sensation of the passage of time.

The exhibition has been organized around three major themes: "Adventures in Bookland" focuses on Niffenegger's artist's books and visual novels; "States of Mind" presents the artist's self-portraits; and "In the Dreamland" explores the territory of dreams and fantasies and the hopeless struggle with what Shakespeare called "this bloody tyrant, Time." (Shakespeare, Sonnet XVI)[2]

ADVENTURES IN BOOKLAND

As a child Niffenegger spent hours alone in her bedroom, dreaming, drawing, reading, and writing. At age sixteen she made her first book, "My Dad and Mr. Rabbit," with drypoint etchings that illustrated the story of a magic rabbit following her father on a business trip. Niffenegger attended the School of the Art Institute of Chicago, and in 1991 received an MFA from Northwestern University's Department of Art Theory and Practice. Although she studied art, she never stopped writing, and she eventually discovered that her interests in art and literature converged in the book arts. In 1994, with several colleague book artists, she established the Columbia College Chicago Center for Book and Paper Arts, where she taught for many years. She is currently a professor in the Fiction Writing Department of Columbia College Chicago.

Niffenegger's strength lies in her ability to craft powerful narratives, which she presents in both pictures and words. She says that her artist's books, which she calls visual novels, were born organically: When she was writing, ideas for images popped into her mind; when she was drawing, words appeared around the pictures. In them, she investigates drama inherent in all relationships: among family, friends, and lovers; among people and animals; among the living and the dead. She explores love, jealousy, sexual attraction, violence, and redemption. Unlike Niffenegger's masterfully written novels, the compelling stories in her artist's books are told primarily through images. They incorporate brief accompanying text, which fully illuminates the plots.

Niffenegger conceived, printed, and handbound *The Adventuress*, her first visual novel, between 1983 and 1985, when she was still a student at the School of the Art Institute of Chicago. This story of a strange, nameless adventuress—the creation of an alchemist father—is typical of Niffenegger's works in weaving a few details of the artist's personal life into a dreamlike narrative. Here, cats (Niffenegger keeps two black cats) and rooms filled with books feature in a story of impossible love, loss, betrayal, and death. It is the most surreal of Niffenegger's visual novels; as she describes, her protagonist's "fortunes are rather random."[3] The adventuress is kidnapped and forced to marry an old man; she escapes and transforms herself temporarily into a giant moth; and she has a love affair with Napoleon Bonaparte and gives birth to a cat, whom she treats as a beloved child. She eventually dies, heartbroken, after a betrayal by the doomed emperor. As in many of Niffenegger's tales, however, the dead and the living coexist and interact with all the joy, despair, and complexity that characterize human relationships. The book ends with a scene of reconciliation and peace.

The masterpiece of Niffenegger's visual novels, *The Three Incestuous Sisters*, was the product of thirteen years' work (1985–98). Stylistically, the images are influenced by Japanese prints and the symbolist art of Aubrey Beardsley. The figures are defined by line, and the compositions' skewed perspectives and characters' exaggerated gestures reveal a full panoply of human emotions: rapturous and tender love scenes; madness, grief, and jealousy leading to murder.

This fairy tale depicts three beautiful young sisters, blond Bettine, red-haired Clothilde, and blue-haired Ophile, living in a lonely lighthouse by the sea. Their story grows complicated as Bettine and Ophile both fall in love with the handsome Paris. Unlike the Greek goddesses who waited patiently for Paris's judgment,[4] Bettine throws an apple to Paris and chooses him, just as any modern woman would. The jealous Ophile subsequently plants a firecracker in the baby carriage of a passerby, letting an innocent and very pregnant Bettine take the blame for a deadly explosion and face a violent crowd's wrath (page 50). Bettine is rescued, too late—she gives birth to a boy and dies in Paris's arms (page 51), and Ophile's sense of guilt drives her to suicide. Niffenegger's smoky color palette, limited to dark, cool neutrals aside from Bettine's and Clothilde's hair, shifts into dark red when depicting blood, dramatizing Bettine's childbirth and her subsequent death. At the plot's resolution, the only still-living sister, Clothilde, distinguished for her extrasensory talents, has returned to the lighthouse with her nephew, who has miraculously survived abandonment. They are joined by Paris, and the tale ends as the ghosts of Bettine and Ophile, alongside the living, merrily picnic in the cemetery, in the shade of old trees.

Niffenegger created *The Three Incestuous Sisters* and *The Adventuress* in small editions of ten copies each, although trade editions of both books were published by Harry N. Abrams, Inc., after the success of her novel *The Time Traveler's Wife*. *The Adventuress* comprises sixty-six aquatints with letterpress-printed text, and *The Three Incestuous Sisters* eighty-six aquatints. The images from both visual novels are displayed in their entirety in the exhibition.

Niffenegger's smallest, most intimate artist's book, *Spring* (1993), was published in an edition of 100 copies and made in collaboration with Marilyn Sward (1941–2008), a paper and book artist. The images and text were printed using stone lithography, and elements were hand-colored. It shares a surreal, whimsical atmosphere with Niffenegger's other works, but this is a story about the rain, about waiting for love, and about disappointment. A young writer types her stories to the rhythm of the rain during March, April, and May, and she meets Mr. Rain, a character from one of her stories, who has sprung to life and knocked on her door.

Niffenegger's interest in the macabre and the symbolism of death does not stop her from being entertaining. Humor often balances the *memento mori* aspects of her work, and this is never more evident than in her artist's book *Poisonous Plants at Table and Prudence: The Cautionary Tale of a Picky Eater* (2006). It includes selections from *Poisonous Plants in Field and Garden*, a guide published by the Reverend Professor G. Henslow in 1901. In the book, four colored giclée prints each unfold accordion-style, featuring seasonal menus of poisonous plants to be served in the spring, summer, fall, and winter. Designed by Trisha Hammer and written and illustrated by Niffenegger, the story features picky eater Prudence Featherweight, who feels "revolted by meat and marshmallows." She attends joyful celebrations—convened at a cemetery by dead souls—as she starves herself into a coma and then to death at home. Initially reluctant to sample the fabulous menu, she eventually joins elegantly dressed skeletons of all ages, feasting, sipping wine, and celebrating life and death.

Raven Girl, Niffenegger's most recent visual novel, is an unusual love story surrounding a girl whose mother was a raven and her father a human postman. A drama of alienation, determination, and courage, it also explores confusion and fixation leading to a murder committed by a madman (like many in the news in recent years). The image of the Raven Girl (page 68), a half-bird, half-human creature who chooses to become a bird with the help of modern medicine, is strangely beautiful and moving. Her intelligent and penetrating blue eyes, framed by a black raven's wing, look straight into the heart of the viewer. *Raven Girl* has been adapted into a ballet by choreographer Wayne McGregor to be performed at the Royal Opera House Ballet in London's Covent Garden in 2013, when the story will also be published by Abrams in the United States and Jonathan Cape in England.

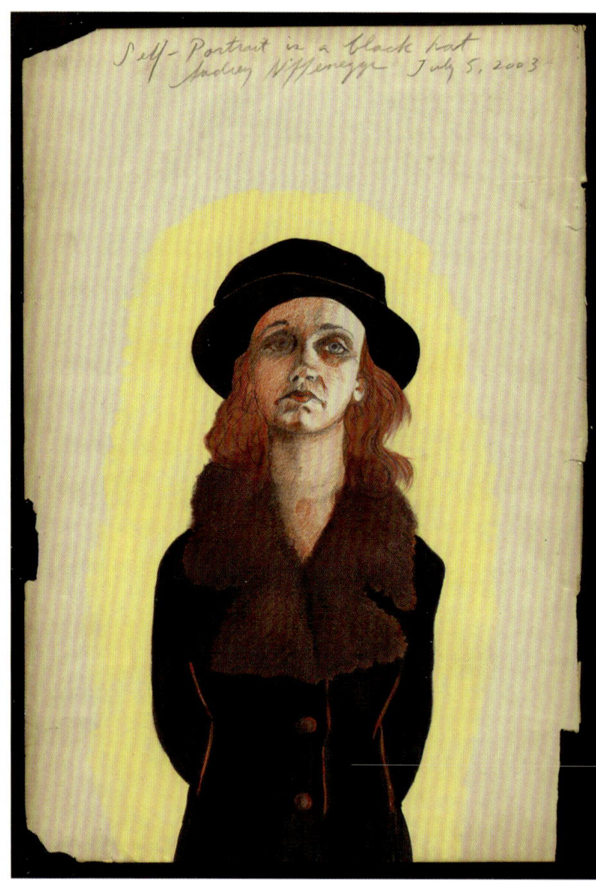

Audrey Niffenegger,
Self-Portrait in Black Hat
(see page 80)

The heroines of Niffenegger's visual novels are usually young women. They are brave, daring, and independent. Sometimes the artist invents their adventures; at other times she draws inspiration from personal experiences, identifying with her characters' trials, attempting to solve their problems, and celebrating their victories. Niffenegger understands the psychology and motivations that drive women to unpredictable encounters, provoking explosions of emotion and unfulfilled desires. Her heroines are occasionally doomed, they misbehave, and they may practice malfeasance, but they are always curious, passionate, and spontaneous. They act, take risks, pay the price if they err, and are a pleasure to meet, if only through Niffenegger's work.

STATES OF MIND

A good portrait always seems to me to be like a dramatized biography, or rather like the natural drama inherent in every man.
—Charles Baudelaire[5]

In his review of portraits shown in the Paris salon in 1846, Baudelaire said that there are two ways of understanding portraiture, either as history or fiction. In the first the artist depicts the model faithfully, and in the second the portrait is transformed "into a poem full of space and reverie." This is where imagination plays a greater role, where the artist creates the portrait of a mind. Baudelaire considered Jean-Auguste-Dominique Ingres and Jacques-Louis David as representative of the "historical" method and Rembrandt, among others, as a master of the "fictional, or romantic" type.[6] It is therefore not surprising that one of Niffenegger's early self-portraits, *Self-Portrait as Rembrandt's Wife, Saskia,* 1992 (page 77), pays homage to the seventeenth-century Dutch painter whose beloved, prematurely deceased wife served as one of his favorite models.

Twenty-two of Niffenegger's self-portraits are included in this exhibition. These inward journeys depict not only her non-idealized likeness but also serve as raw visual accounts of her moods, feelings, dreams, and desires. Niffenegger's somber, questioning face confronts the viewer; her forceful gaze surprises those who are familiar with her even temper and rather cheerful personality. The paintings simultaneously reveal self-assurance, whimsy, and humor alongside anxiety, loneliness, and melancholy. The artist presents herself in many guises—as Medusa, a jailbird, and a bad fairy.

In her self-portraiture, Niffenegger uses her hair as a tool to communicate angst and recklessness. It is alternately a traditional attribute of feminine beauty and a manifestation of rebellion and personal independence. In *She Was Vain of Her Hair,* 1986 (page 75), her ambiguous depiction of a rebellion or punishment shows her hair cut very short, a razor floating above her head. *Hairpiece*, 1986 (page 74), presents the artist completely bald, though a small strand of her hair is collaged to the drawing as a reminder of her former self. In contrast, *Bad Fairy,* 2005, (page 81) brings our attention to a cascade of red long hair reminiscent of Edvard Munch's vampire women, framing a face full of existential angst: This fairy will not perform helpful miracles with her magic wand. Another depiction suggesting chaos, *Tornado Head*, 1987 (page 78), is a monochromatic drawing of the back of Niffenegger's head, her knotted hair resembling the powerful twist of a tornado. A tiny, storm-devastated landscape in the drawing's lower section complements the primary image, akin to predellas in classical altarpieces.

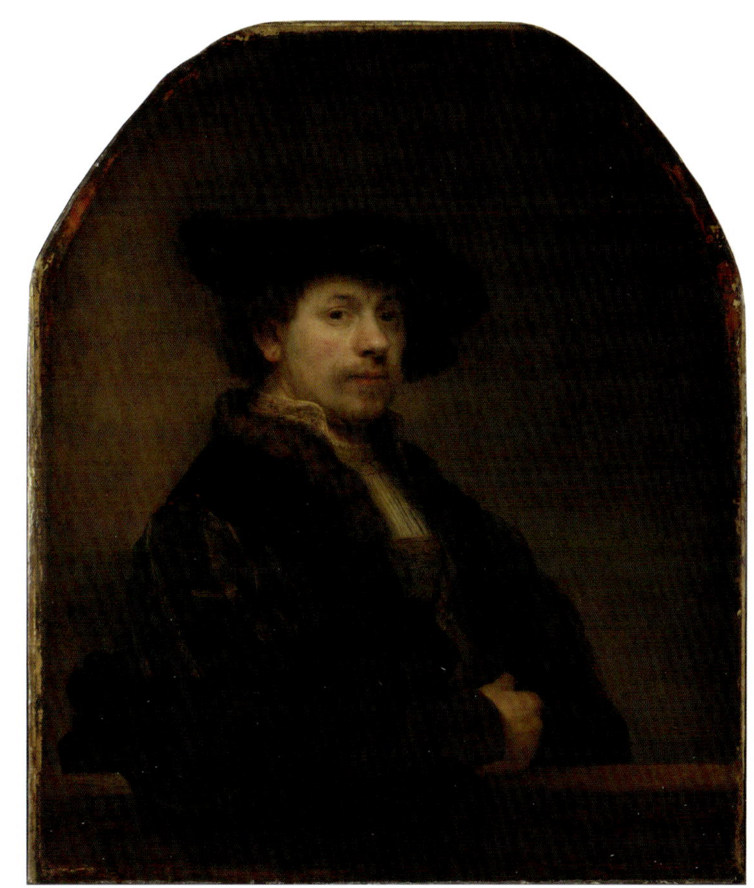

Rembrandt Harmensz van Rijn, *Self Portrait at the Age of 34*, 1640
Oil on canvas
40 1/8 x 31 1/2 in.
National Gallery, London, Great Britain;
Bought, 1861 (NG672)

CREDIT:
© National Gallery, London /
Art Resource, NY

Hats appear in Niffenegger's self-portraiture as reflections of her states of mind. The psychological depth, doubt, and self-knowledge expressed in her *Self-Portrait in Black Hat*, 2003 (page 80), confirms her allegiance to Rembrandt's profound self-portraiture goals, particularly in works such as his hat-wearing *Self Portrait at the Age of 34* (1640, National Gallery, London). *Self-Portrait with Philip Treacy Hat*, 2007 (page 84), presents the artist realistically, as a self-assured, elegant young woman wearing a hat from the fashionable London millinery shop. In *Skull Hat*, 1998 (page 76), twelve skulls, one on top of the other, make up the conical top of a wide-brimmed hat, reminiscent of witches' hats sold for Halloween costumes.

Several self-portraits reflect the artist's profound interest in the natural world, depicting her accompanied by monkeys, cats, moths, and butterflies. (In addition to the two cats, Niffenegger lives with a menagerie of taxidermy animals and birds, which sometimes serve as her models, and a library including many science texts.) Niffenegger's self-portraits with monkeys call to mind such Frida Kahlo self-portraits as *Fulang-Chang and I*, 1937, and *Self Portrait with Monkey* (1938, Albright-Knox Art Gallery, Buffalo). In spite of the visual similarities, however, Niffenegger says that her works were inspired by unrelated encounters and ideas: her *Lady with Monkey*, 2005 (page 82), sprang from her view of a San Francisco elevator mural, and *Monkey Mind*, 2010, from a Buddhist term for a capricious, unsettled mentality. Both Niffenegger and Kahlo include skull iconography in their self-portraits, and they also depict themselves in close union with nature—Niffenegger borrows butterfly wings to fly away and two antennae to help her navigate in *Flying*, 2005; Kahlo's *Roots*, 1943, depicts her lying on the ground with plants growing from her body.

Remedios Varo is another influence and spiritual kin of Niffenegger. Both artists inhabit imaginary realms ruled by magic; both are fascinated by animals, birds, and insects; and both depict hybrid creatures in unstable, atmospheric worlds. The artists' common interests can be seen in Niffenegger's work such as *Reader, Spider* (page 63), *Raven Girl*, and her self-portrait *Moths of the New World* (page 79 and cover).

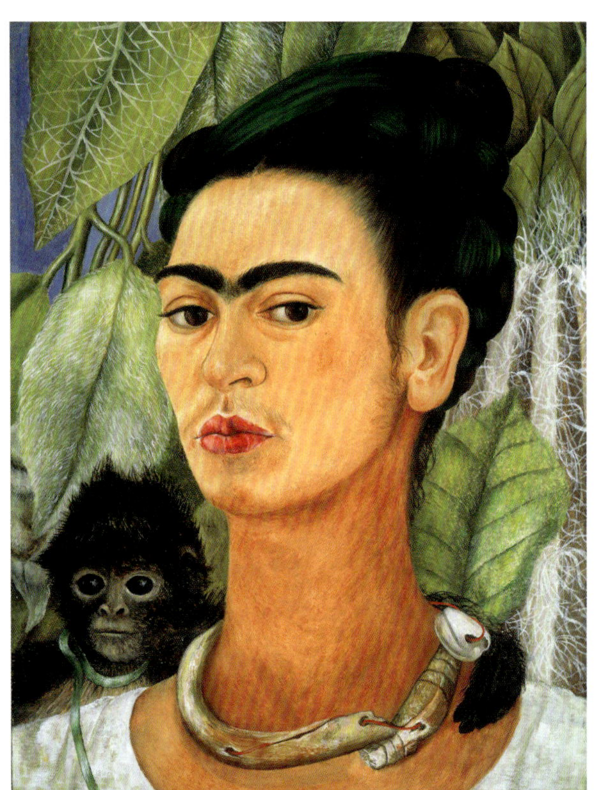

Frida Kahlo, *Self Portrait with Monkey*, 1938
Oil on Masonite support
16 x 12 in.
Albright-Knox Art Gallery; Bequest of
A. Conger Goodyear, 1966

CREDIT:
Image courtesy of Albright-Knox Art Gallery / Art Resource, NY; © 2012 Banco de México Diego Rivera Frida Kahlo Museums Trust, Mexico, D.F. / Artists Rights Society (ARS), New York

Niffenegger's self-portraits *Observation*, 2010 (page 85), *Jailbird*, 1993, and *Moths of the New World*, 2005, serve as metaphors for freedom and constraint. *Observation* presents Niffenegger's head surrounded by a multitude of eyes watching her every move; in *Jailbird*, a cage is lowered over her head, which keeps her in an imposed or self-inflicted prison. *Moths of the New World* portrays the artist surrounded by moths at night, consumed by a mystical love of beauty, as poet Don Marquis described in "The Lesson of the Moth": "Fire is beautiful / And we know that if we get / too close it will kill us / but what does that matter / it is better to be happy / for a moment / and burned up with beauty / than to live a long time / and be bored all the while."[7] With their wings, artists have the power to escape being burned.

She depicts birds' nests in two self-portraits, which she describes as symbolic of minds, "incubators of ideas."[8] An egg rests, protected, within a nest in Niffenegger's hair in an early *Nest*, 1985 ; in a later Nest, 2000 (both, pages 72–73), a baby bird cries with an open beak.

For years, Chicago artists have been renowned for narrative and surreal art. Niffenegger emerges from this tradition, which includes Riva Lehrer, Ellen Lanyon, Hollis Sigler, and Phyllis Bramson, among others. These artists extol subjective, personal approaches to art-making and employ their unbound imaginations to feed fantastical imagery.

Niffenegger considers self-portraits a form of magic. As she says, "something is created from nothing as though I myself were a magician." She describes them as illusions providing her with experiences that would be impossible in real life. Her paintings and drawings endeavor to reveal and conceal—in the manner of the best magicians—her self-revelations and self-discoveries.

IN THE DREAMLAND

—Nobody wants to die;
tell me it is a lie!
But no, I know it's true.
It's just the common case;
there's nothing one can do.
—Elizabeth Bishop, "Breakfast Song"[9]

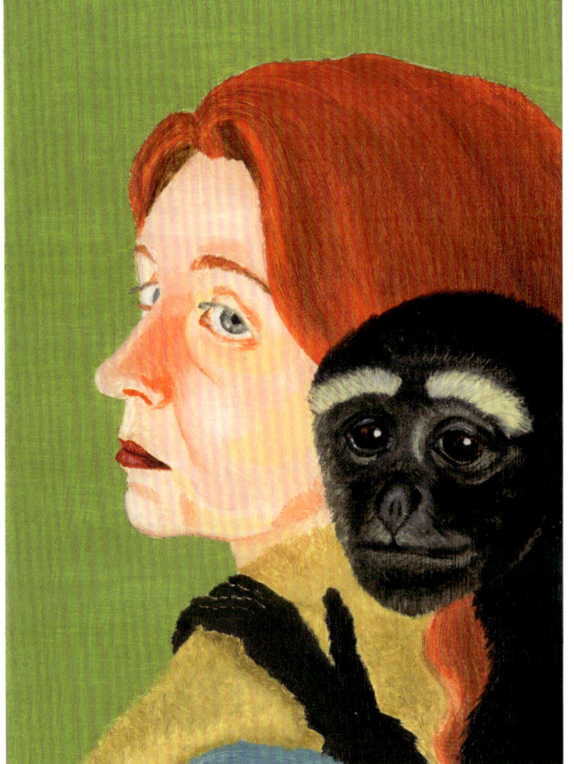

Audrey Niffenegger,
Lady with Monkey
(see page 82)

Sigmund Freud's *The Interpretation of Dreams*, 1900, opened dreamland to artists. Armed with scientific theory, Symbolists, and later Surrealists, felt free to explore the subconscious and to travel beyond the visible. The mystery of the human psyche, dreams, erotic fantasies, and the connection between life, love, and death became rich sources of inspiration. Both movements considered literature a true sister of the visual arts. Symbolist painter Odilon Redon illustrated Gustave Flaubert's *The Temptation of St. Anthony* (1896), and Aubrey Beardsley created exquisite drawings for the first English edition of Oscar Wilde's *Salome* (1894). Doubly talented Surrealists Leonora Carrington and Dorothea Tanning are celebrated for their paintings as well as for their poetry and novels.

Niffenegger has been a spiritual heir to both movements. She shares with Symbolists and Surrealists a fascination with dreams, abundant imagination, and curiosity about the dark corners of the soul. She is also a Romantic, however, and her work is permeated by the subjects of doomed love and love stronger than death, whose histories in world art and literature have extended from *Orpheus and Eurydice* through *Romeo and Juliet*, and to Niffenegger's own novels, *The Time Traveler's Wife* and *Her Fearful Symmetry*.

The presence of death in our lives, the ephemeral nature of human existence, and the connection between love (Eros) and death (Thanatos) are the subjects of *Vanitas*, a 1989 portfolio of prints. Niffenegger's images are accompanied by poetry written by some of the greatest poets of the English-speaking world. The artist acknowledges the influence of seventeenth-century Northern European still lifes, but instead of presenting wilted flowers and clocks—symbols of the brevity of life—Niffenegger's *memento mori* prints celebrate birth, love, and death from a female perspective. Juxtaposed with *Death Comforts the Mother* (page 88), Anne Bradstreet's poem "Before the Birth of One of Her Children" expresses the fear of a young woman whose life may be threatened by childbirth. *Lovers' Embrace* (page 90), a sensuous portrayal of a woman tenderly embraced by death, corresponds with Thomas Campion's "Dismissal."

As Niffenegger describes one of her main concerns, "With the passage of time we are losing everything all the time. We are changing from moment to moment." A drawing, *Allegory of Time*, 2005 (page 98), depicts a naked young woman in a landscape, holding a watch and a whip. She stands on the back of a turtle, which in turn is pulled by a skeleton. It seems that the turtle must move slowly, making the young woman impatient and perhaps later regret her hurry.

Niffenegger's Dreamland is not a landscape of mourning but a lively place of strange and unusual occurrences, where life and death are intertwined and where the rituals of death are celebratory occasions. A delightful etching, *The Starling's Funeral*, 2008 page 100), depicts a glass hearse carrying a dead starling. It is being driven to a cemetery by birds and two horse skeletons wearing festive attire. A flock of butterflies announces the procession, and the starling's bird-friends seem to gather on the roadside to watch the fanciful passing caravan, which is driven by an undertaker dressed in top hat and a cape.

In Dreamland, ghosts, the dead, and the skeletons interact with the world of the living; they dress up for special occasions and sing. *Black Roses (In Memory of Isabella Blow)*, 2007 (page 104), features one of the "special occasion" dresses that Niffenegger created for the British journalist and fashion personality who committed suicide in 2007 at age forty-eight. The artist dresses a skeleton in a long skirt made of black roses, creating an ensemble fit for the best-dressed ghost in Gloucestershire. The melody in *Song of the Womb*, 2005 (page 99), is performed by a skeleton who "sings a little song of the womb...like a roar of the sea in a shell," as Niffenegger writes on a page covered with musical notations.

Niffenegger admits to a preoccupation with death. "To me, death is just totally normal," she says. "It is part of us from the moment we are born." She shares Heraclitus's philosophy of *carpe diem*. "We need to seize the day," she says, "and pay attention.... We should look carefully at ourselves and things around us, and not be oblivious to life as it passes us by. I use fantastic elements in my art to startle people into noticing and paying attention...strangeness makes us see more acutely."

NOTES:

1. Andre Breton, "Excerpts from *The Second Surrealist Manifesto*," in *Surrealists on Art*; ed. Lucy Lippard, (Englewood Cliffs, NJ: Prentice Hall, 1970), 28.

2. William Shakespeare, *The Complete Works of William Shakespeare*, (New York: Gramercy Books, 1975), 1194.

3. Audrey Niffenegger, Afterword, in *The Adventuress* (New York: Abrams, 2006).

4. According to Greek mythology, at a wedding, Eris, the goddess of discord, threw a golden apple into the midst of partying goddesses with the words "For the Fairest" attached. Hera, Athena, and Aphrodite claimed the apple and asked Zeus to decide which was most beautiful. Zeus refused and asked Paris, a mortal, to judge. Each goddess tried to bribe Paris, but Aphrodite promised him the most beautiful woman in the world, Helen, wife of the Greek King Menelaus, and won the apple. The abduction of Helen by Paris was the cause of the Trojan War.

5. Charles Baudelaire, "The Salon of 1859," in *The Mirror of Art: Critical Studies by Baudelaire*, (Garden City, NY: Doubleday Anchor Books, 1956), 274.

6. Charles Baudelaire, "The Salon of 1846," in *The Mirror of Art: Critical Studies by Baudelaire*, (Garden City, NY: Doubleday Anchor Books, 1956), 92–97.

7. Don Marquis, "The Lesson of the Moth," in Dinitia Smith, "From Humble Insect to Hallucinatory Art; Printmaker Turns Moths Into Objects of Beauty," New York Times, August 14, 2002, http://www.nytimes.com/2002/08/14/arts/humble-insect-hallucinatory-art-printmaker-turns-moths-into-objects-beauty.html.

8. All quotes from the artist are from a series of email messages to the author, March–September 2012.

9. Elizabeth Bishop, *Elizabeth Bishop: Poems, Prose and Letters* (New York: Literary Classics of the United States, Inc., 2008), 256–57.

Mark Pascale

AUD
NIFFENEG
A PRI

An educator's primary duty is to coax a person out of raw, immature material.
People educate themselves if provided the opportunity to do so. At the School
of the Art Institute of Chicago (SAIC), where Audrey and I began our personhood
in 1981, the idea of education was basically defined by existentialism.[1] There were
no grades, and little if any structure. I was her professor, instructing a beginning
lithography class, and although I cannot remember the first time I met Audrey, or
our first conversation, I do remember the impression she made on me. She was
born more or less fully formed. What to do with her?

Years later, I asked her high school mentor, William Wimmer, if he agreed that
Audrey bounced out of the womb an adult. He replied, "Audrey was never a child."[2]
Apparently, she struck Mr. Wimmer very much the same way that she did me. She
was always eager—to work, to try anything, to listen and share stories. She was and
is the kind of person who reads a lot—certainly more, and more broadly than me—
but she never rubbed it in. Instead, if there were no chance to discuss a particular
text, in her very adult way, she would find a topic of mutual interest.

In the early 1980s, SAIC was less like a college than anything I had experienced.
There was a nearly complete lack of convention—in social circles, fashion, or the
curriculum. It was fairly typical to have a first- or second-semester freshman with
little or no drawing experience taking a beginning lithography class—a medium
that fundamentally requires drawing skills.
Nothing prepared me for this, and nothing
prepared me for the rather indifferent
attitude that students often adopted
toward "requirements." Audrey stepped
into one of my early classes at SAIC,[3] and
I saw in her a depth beyond what her work
indicated in that class. She liked drawing
with line—she was already quite adept at
etching—and, as etching folks often do,
she quickly developed an anathema to the
lithography process, not least because of
the relative difficulty of making a drawing
with as sharply defined a line as one
created through line etching.[4] Yet, she
found sufficient interest in playing with
the technique that she repeated the class
twice more at the advanced level.[5]

Indeed, Audrey, along with several of her high-school peers, repeatedly took classes with me at SAIC during the early 1980s.[6] As a group, they were high-spirited, intensely funny, and intelligent, and they always pushed the boundaries of what I thought acceptable as a print. When I go back through my teaching portfolio, I am struck by how many prints by this group of students I still use as examples.

They are all different, but similar in the extent to which they willfully undermined my attempts to make them conform to my expectations. This, of course, is a time-honored methodology in college-level teaching: to provide instruction with a cause and effect, purposefully inviting disagreement and contrary results so that students expand beyond their own expectations.

Thinking about what remains in my holdings of Audrey's early work, I am struck by the consistently depressing or dark subject matter. That, often coupled with an impish sense of humor, seemed to define this period in her life.[7] I could relate; as an undergraduate, I commuted from home, just as Audrey did. There is a special social pressure for college commuters, compared to their apartment- or campus-dwelling peers, who are fairly free from parental scrutiny. It's quite a bit more difficult to establish independence when you know that you'll be sleeping in your childhood bed, and taking meals with your family at the very moment when you are trying to detach and become self-sufficient. Looking inward, finding places of fantasy life, and other methods of ratcheting oneself out of the preceding eighteen years of life are fairly common ground. Audrey's fantasy life was enriched by her reading as well as her discovery of artists such as Aubrey Beardsley and Egon Schiele. In Beardsley she discovered an artist who drew in a familiar but more sophisticated way than she did, and who also was dedicated to text. Combining words and pictures was an early motif within Audrey's work—in fact, I can hardly think of a lithograph she made without a text of some kind. Thinking of her visual novels, illustrated with etchings, illuminates the significance of her early discovery of Beardsley, as well as of Victorian mores. William Wimmer even characterized her early work as featuring floating women

Aubrey Vincent Beardsley, *Virgilius the Sorcerer*, c. 1893
Pen and brush and black ink, over traces of graphite, on ivory wove paper, laid down on board
9 1/8 x 5 5/8 in.
Gift of Robert Allerton, 1925.928, The Art Institute of Chicago

CREDIT:
Photography © The Art Institute of Chicago

garbed in flowing frocks, not unlike the rather elaborate costume worn by Virgilius in the Beardsley drawing at the Art Institute which Audrey would have seen as a student (opposite).

Among Audrey's other early influences were drawings by Egon Schiele and Horst Janssen. Like Beardsley, Schiele probably has shocked many teenage artists first stumbling upon his work (he certainly shocked me out of my Ingres-worship). His sad biography and short life, coupled with the eroticism and acute vision he expressed, are still stunning discoveries for anyone who happens upon or seeks out his work. In addition, Schiele's line and color were so expressive, and his repetitive format likewise is appealing to younger artists accustomed to drawing in sketchbooks. The Art Institute of Chicago has only two sheets of Schiele's mature drawings, both double-sided and typical of his method. Each depicts at least one self-portrait—which, given her penchant for revealing self-portraiture, would have been of great interest to Niffenegger— with completely different characteristics. In one Schiele, we see the artist's head alone with a sleepy or sickly gaze, held up by his long, thin hand and partially rendered with oil paint (page 24). The second, the verso of a major composition, is a more typical, vaguely erotic self-portrait of the artist's emaciated nude body embracing a nude model; both figures' genitals are bare and generalized. Both drawings are executed with a powerful contour gesture—one rather gloomy and the other desperate and urgent. What makes these discoveries so vital to Niffenegger is that both Beardsley and Schiele made images either as illuminations for other texts or made images fraught with innuendo that was picaresque or simply literary. Both conditions continue to inform her visual and literary work.

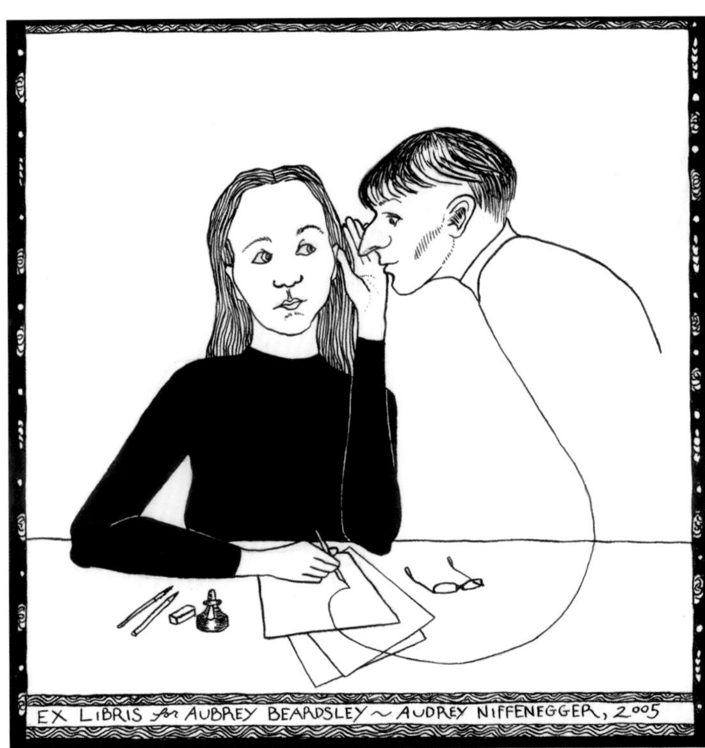

Audrey Niffenegger, *Aubrey Beardsley Ex Libris*, 2005
Ink on paper
6 1/8 x 6 in.
Collection of Audrey Niffenegger,
Chicago, Illinois

In Janssen, Audrey discovered one very important lesson. When she saw the Art Institute's exhibition *Horst Janssen: Drawings & Etchings*,[8] she witnessed, perhaps for the first time, an overview of work by a contemporary artist whose major contribution and corpus of work was on paper. The exhibition featured a large, long wall of colorful self-portraits. One showed the artist with a bespectacled, tortured face seen from below, eyes and mouth a bruised red-purple, announcing his initials "H" and "J," which float past and above his head. It is a desperate image, urgently revealing the artist's psyche and willingly showing his vulnerability (opposite). Janssen drew the work in 1982, the same year it was acquired by the museum. All of these factors must have impressed the young Audrey Niffenegger, particularly the realizations that it was possible to be recognized by a major museum during one's lifetime and to have a recognized career based primarily on works on paper. Janssen was an excellent printmaker as well, and the majority of his intaglio prints seen in the exhibition were direct, using the hand-drawing processes of drypoint and etching deliberately and minimally, so that the images were not augmented by printmaking tricks.[9]

During her career, Niffenegger has made a significant number of self-portraits. It is a time-honored motif, dating to at least the Greek myth of the hunter Narcissus, who died after seeing his reflection, committing suicide because he was unable to live with the knowledge of his own beauty. All of the artists whose work Audrey studied at the Art Institute made self-portraits; indeed, the museum focuses on artists' self-portrait drawings. Another significant example of the motif, Jean Siméon Chardin's pastel *Self-Portrait with a Visor* (1776; page 26) entered the collection and was exhibited during Audrey's student years.[10] The image of the painter, aged, feminized by the scarf that ties his visor to his head, must surely have been interesting to her. The passing of time has long been a theme in her work, as have been the qualities of persona and physiognomy. One can see this in her books, as well as her treatments of herself (several of which are included in this exhibition), not to mention her first published novel, *The Time Traveler's Wife*.

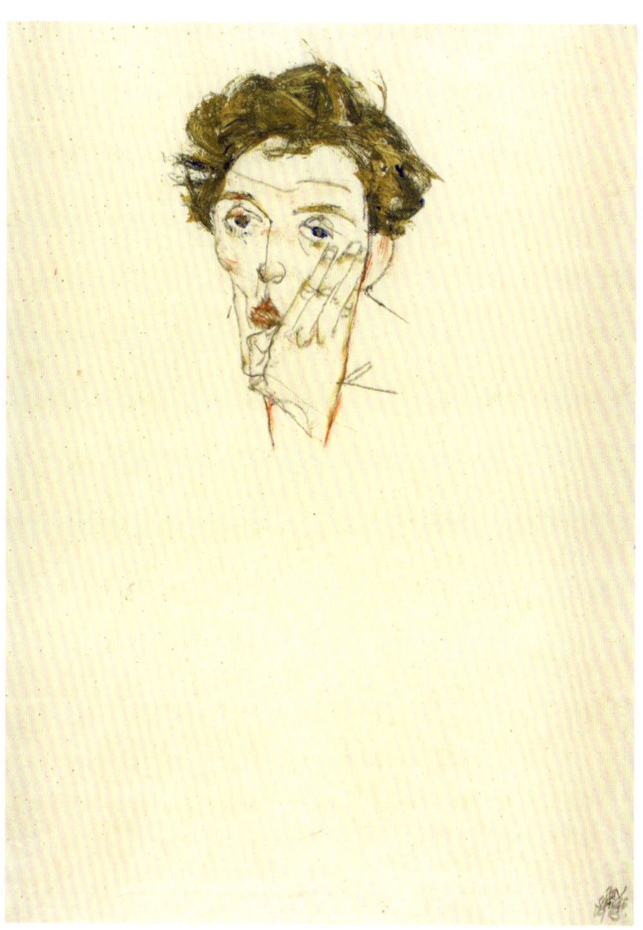

Egon Schiele, *Self-Portrait*, 1913;
Graphite, with touches of oil,
on wove paper
12 1/2 x 18 1/4 in.
Restricted gift of Mr. and Mrs. William
O. Hunt and Prints and Drawings
Purchase Account, 1966.186R; The Art
Institute of Chicago

CREDIT:
Photography © The Art Institute
of Chicago

There were other exhibitions during Audrey's student years that may have influenced her, or given her permission to continue working in the style she established early on. In 1982, the Art Institute mounted *Incunabula of Etching*, which included many fine examples of the medium in its earliest iteration. Among the works were examples by Dürer, whose early attempts at etching were rudimentary compared to his elegant engravings. Also, in 1984, *Bindings from Ryerson and Burnham Libraries* was available in the library's vitrines in the reading room. Among the special collections within the library is the Mary Reynolds Collection, which contains works that have influenced many generations of SAIC students. Reynolds was an intimate of Marcel Duchamp, and close with all of the major Surrealist artists in Paris. She was a bookbinder who created special, one-of-a-kind bindings for certain artist's books—one included the skins of two toads.[11] Audrey certainly learned how to bind her own books as a student, but one has to consider the powerful conceptual influence on the young artist by the whimsicality of a woman like Mary Reynolds.

Finally, what has always stayed with me as one of Audrey's many influences and something she introduced me to is the great serial comic strip by Lynda Barry, "Ernie Pook's Comeek," that appeared in the *Chicago Reader*, a weekly newspaper.[12] I still recall how, on Thursdays, students and faculty alike waited for the weekly *Reader* delivery in the lobby of SAIC's Columbus Drive building. Audrey probably went straight for "Ernie Pook"—she had an appetite for it, as de Kooning and other artists did for George Herriman's "Krazy Kat." What Barry's strip lacked in daily-comics slapstick and gags, it delivered in spades in the realm of adolescent interior life. The main characters of "Ernie Pook" were Marlys and Arna (great names for a young artist with deep literary interests and imagination), whose experience of life was filled with acute pathos and psychology. A young adult like Audrey could easily relate to their daily tribulations and observations of everything from the banal to the fabulous. Now truly adult in years, she has published her own volume of comics. It is a serialized graphic novel in the manner of "Ernie Pook's Comeek," *The Night Bookmobile*, which she began publishing in 2008 in *The Guardian*, and subsequently published in book form in 2010.

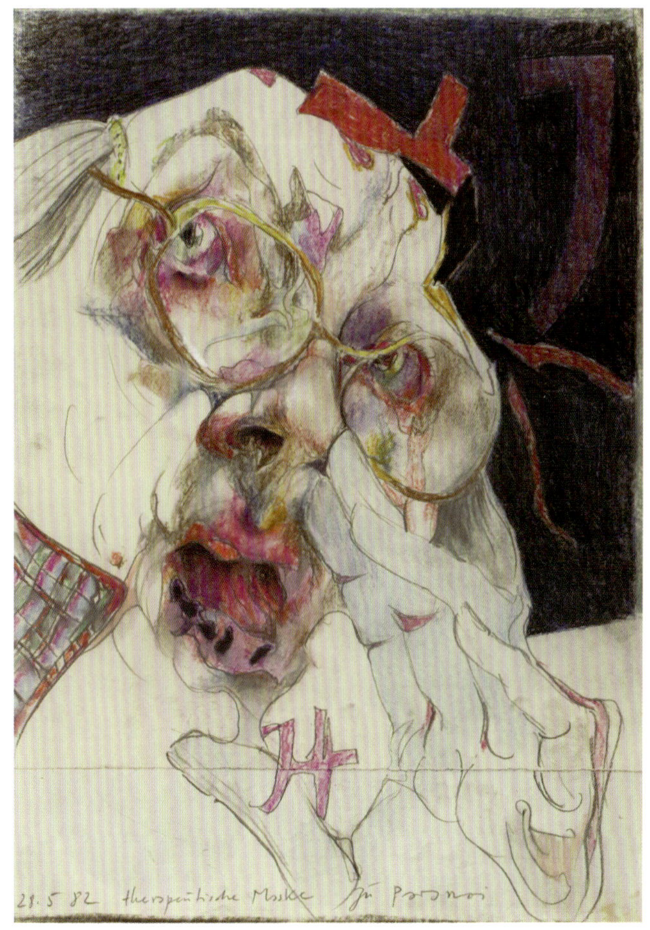

Horst Janssen, *Therapeutic Mask*, from *Paranoia Series*, 1982
Pastel and graphite on cream wove paper (pieced at bottom)
14 7/8 x 10 1/4 in.
Restricted gift of Dr. Eugene A. Solow, 1982.1488; The Art Institute of Chicago

During the years that Audrey has exhibited her work, I have observed her vacillate between her lyrical, linear style of making figures and her sincere exploration of carefully observed drawings and paintings, rendered in an Old Master style. What I often sensed was missing from these is her terrific ability to articulate a story in a pithy visual manner, but one that combined her storytelling ability with her evolving graphic and painterly interests. In her earlier books, such as *The Three Incestuous Sisters*, she certainly exhibits a concise graphic vocabulary—good enough for a trade edition to be produced based on what is an extraordinarily deluxe, hand-bound *livre d'artiste*. The book's illustrations follow a stylistic pattern that Audrey

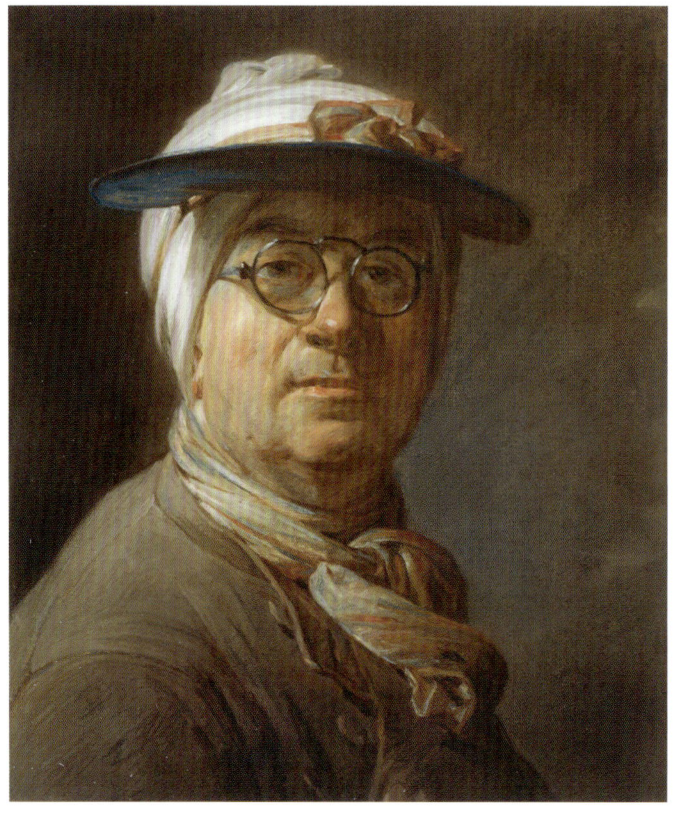

Jean Siméon Chardin, *Self-Portrait with a Visor*, c. 1776
Pastel on blue laid paper, mounted on canvas
18 x 14 3/4 in.
Clarence Buckingham Collection and the Harold Joachim Memorial Fund, 1984.61; The Art Institute of Chicago

CREDIT:
Photography © The Art Institute of Chicago

instigated very early on—a fluid, unembellished line to describe figures, in concert with generally flat planes of aquatint tone. The images have a quotidian quality that remains to this day in her etched work, even in her most recent publication, *Raven Girl.*

When she exhibited the drawings for *The Night Bookmobile* (not in this exhibition) a few years ago, a forceful change in her visual syntax struck me. She had illustration sufficient for reproduction, but enough of her usual manner remained to remind me that it was Audrey. There was color, but the color was less self-conscious than her painting palette. In short, I felt that she had established a relaxed style, joyful, sophisticated, and full of the love and wonder she has for the world of books and knowledge, expressed in a graphic form. I have ruminated about this for a few years without broaching it with her—Why would she care what I think, now that she has far surpassed me in the field? It leaves me happy and satisfied to have had a chance to express these thoughts publicly, in a book celebrating her rich career. I am so fortunate to know Audrey and always have felt blessed that for a few years we shared our growth in close proximity.

NOTES:

1. I mean that "beginning personhood" refers to attaining independence. For me, the experience at SAIC freed me from the bonds of academia as I experienced them in state universities. It was not so much a lowering of my standards as establishing new priorities. For Audrey, it was more literal—leaving behind requirements and establishing her own course and choices.

2. Phone conversation, August 10, 2012.

3. She enrolled in Beginning Lithography during the spring 1982 semester. It was the second semester at SAIC for both of us.

4. I am reminded of something Jasper Johns, a master of lithography once said about his initial attempts at etching: "Within a short unit of an etching line there are fantastic things happening in the black ink, and none of those things are what one had in mind." Johns, too, went on to master the combined etching processes.

5. Niffenegger enrolled in advanced classes with me in the fall 1982 and spring 1983 semesters. For her experience with etching, see the "Chronology" (page 114) in this book.

6. Among them were David Kelly, Allen Levinson, Tina Onderdonk, and Margret (Peggy) Wade—all students of William Wimmer at Evanston Township High School.

7. Among the prints that I still have is one that she made with an etching needle, scratched into a black tusche ground to produce a white line on black. The image is a somewhat comical drawing of a car driven by a hooded figure along a lonely road at night. It's a bit like a *New Yorker* cartoon.

8. Exhibition at The Art Institute of Chicago, November 17–December 30, 1984.

9. These were referred to as "frivolous effects" by my professors.

10. In addition to being a self-portrait, the work is a pastel drawing—another graphic medium that was once considered a form of painting, and another specialty of the Art Institute's collection. The Chardin, one of five pastel self-portraits, is a pendant to another pastel portrait he made of his wife, and they were exhibited together in the Salon of 1775. The Art Institute acquired the portrait of Madame Chardin in 1962, and waited patiently for the companion pastel to become available. They were first exhibited together in the Art Institute's galleries in the spring of 1984, during Audrey's student years at SAIC.

11. The binding by Reynolds was created for an earlier publication, Jean-Pierre Brisset, *La Science de Dieu ou La Création de l'homme* (Paris: Chamuel Editeur, 1900). For more on Reynolds and the holdings at the Art Institute, see *Surrealism and Its Affinities: The Mary Reynolds Collection, A Bibliography Compiled by Hugh Edwards* (Chicago: The Art Institute of Chicago, 1973), 84; and "Mary Reynolds and the Spirit of Surrealism," *The Art Institute of Chicago Museum Studies* 22, no. 2 (1996).

12. Barry started publishing "Ernie Pook's Comeek" in the *Chicago Reader* in 1979, which encouraged her to move to Chicago, where she lived for many years. Her presence in Chicago, as well as her career in publishing, was surely inspirational to Audrey.

Audrey Niffenegger

AWAKE IN DREAM WO

My first memory is of color. I am a year old. I stand up in my crib, clinging to the rails. I'm looking at a corner of my room. It is painted blue. Light, slightly greenish blue. There is nothing in the corner, only two walls meeting each other, but I see it and remember it.

I'm sitting at the dining room table in our old apartment on Maple Street. It's a summer afternoon. I am just four years old. My mother is in the kitchen. The radio is on. I have a small stack of white typing paper in front of me. I have some crayons. I make a drawing. It is of two people, side by side. One is blue, the other is orange. The blue one is larger and I draw a mark on his chest. My mother comes by and I show her the drawing.

    It's Superman, I tell her. And Robin.

    Why do they have square heads? she asks me.

    I puzzle over this. I realize that real people don't have square heads. I realize that pictures can be something else—reality can go one way and the world in the picture can veer off into—well, I don't know what, yet.

    But I am going to do my best to find out.

In fourth grade I win a prize for a drawing. We don't have regular art class but occasionally we get to do something like art, usually to keep us busy and quiet on a rainy day when we cannot be decanted onto the playground during recess. For some reason the class is told to draw the TV character Fat Albert.

I don't quite know who Fat Albert is (he is a cartoon character on a show created by Bill Cosby) but I have a notion of what he looks like (overweight, black, friendly). All the kids in my class are white. All the kids in the whole school, in fact, are white. We all sit there industriously drawing Fat Albert. The other kids draw him alone, hovering in space on manila paper. I draw him in a barnyard chasing a chicken and being chased by a blond white girl who looks like Elly on *The Beverly Hillbillies*. Chickens look alarmed. Fat Albert is holding a knife and fork. Fat Albert is hungry. He is going to catch the chicken and have her for dinner.

The substitute teacher looks over all our drawings and chooses mine. He explains to the class that my drawing is the best because I have told a story, the drawing is interesting because there are characters and we are curious about what will happen to them.

I always tried to tell stories with pictures, and it was the first time anyone told me that was unusual. To me it seemed like the most normal and absorbing thing in the world.

I am fourteen and have been attending high school for only a few weeks when I come down with an ear infection. I used to get these all the time. This one is especially bad and I spend a week on our couch, heating pad pressed to my horrible ear, reading. My mom kindly goes to the library and brings home a huge stack of art books. One of these is Brian Reade's catalogue for the Victoria & Albert Museum's Aubrey Beardsley exhibition. I fall in love.

It is not Beardsley himself I am in love with: he is beaky and gawky, tragic and tubercular. Even at fourteen I understand that he is one of Art's Bad Boys, impudent, precocious, precious. The thing I love is his line. His work is almost Japanese in its minimalism, black and white, line and wash, ink and empty paper describing worlds. He is an illustrator but he is not subservient to any text. I want this line and this freedom for myself. I begin to imitate Beardsley's work. I don't copy, but I make drawings with a dip pen; I work in his style. I have fallen out of my own time and into the 1890s.

At the end of the school year my friend Becky Heydeman tells me, If you're going to draw like that you should go talk to Mr. Wimmer. He'll teach you etching.

I knock on the door of the Art Office and William Wimmer opens it. He is a tall bespectacled kind-looking man who smiles and asks, Can I help you? I explain that I want to learn etching (though I don't quite know what etching is). And he does help me; Bill Wimmer spends the next three years carefully teaching me the art of intaglio. I realize even at the time that this is an enormous gift.

So much of what forms us is accidental, ephemeral-seeming. When I was young I knew I wanted to be an artist. Sometimes I wanted to be a writer, too, and make books; sometimes I wanted to be a singer. For a brief period when I was twelve I wanted to be a jockey (and twelve was the last time in my life I would ever be small enough for that job). I wanted to be an artist because my mother, Patricia Tamandl Niffenegger, is an artist, and no one ever told me grown people don't sit around making things all day. From the time I was very small I told stories and stories were told to me. Books were read to me and I could see that books equaled worlds. Somewhere along the way I realized that the trick is never to stop. I understood intuitively that art (or what John Cage called "purposeless play") was important in ways that had nothing to do with "what do you want to be when you grow up?" I knew there was probably no career in it.

Art was a method of manifesting bits of myself and sending them off into the world to fend and make their own way. Art was a vocation.

In my application essay for art school I wrote that I wanted to be an Art Nun. I don't know if anyone else at the School of the Art Institute of Chicago in the early 1980s felt that way, but there was a dark intensity to the place that felt like home. Punk had blossomed into a spiky, nocturnal scene; Chicago felt more dangerous then. Being an Art Nun didn't mean giving up sex. Sex has always been part of art, somehow, just like every other vital human experience. My friends at SAIC were often whimsical and absurd, but dead serious in their approach to making art. The thing I had in common with them was intensity. I often felt insufficiently Romantic around my friends. I was living at home in suburban safety (it was the only way we could afford such an expensive school). My purple hair was dyed at a salon. My parents gave me an allowance to buy art supplies. My friends were grittier and had more worrisome tastes than I did. But we were all determined to take this art thing as far as it would go.

In the summer before my third year at SAIC I made a series of drawings of a woman who wore elbow-length gloves and a long skirt. Her breasts were exposed but she seemed not to mind. She appeared unfazed in the drawings although she was transforming into a giant moth, giving birth to a cat, unraveling as though made of string. I could see that this was a story, though not a very linear one; it had dream logic, fairy-tale structure. It became *The Adventuress*. To make it I learned letterpress printing and hand bookbinding. Elsewhere on the planet personal computers had been invented, but their type was pixilated and they couldn't handle handmade paper. So I acquired more five-hundred-year-old skills.

After I graduated I became deeply involved in the book world, though not in the usual sense. I wanted to publish "normal" books, but my books didn't fit any category in trade publishing. I received some interesting rejection letters ("this is brilliant but we can't publish it"). So I happily continued to write, make prints, hand-set the words in lead type, and bind my books in small editions. I joined the Chicago Hand Bookbinders, a group that included book conservators and fine binders. I studied fine bookbinding with Heinke Pensky-Adam, learning from her to work with leather and vellum and to repair books. I met Pamela Barrie and we established a letterpress studio, Green Window Printers. We took on some commercial projects, mostly wedding invitations, but we usually worked on our own book projects. A great deal of my letterpress knowledge I learned from Pam. We happened to be forming our studio just as the last generation of commercial letterpress printers was retiring, so we often found ourselves buying type from old men who found the very existence of female printers a little disturbing. We used to refer to ourselves as Girl Printers. At various times other Girl

Printers were part of Green Windows. Teresa Pankratz and Mary Kennedy were both members of the studio for years.

In 1989 I went to graduate school at Northwestern University. At the time it was a haven for realists who wanted to draw; Phillip Chen and James Valerio taught there and both of them had a lot of impact on my drawing and painting abilities. It was a good place for someone who wanted to make narrative art. I was working on my second large book, *The Three Incestuous Sisters,* and though I was the only printmaker and somewhat isolated it was a formative period for me.

Chicago was a good place to be during the 1980s and 1990s if you were interested in the book arts. Paper Press and Artists Book Works offered classes and studio space. Aiko's was a Japanese paper shop that imported marvelous useful papers no one else carried. Jack Frank had a massive warehouse in Pilsen full of letterpress equipment, where you could buy a Vandercook for $500. Graphic Chemical was a printmaker's delight.

There were many people making exciting book work in Chicago. A bunch of us got together in 1993 and began to create the organization that became the Columbia College Chicago Center for Book and Paper Arts. I was the assistant director. There were only two staff members; the inimitable Marilyn Sward was the director. One of my many tasks was to write catalogue copy for our class brochures. This was very boring, and I started to make the class descriptions more and more outré. The weirder the brochures became, the more I got interested in writing. I began working on a novel.

The idea for *The Time Traveler's Wife* came to me while I was making a drawing. Drawing is a good thing to do when you are writing because the language-wielding part of the brain isn't in use, so ideas drift along while you are looking and making marks. The idea was just the phrase: the time traveler's wife. I wrote it down and began to think about it. Who was this wife? Why had she married a time traveler? That must be rather lonely.... The more questions I asked, the more the story evolved. Five years later I had written a 600-page manuscript.

Almost everything I have made falls outside the recent trends of art and literature. Chicago prizes outsiders and oddballs; I do too. But being outside of categories sometimes makes it more difficult to be exhibited or published. I have been lucky to have worked with one gallery for more than twenty-five years, Printworks Gallery in Chicago. Bob Hiebert and Sidney Block have made their gallery a home for my art and they have found good homes for each piece. I have also been blessed with brilliant collectors who don't mind strangeness, who, in fact, really like the unusual. But when I approached the world of publishing it took time to find people who were interested in the odd and uncategorizable. *The Time Traveler's Wife* was saved from life in a drawer by Joseph Regal, who became my agent and found it a home in tiny MacAdam/Cage, an independent publisher in San Francisco. They were fine with quirkiness. The book became a bestseller, which was the strangest thing that has happened to me. The outer realms of art were very familiar and comfortable; to suddenly have millions of readers was unsettling. In the art world popular things are suspect, so it took me a while to adjust to the new scale of my audience.

Since I was very young I have been making art about death and decay, the passing of time, the inevitability of change. It was an abstract idea for me in my teens, twenties, thirties, but now that I am about to turn fifty it feels like an old friend. The self-portrait was originally a means for me to examine loneliness, sadness, skepticism, fury, delight, dreams, all the uncomfortable mental furnishings I didn't want to load onto to someone else in a portrait. It has become a record of my past emotions and thoughts, sometimes diaristic, sometimes fictional. My curiosity about death, love, the irrational, the fleeting nature of everything: it will never be satisfied. My work is not meant to comfort or pacify; it is always a question and the answer is always immanent, never arriving. Gathering this art together for this exhibition at the National Museum of Women in the Arts has made me reflect and take stock of the progress of long lines of enquiry. Art is not a science of emotion, there will be no incontrovertible results. But the mysteries still ask to be given forms, the stories I tell shape my thoughts. I am still on the same path I first took when I was a child, awake in the dream world, making and unmaking that world with black lines on pieces of paper, never knowing, always wondering.

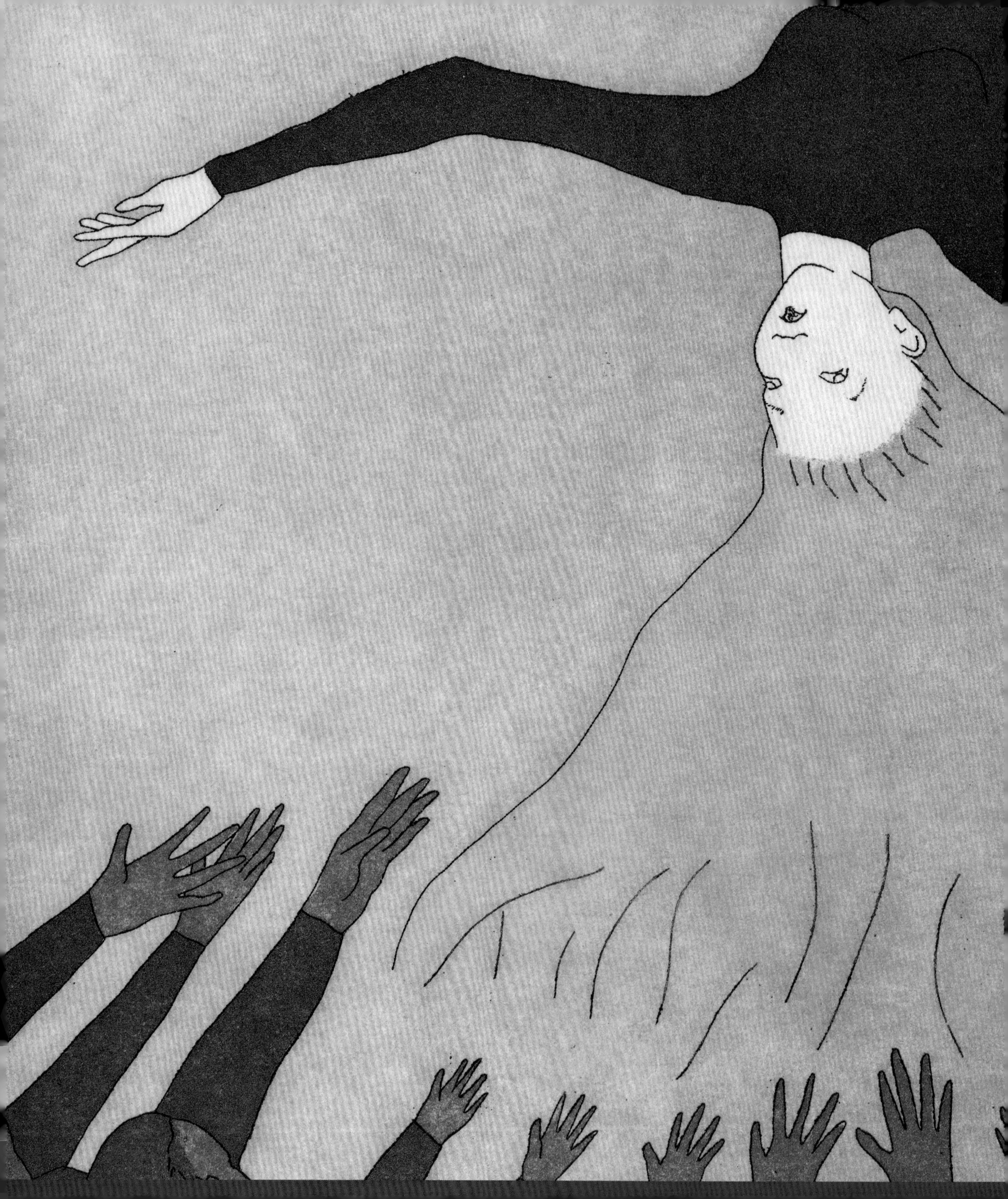

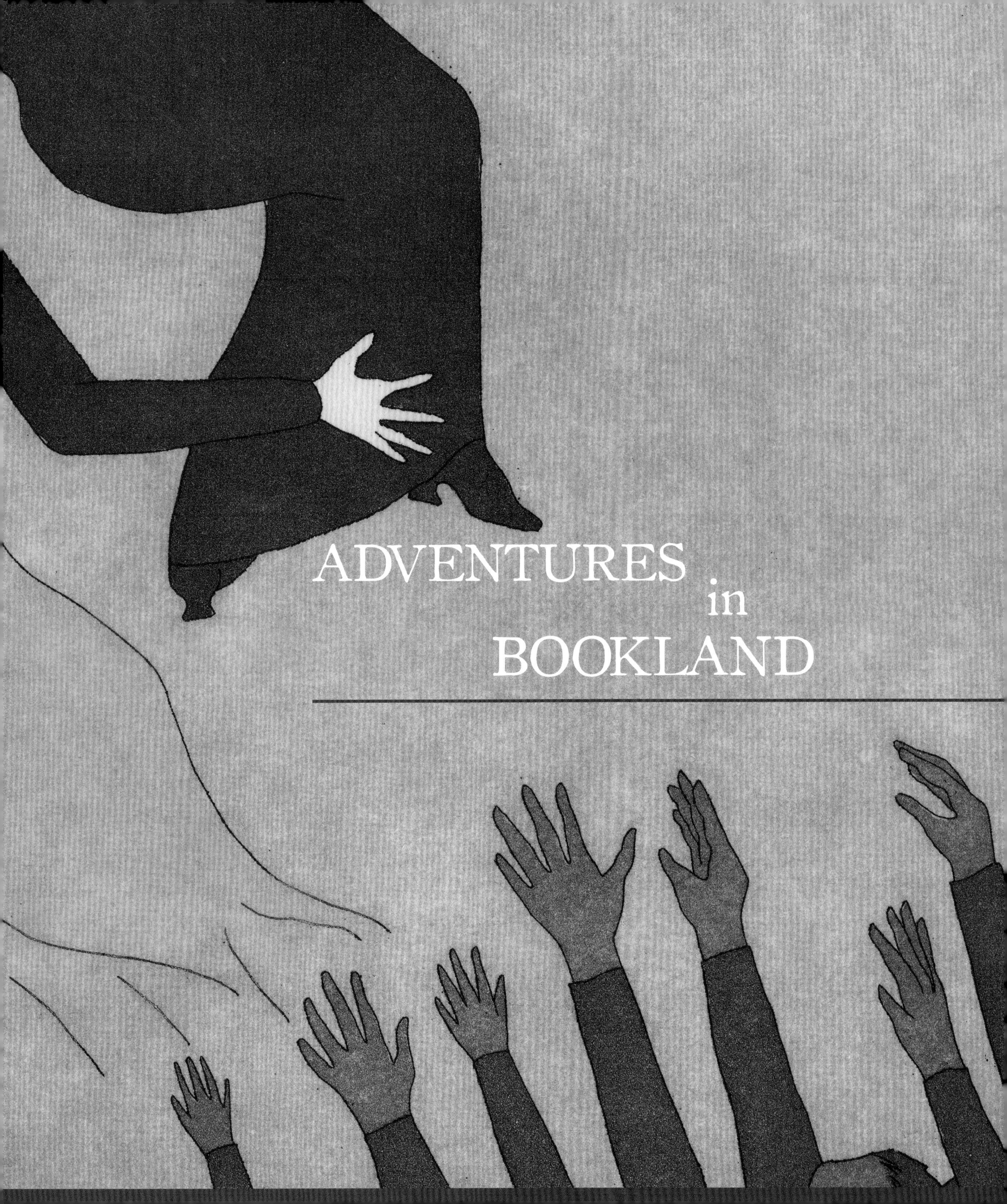

ADVENTURES
in
BOOKLAND

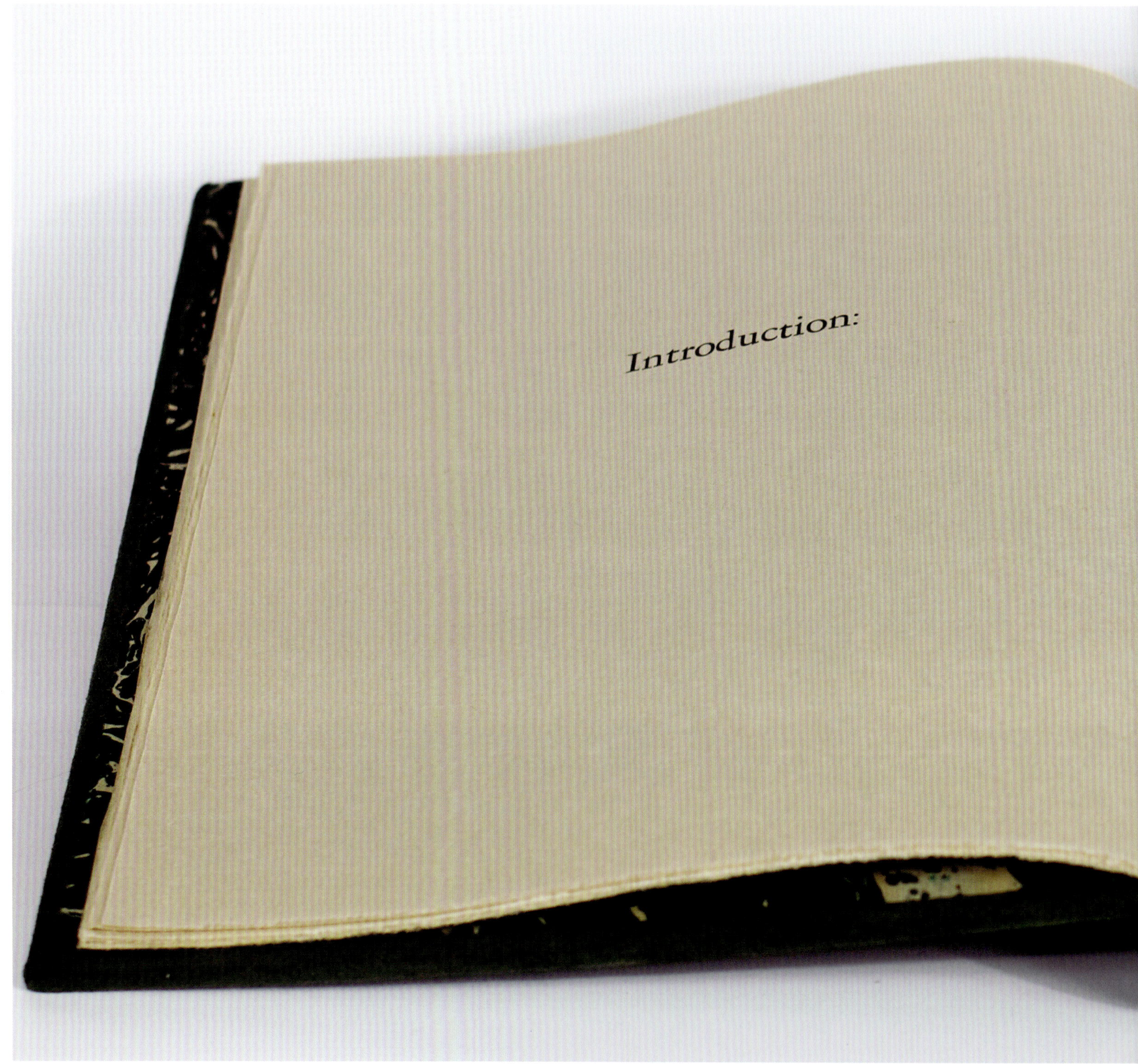
Introduction:

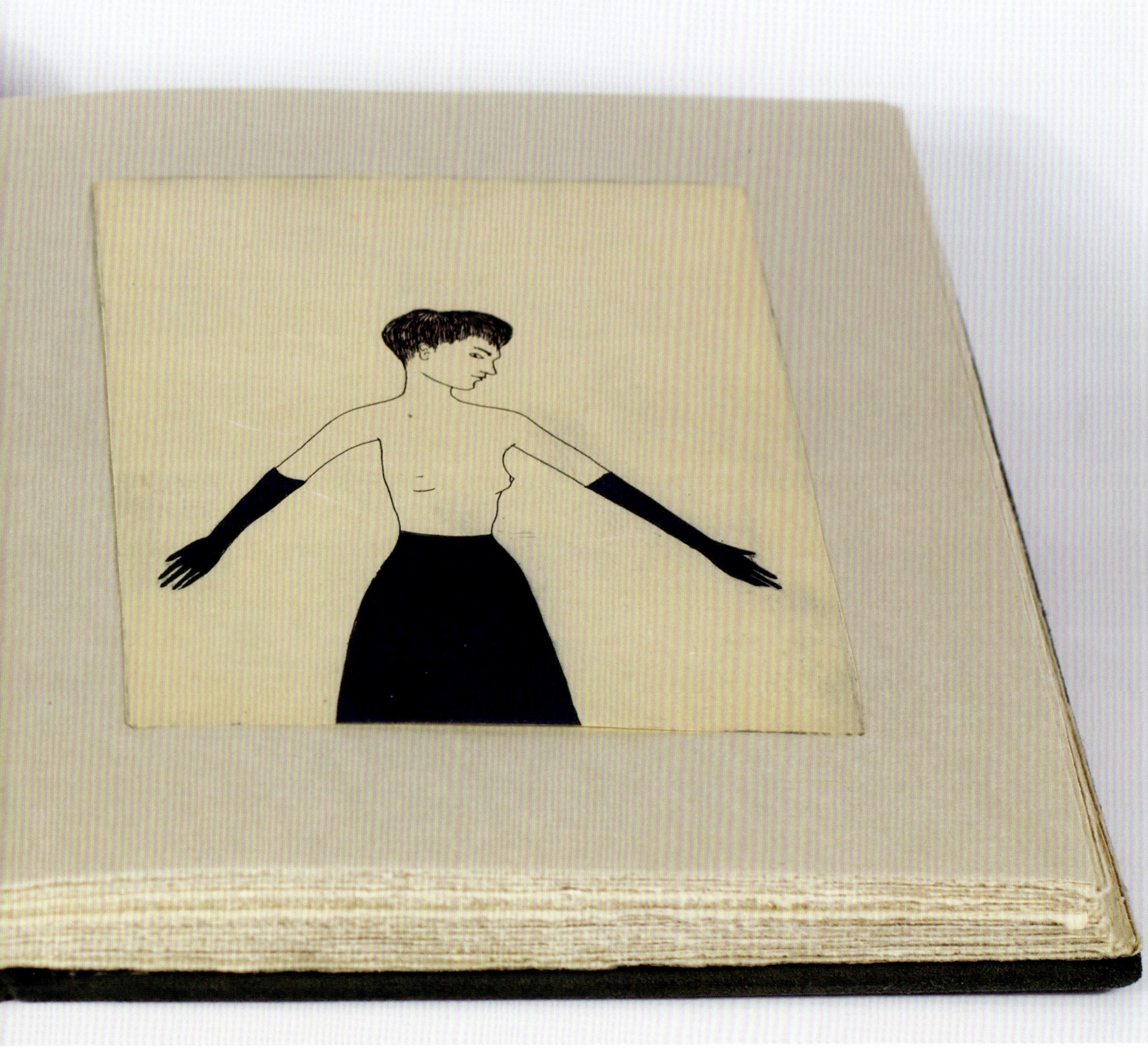

Introduction, from *The Adventuress*

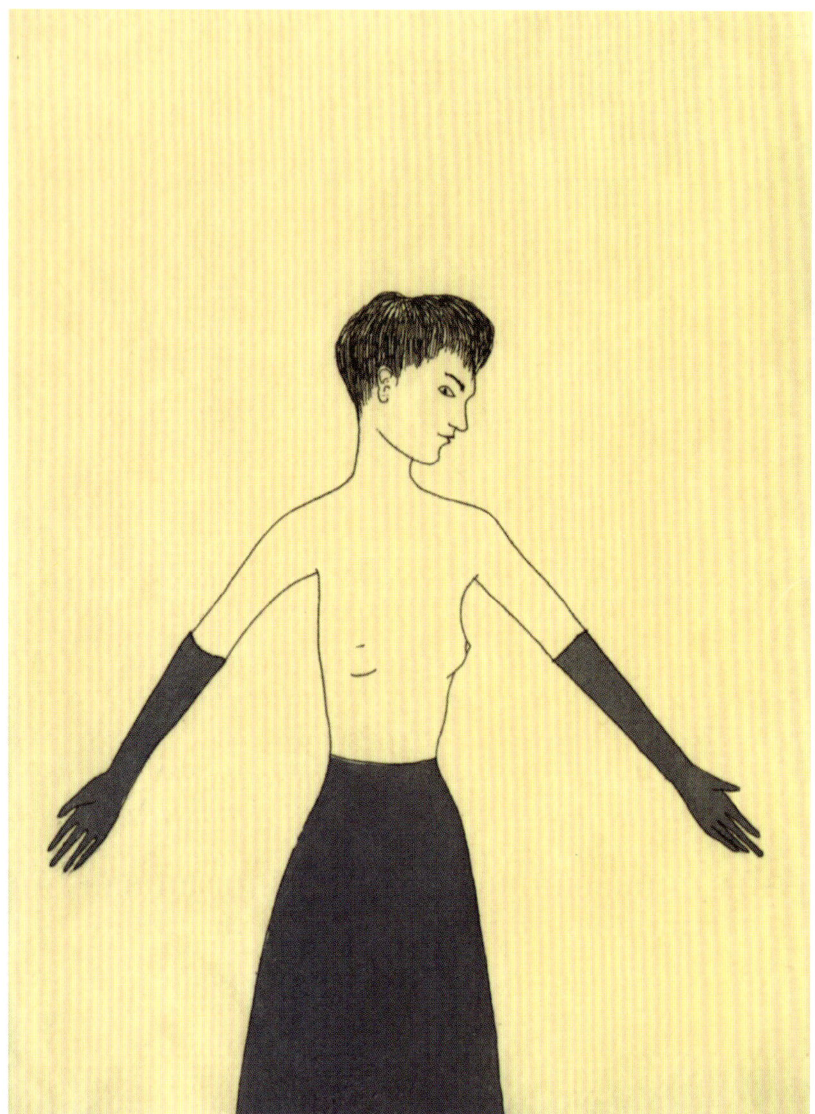

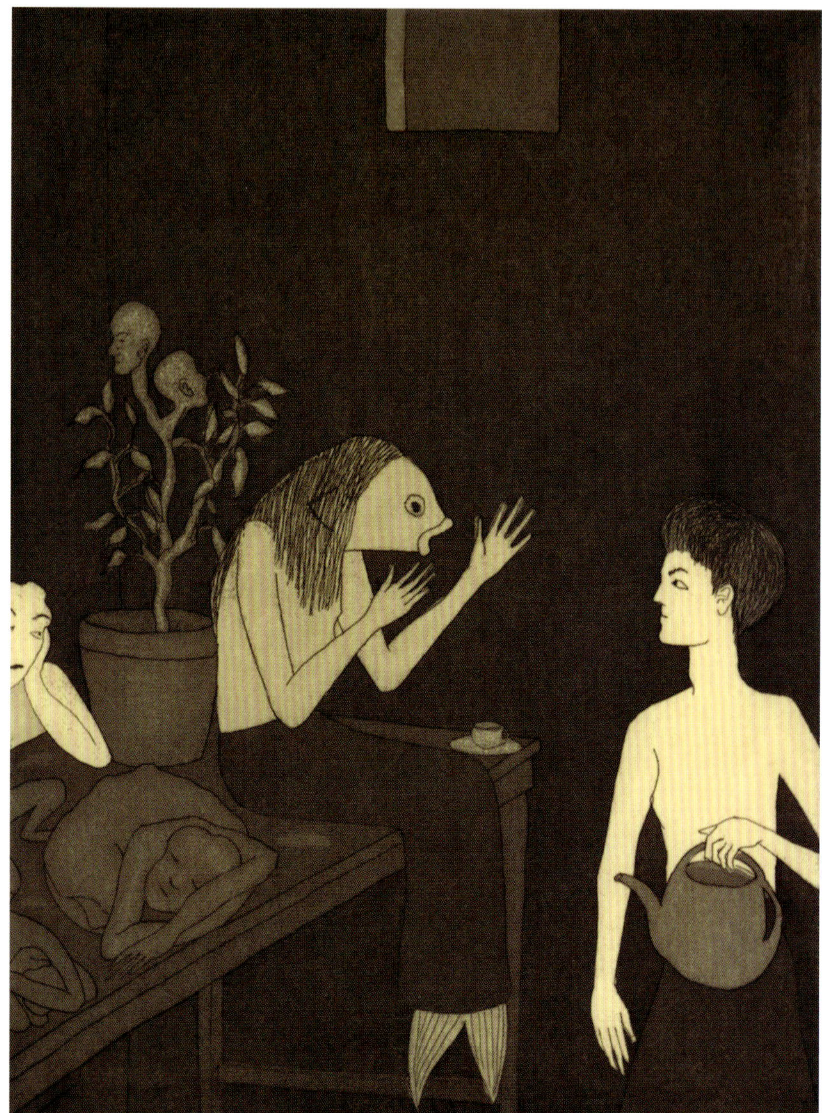

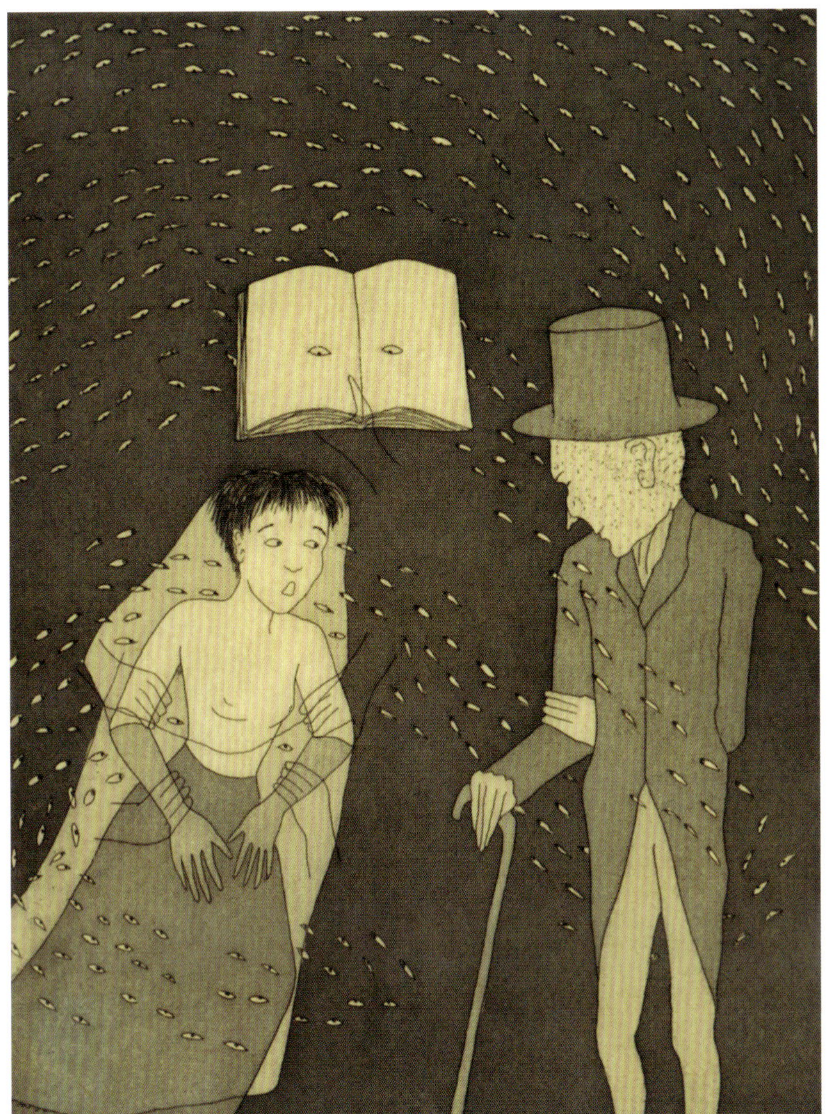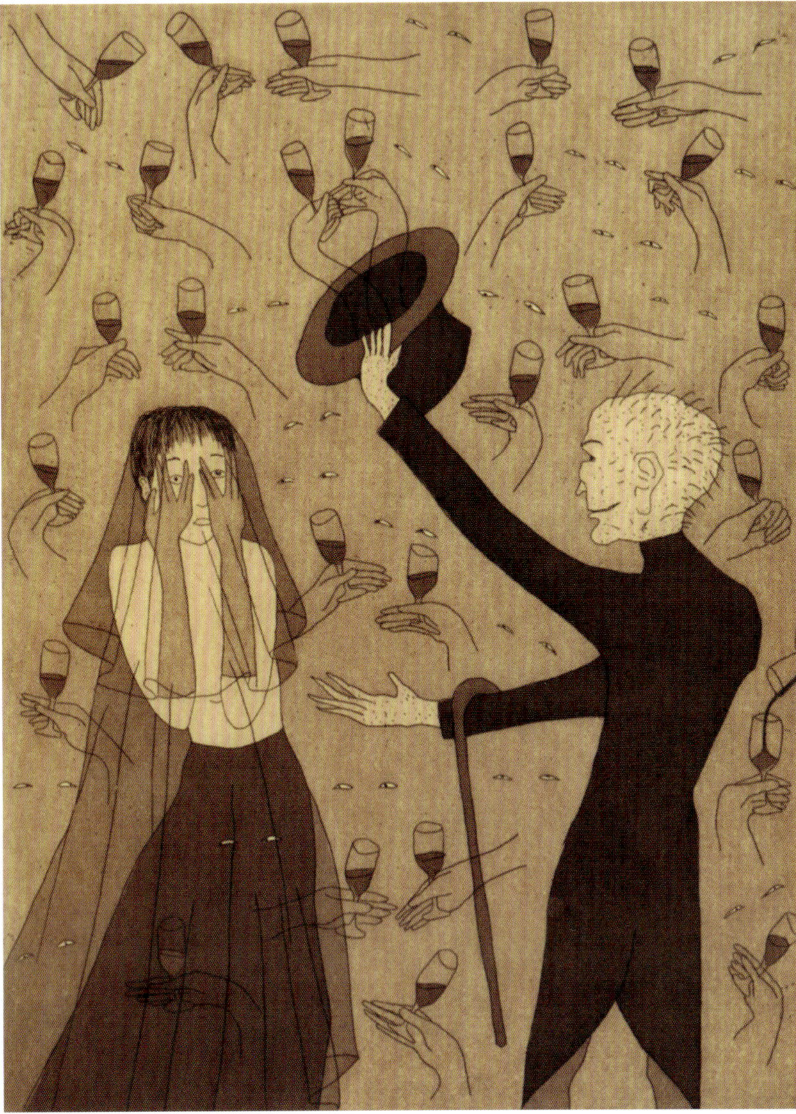

LEFT:
The wedding, from *The Adventuress*

RIGHT:
Revelry, from *The Adventuress*

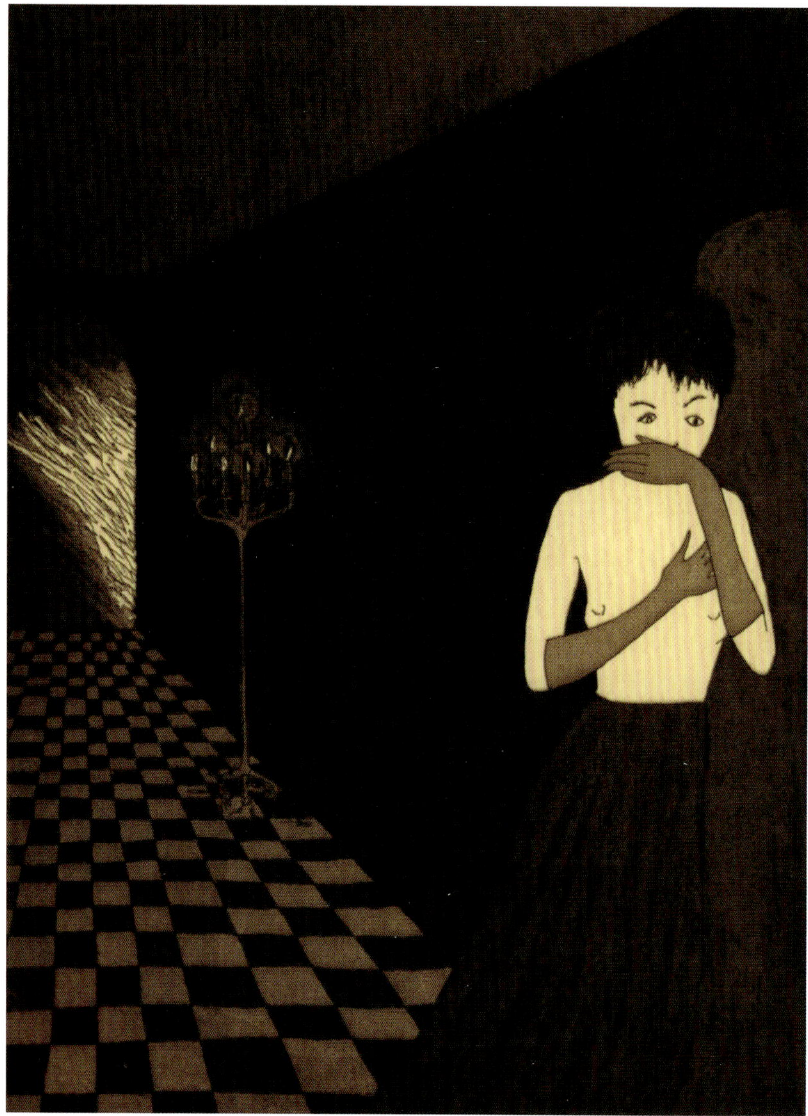

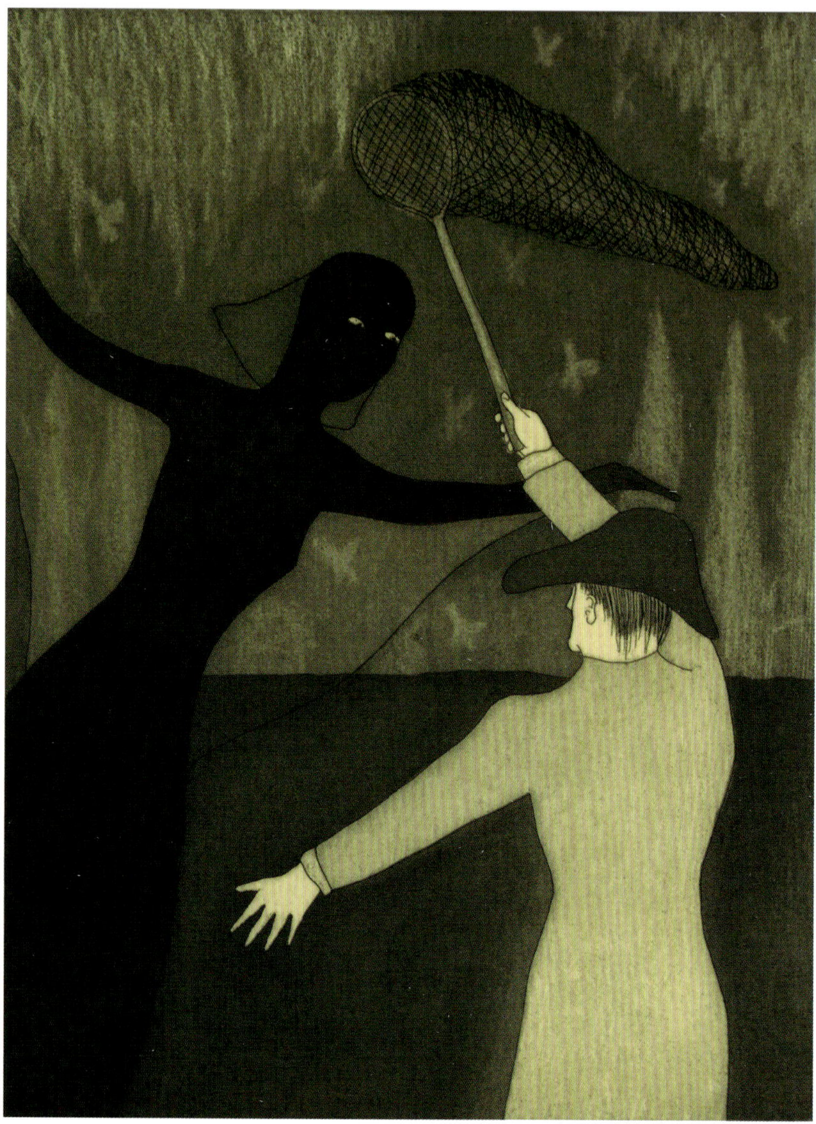

LEFT:
Running away, running away, Running while everything burned,
from *The Adventuress*

RIGHT:
She flew into the garden Of Napoleon Bonaparte; He was a butterfly collector
And tried to capture her., from *The Adventuress*

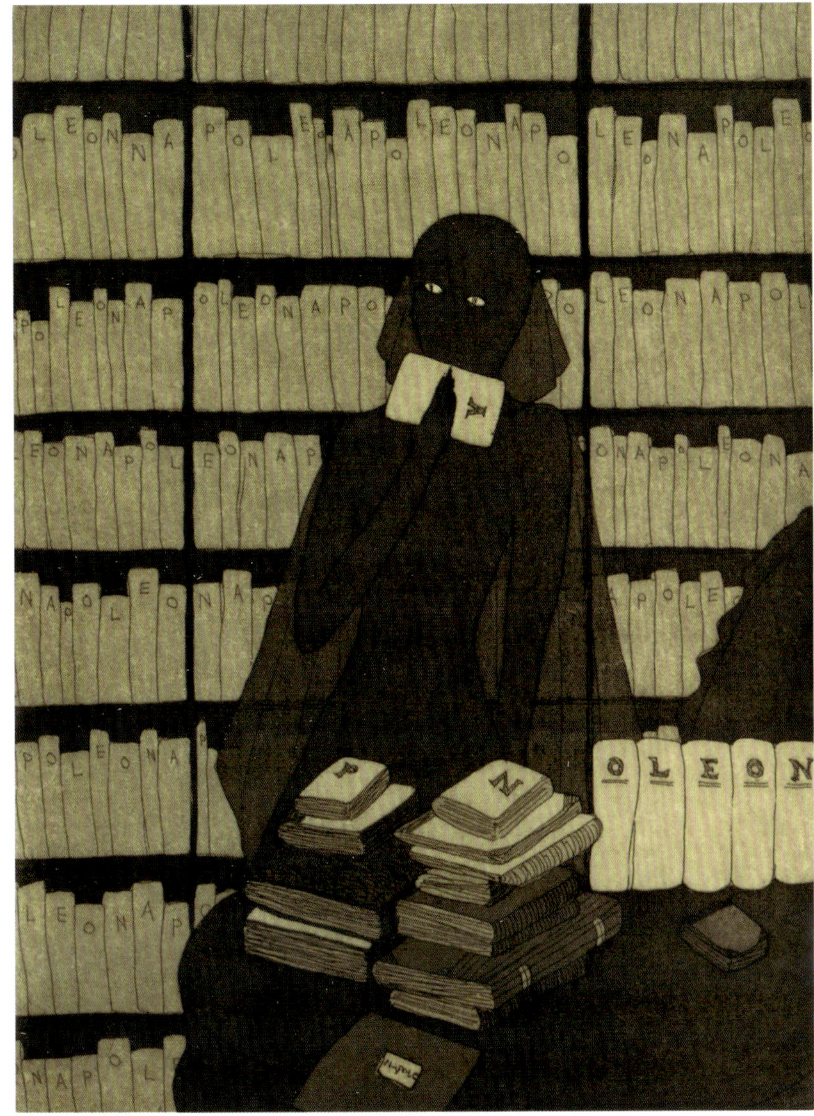

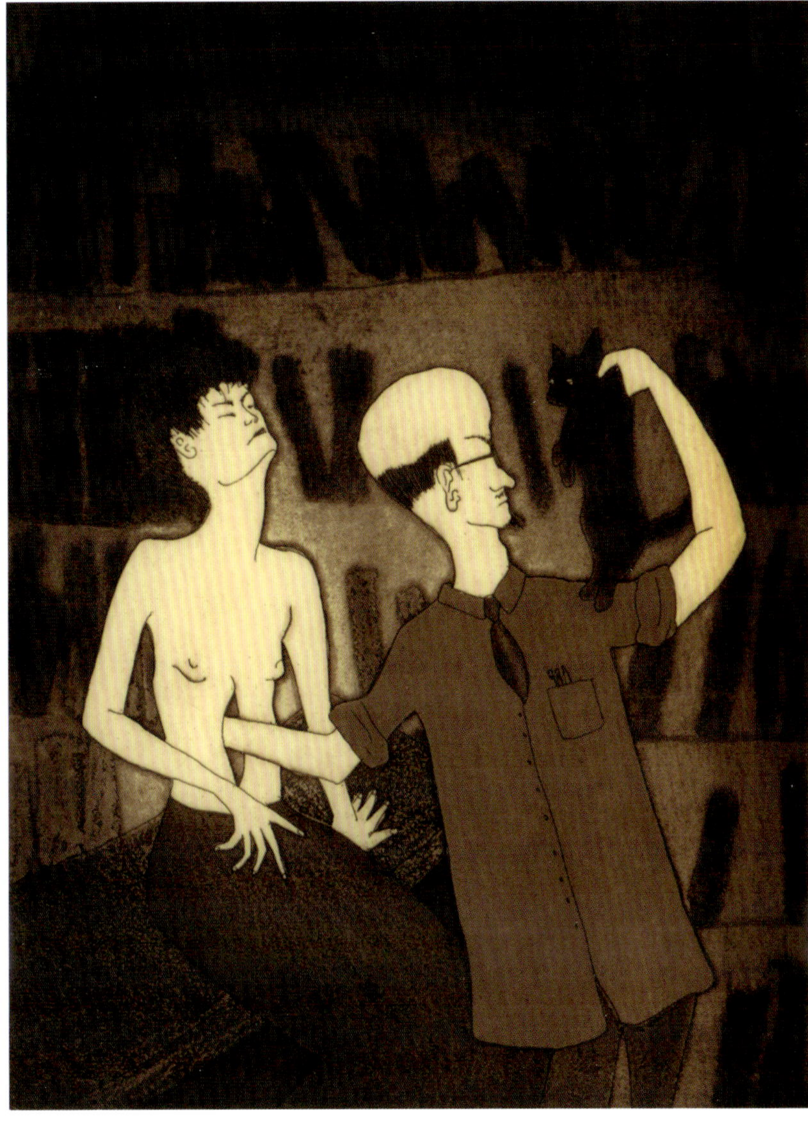

LEFT:
All the books were about Napoleon; Being a moth, she ate them all.,
from *The Adventuress*

RIGHT:
The birth of Maurice, from *The Adventuress*

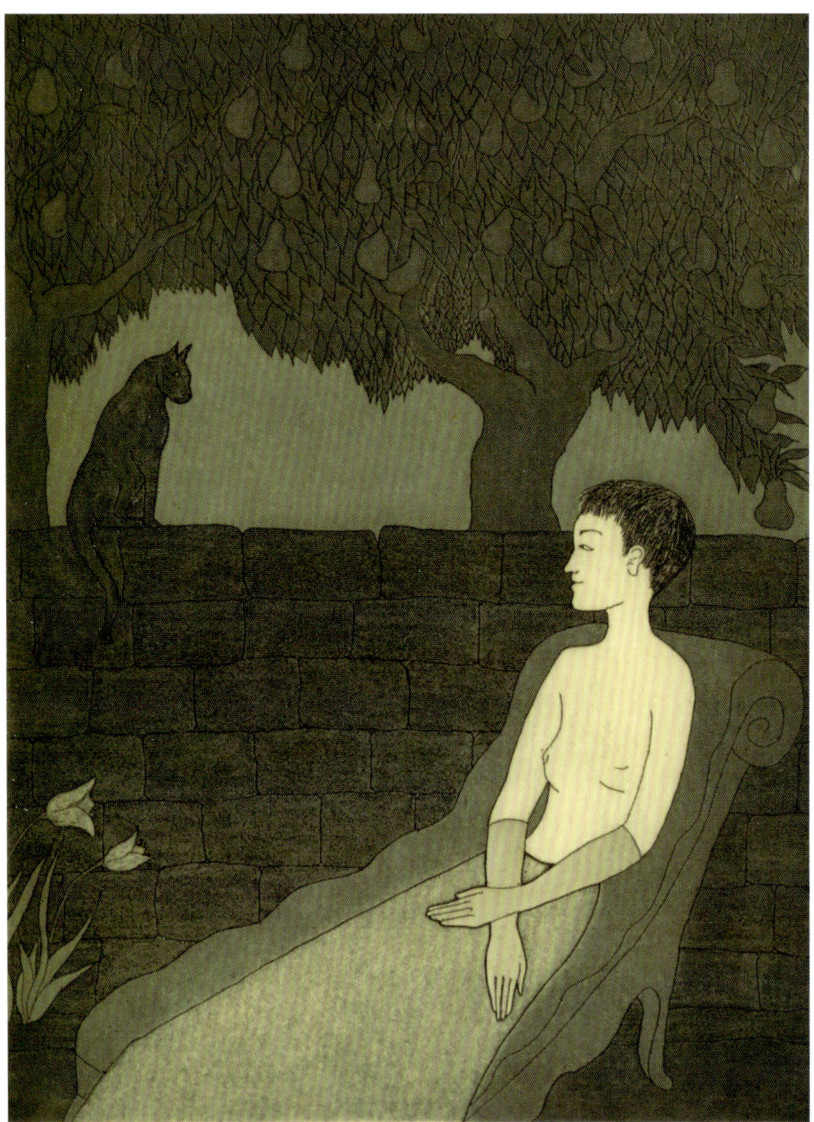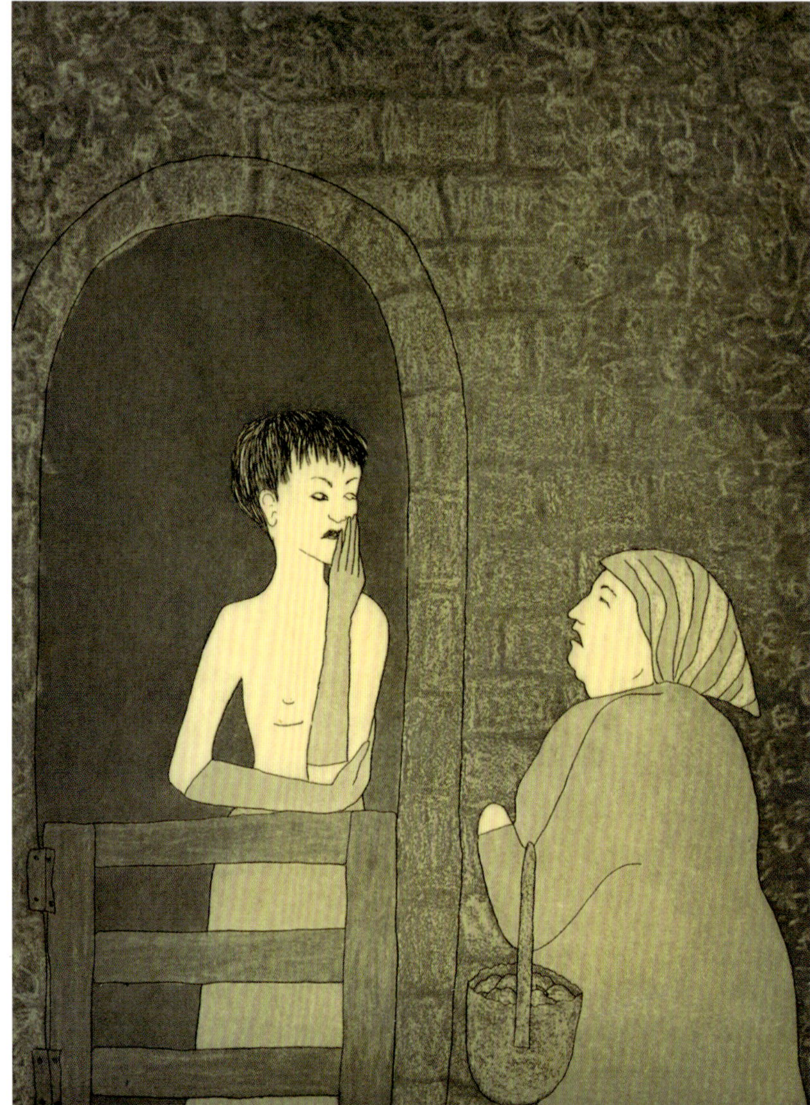

LEFT:
Sometimes, They sat for hours In the garden., from *The Adventuress*

RIGHT:
One day an apple seller came, And in her gossip conveyed that Napoleon was not in Russia at all, But was in the town, with a woman., from *The Adventuress*

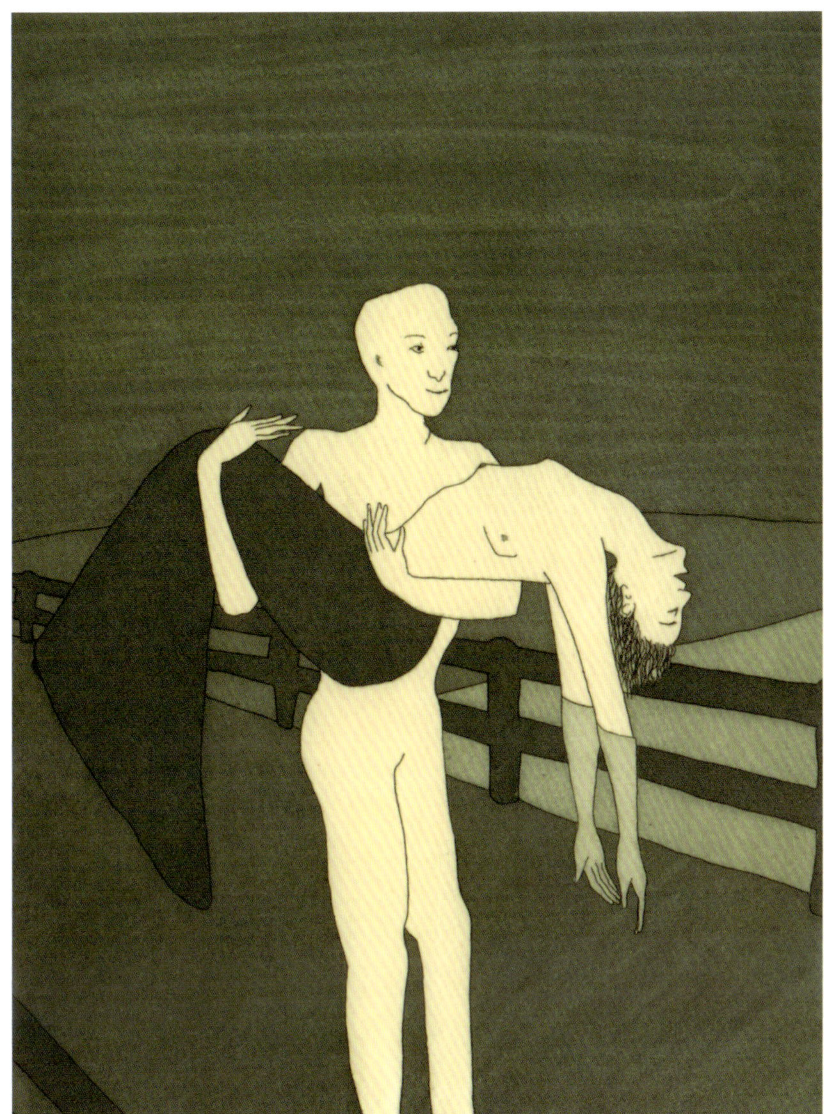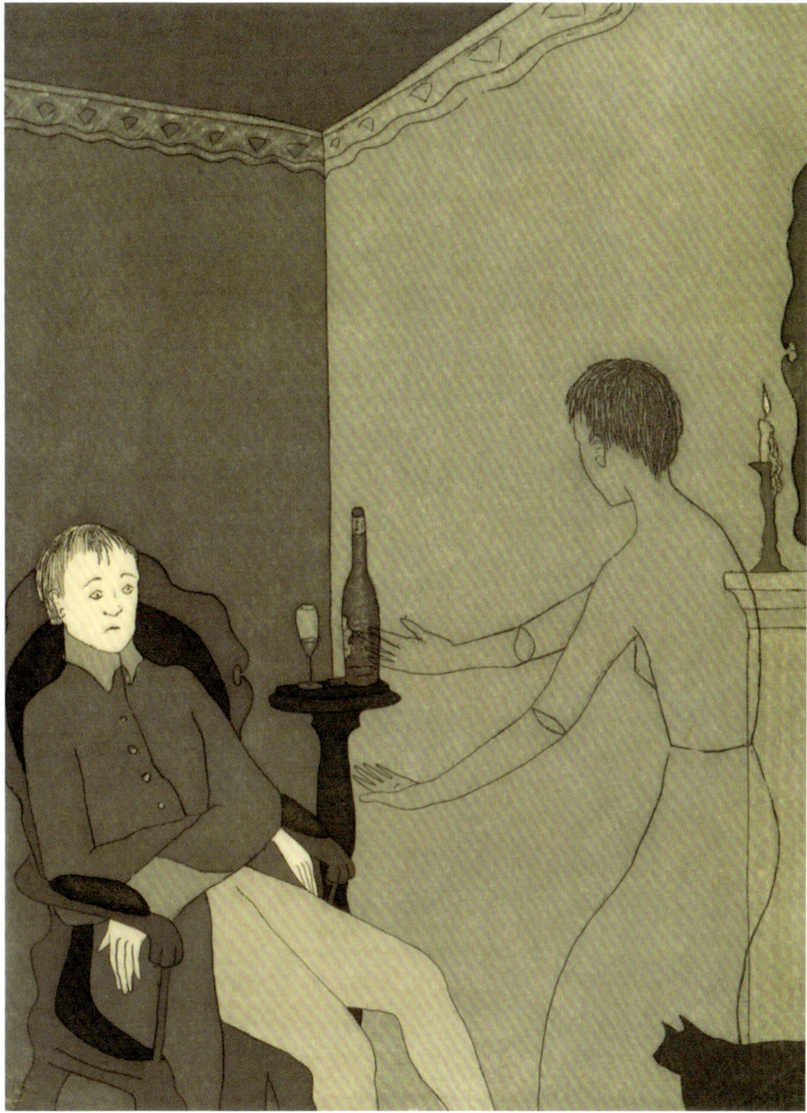

LEFT:
This chameleon, using his own alchemy, Transformed himself and carried her Out of the woods to a nunnery Which stood on a hill., from *The Adventuress*

RIGHT:
Forgiveness, from *The Adventuress*

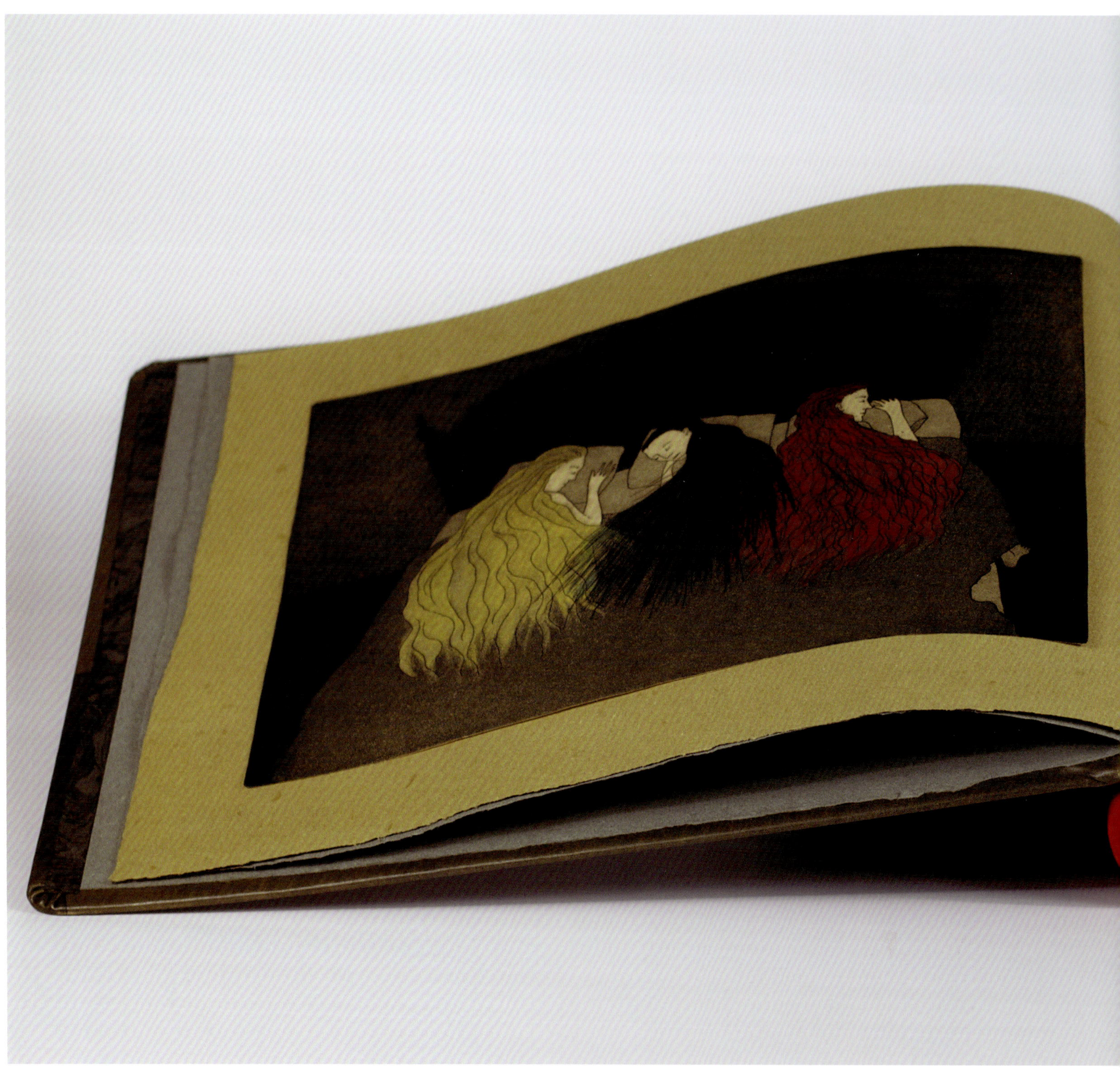

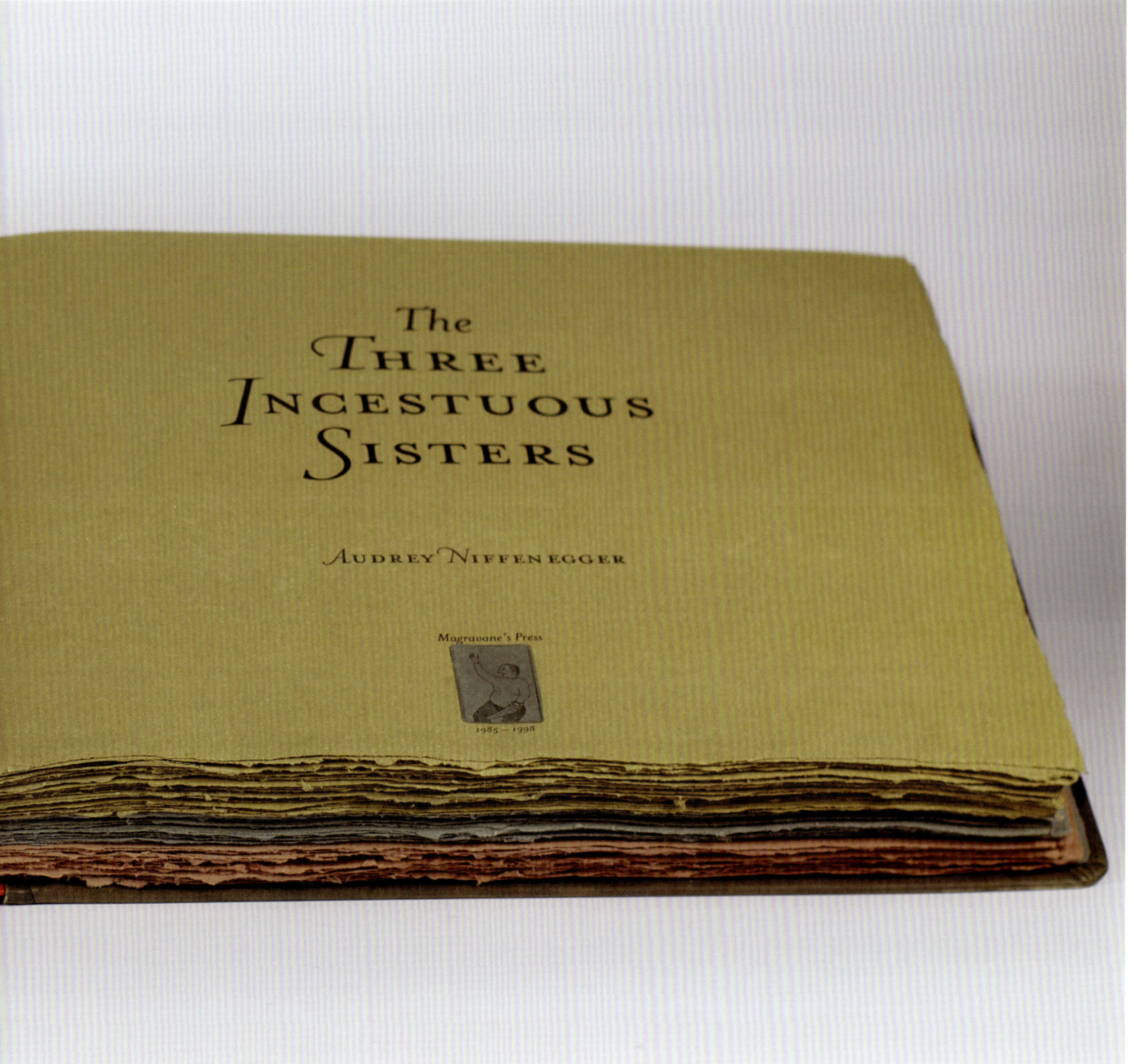

Frontispiece from *The Three Incestuous Sisters*

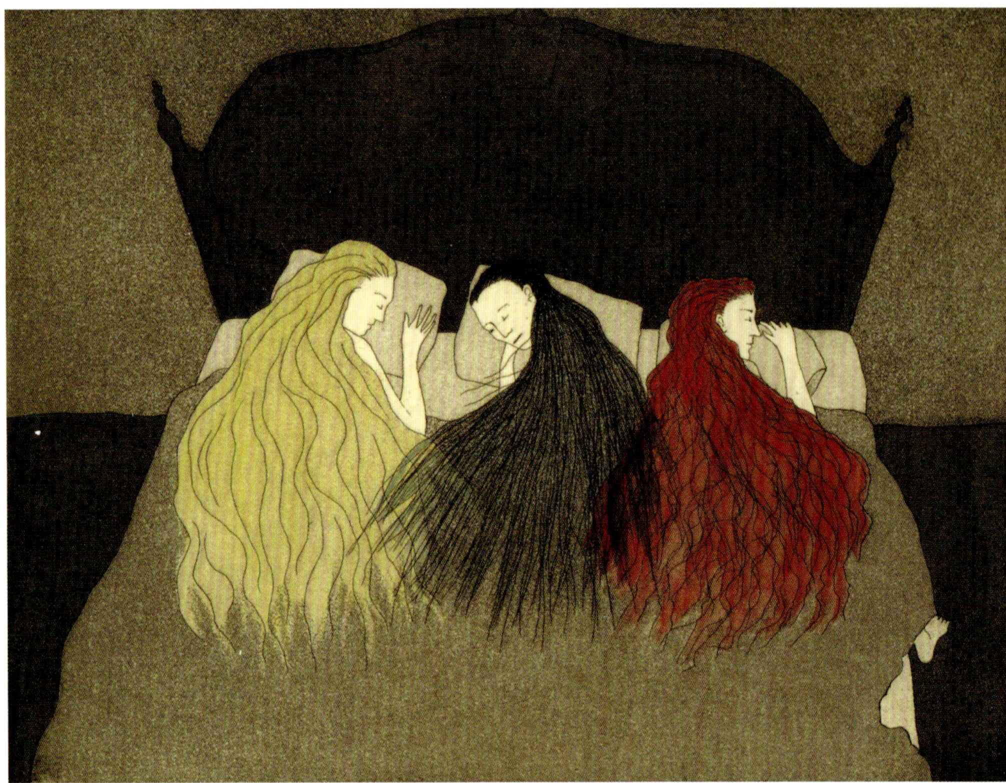

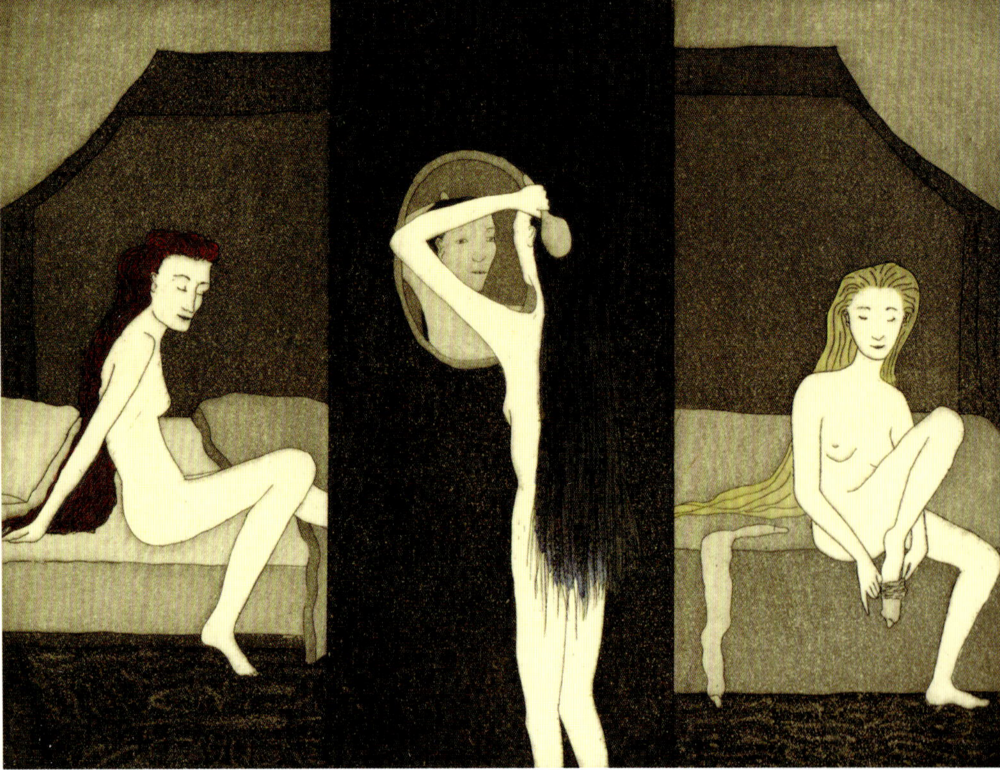

TOP:
Frontispiece from *The Three Incestuous Sisters*

BOTTOM:
Bettine, the youngest, had blond hair and was considered the prettiest sister.
Ophile, the eldest, had blue hair and was often thought to be the smartest sister.
And Clothilde, who had red hair, was in the middle, and was the most talented sister.,
from *The Three Incestuous Sisters*

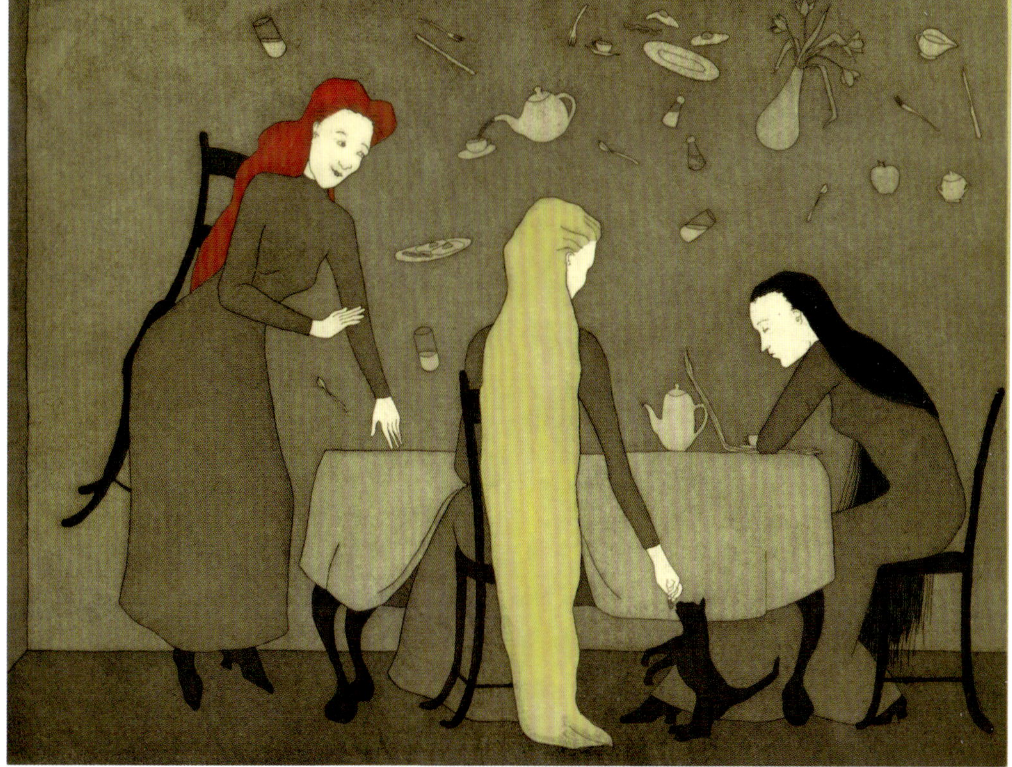

TOP:
Bad luck: Clothilde., from *The Three Incestuous Sisters*

BOTTOM:
A few days later; Clothilde practices levitation at breakfast.,
from *The Three Incestuous Sisters*

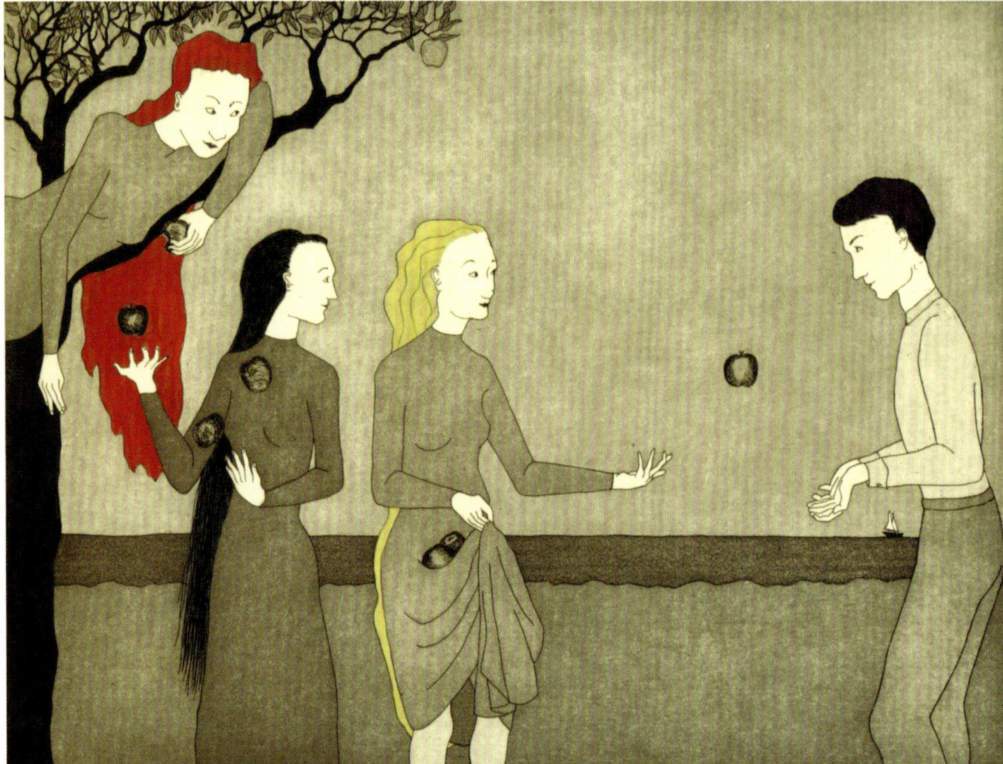

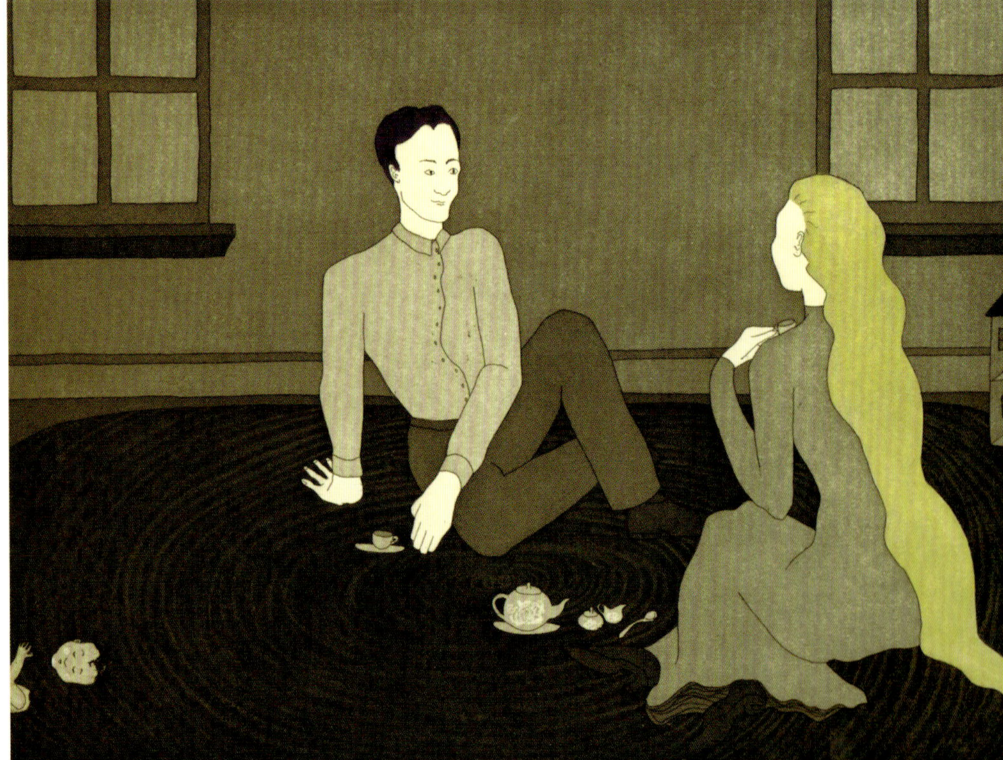

TOP:
Paris's Choice, from *The Three Incestuous Sisters*

BOTTOM:
Tea in the old nursery., from *The Three Incestuous Sisters*

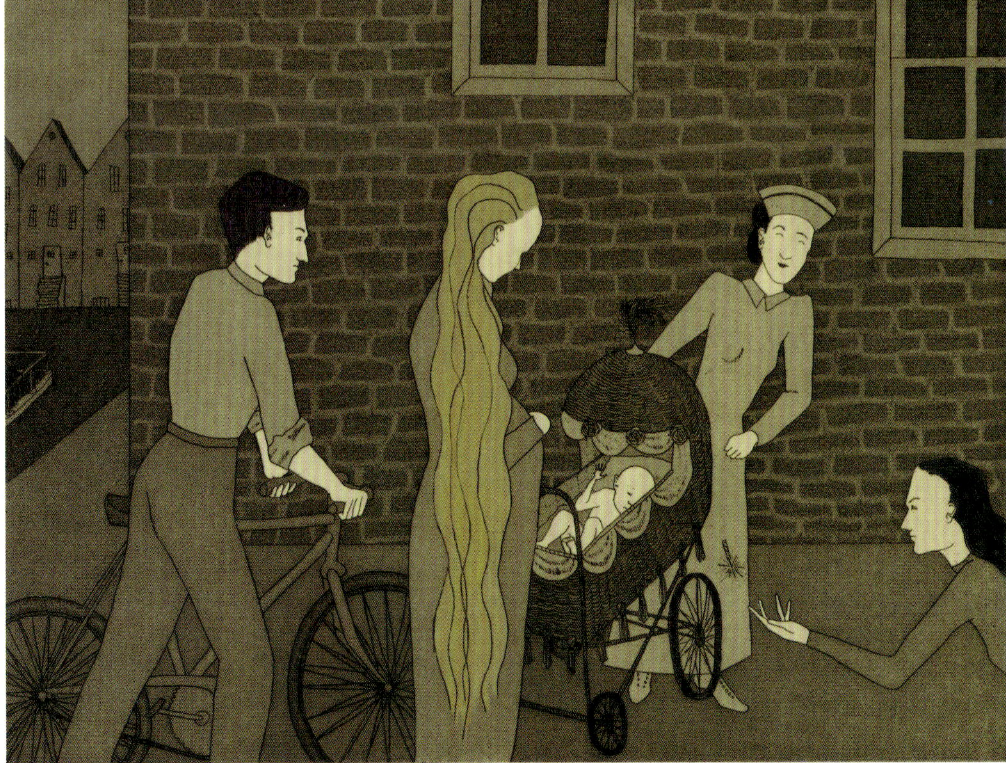

TOP:
Clothilde's headache, from *The Three Incestuous Sisters*

BOTTOM:
Ophile's revenge, from *The Three Incestuous Sisters*

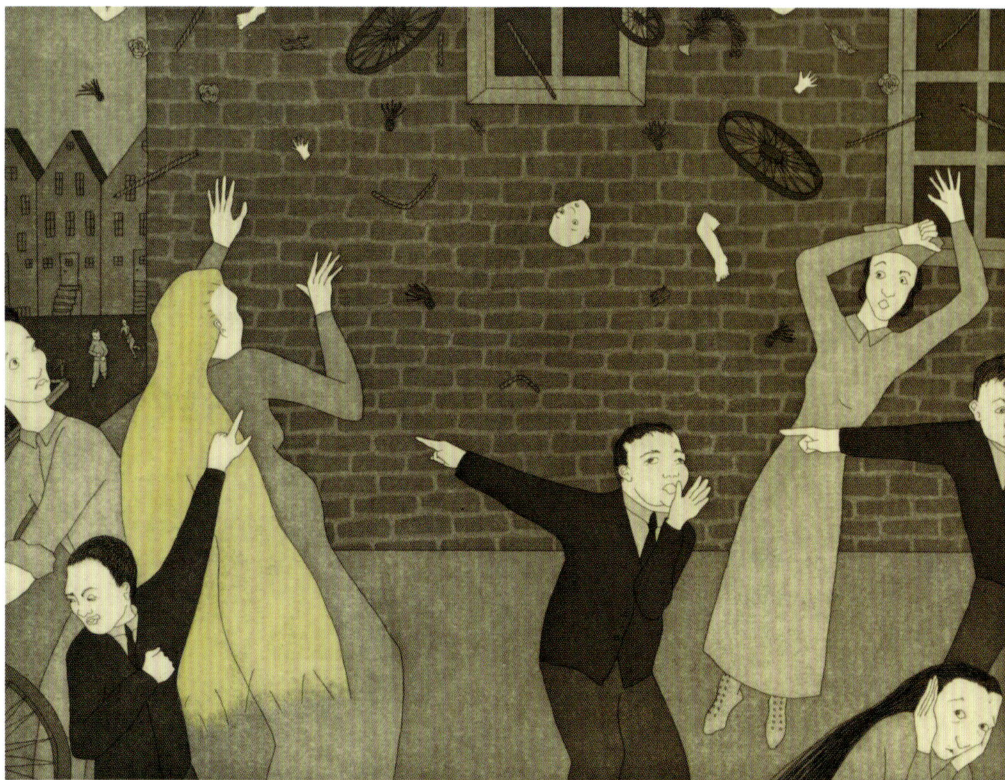

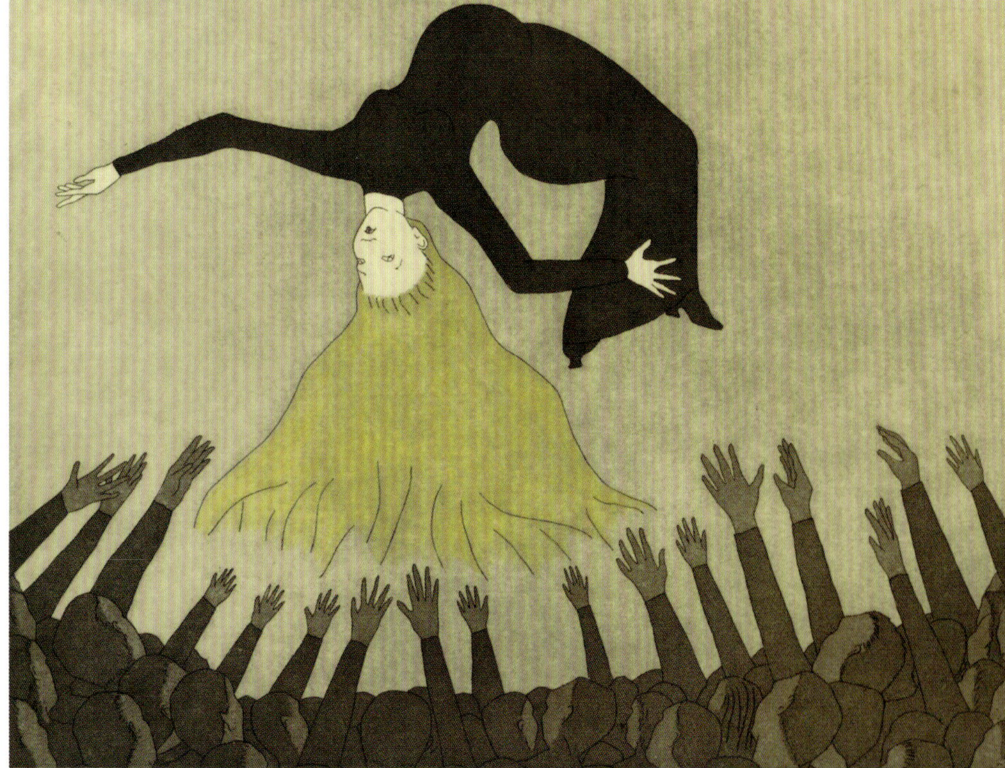

TOP:
A firecracker in a baby carriage!, from *The Three Incestuous Sisters*

BOTTOM:
Mistaken identity., from *The Three Incestuous Sisters*

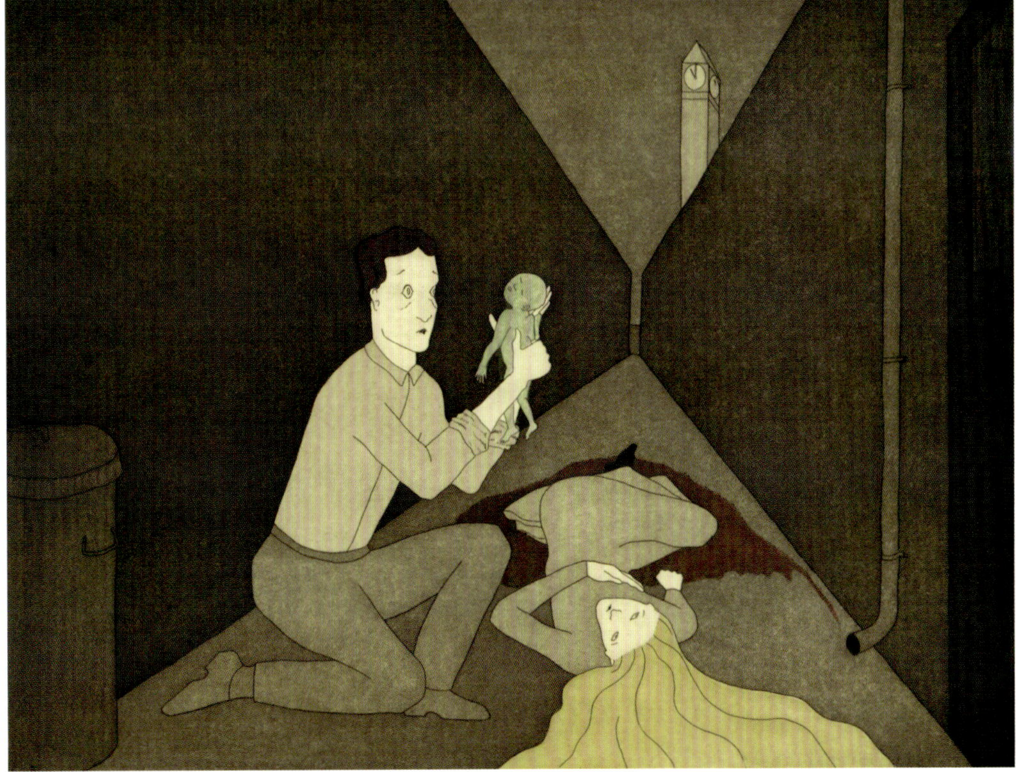

TOP:

Rescued, but too late., from *The Three Incestuous Sisters*

BOTTOM:

The birth of The Saint., from *The Three Incestuous Sisters*

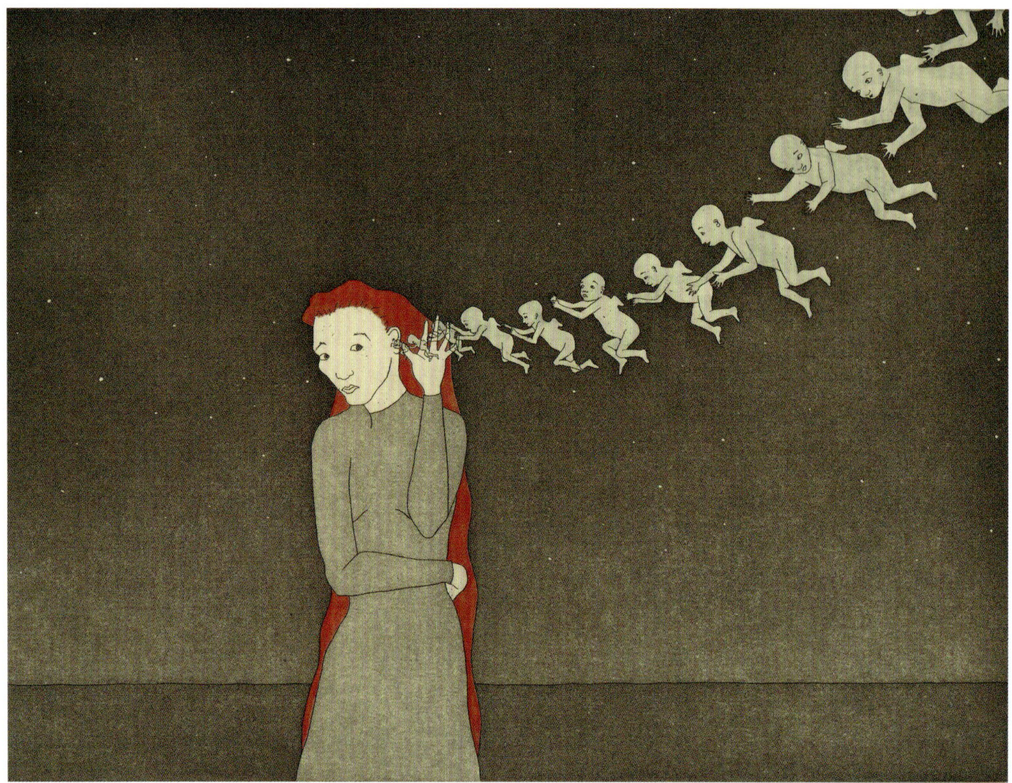

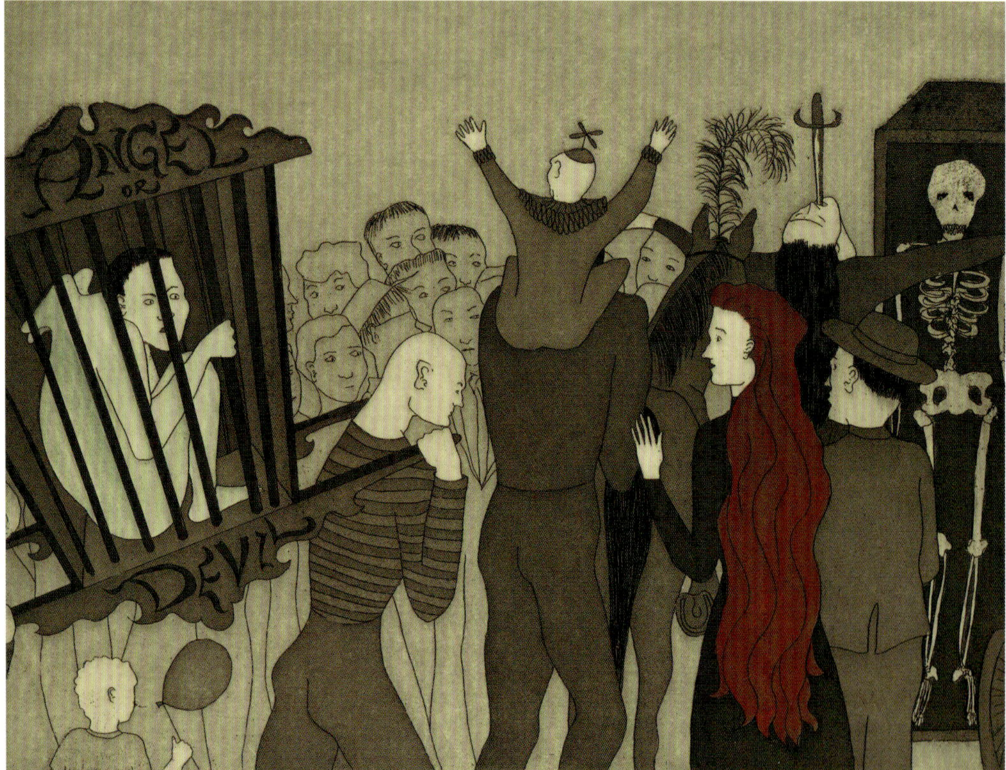

ANGEL
OR
DEVIL

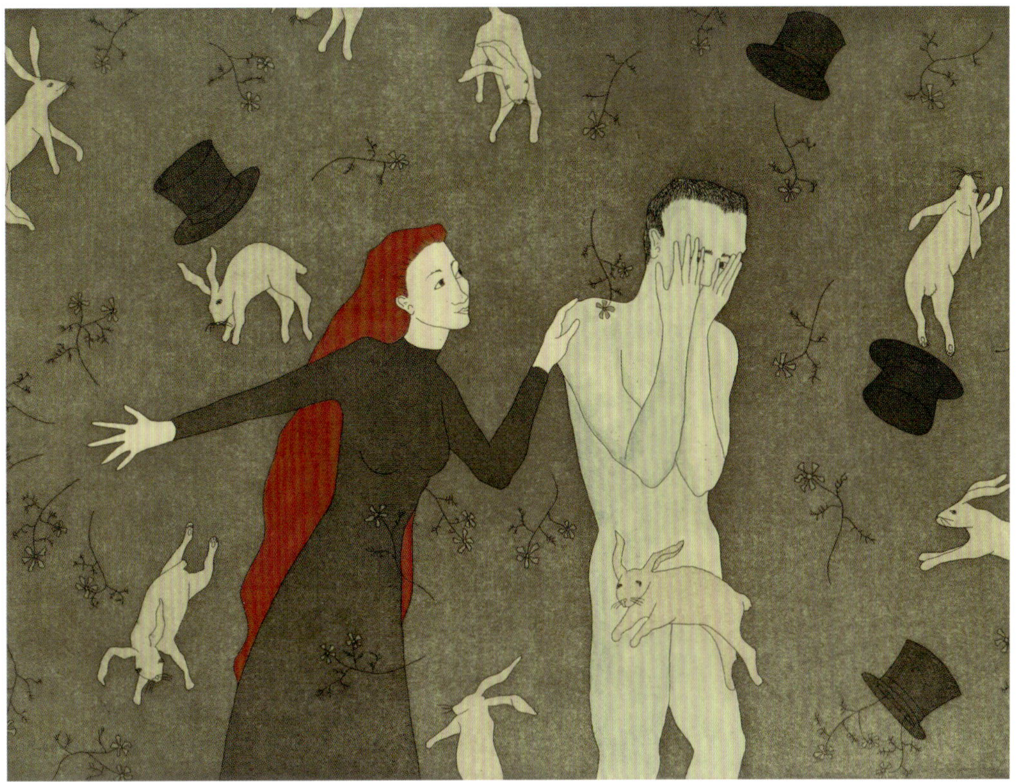

OPPOSITE, TOP:
Suddenly one day, she hears a voice: Here I am, here I am! Not dead at all! Come to the City, Clothilde!, from *The Three Incestuous Sisters*

OPPOSITE, BOTTOM:
A Circus Parade., from *The Three Incestuous Sisters*

TOP:
Don't be sad; look!, from *The Three Incestuous Sisters*

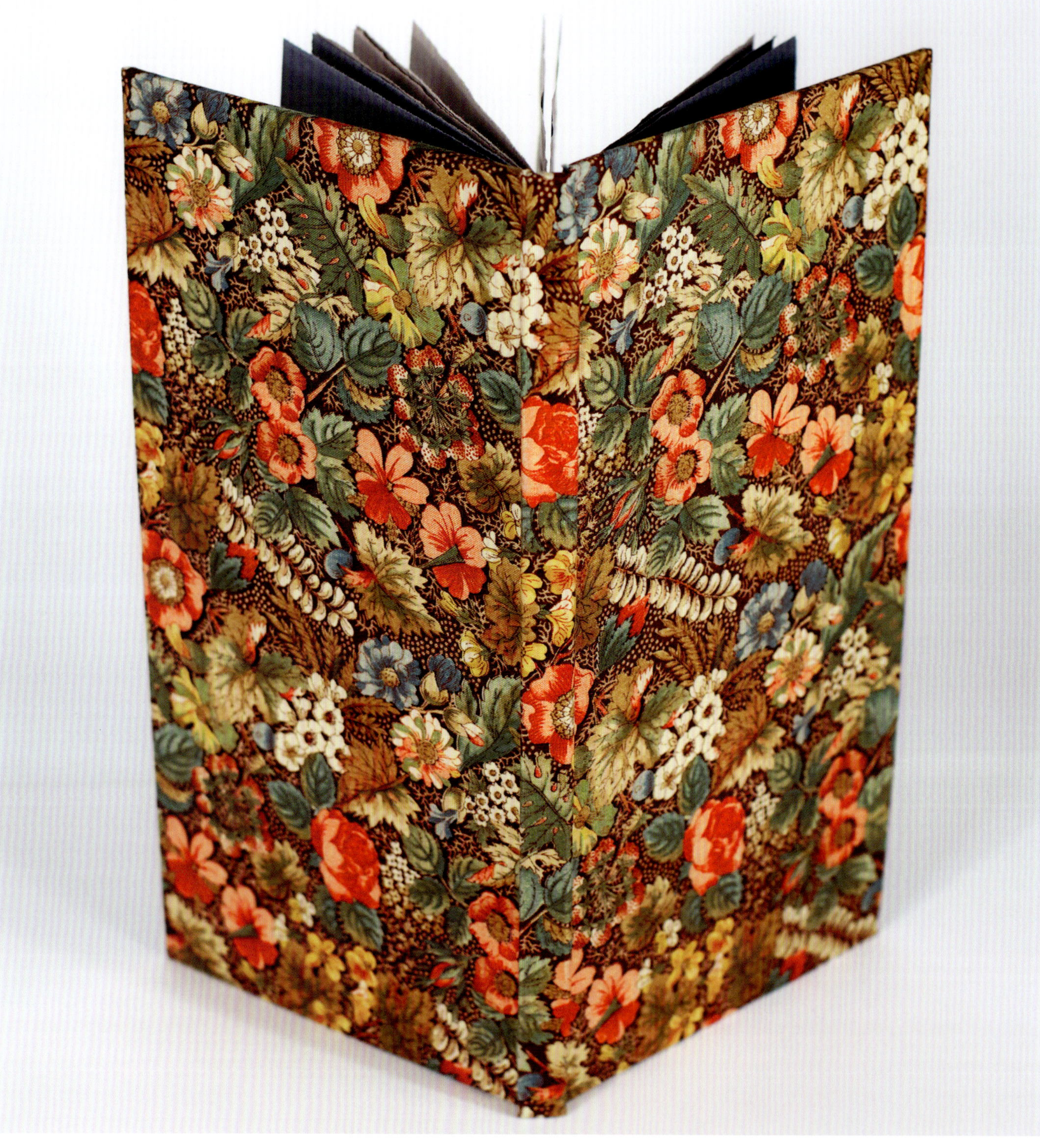

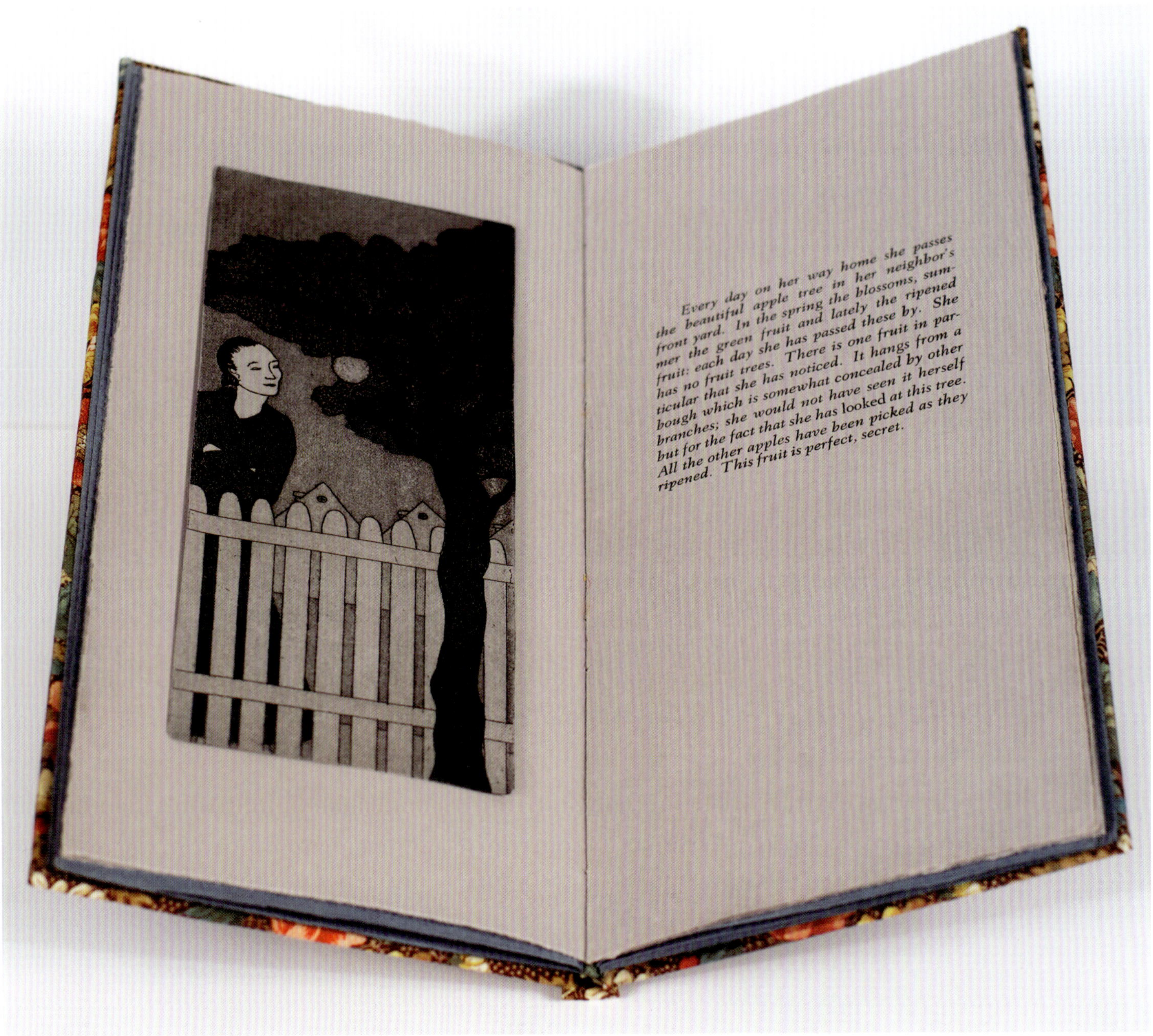

OPPOSITE:
Cover of *The Spinster*

ABOVE:
Every day on her way home she passes the beautiful apple tree in her neighbor's front yard..., from *The Spinster*

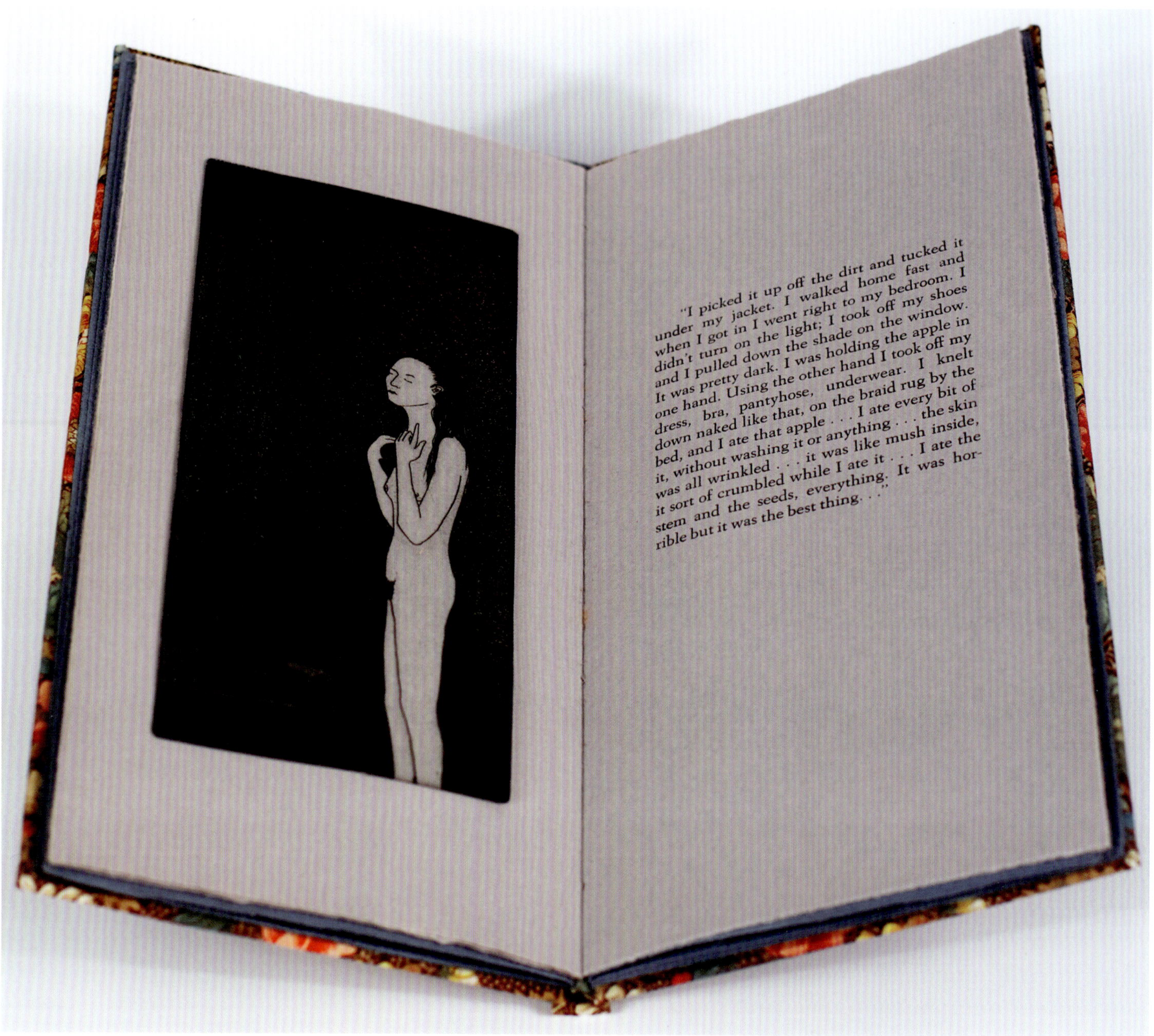

"I picked it up off the dirt and tucked it
under my jacket. I walked home fast and
when I got in I went right to my bedroom. I
didn't turn on the light; I took off my shoes
and I pulled down the shade on the window.
It was pretty dark. I was holding the apple in
one hand. Using the other hand I took off my
dress, bra, pantyhose, underwear. I knelt
down naked like that, on the braid rug by the
bed, and I ate that apple . . . I ate every bit of
it, without washing it or anything . . . the skin
was all wrinkled . . . it was like mush inside,
it sort of crumbled while I ate it . . . I ate the
stem and the seeds, everything. It was horrible but it was the best thing. . . ."

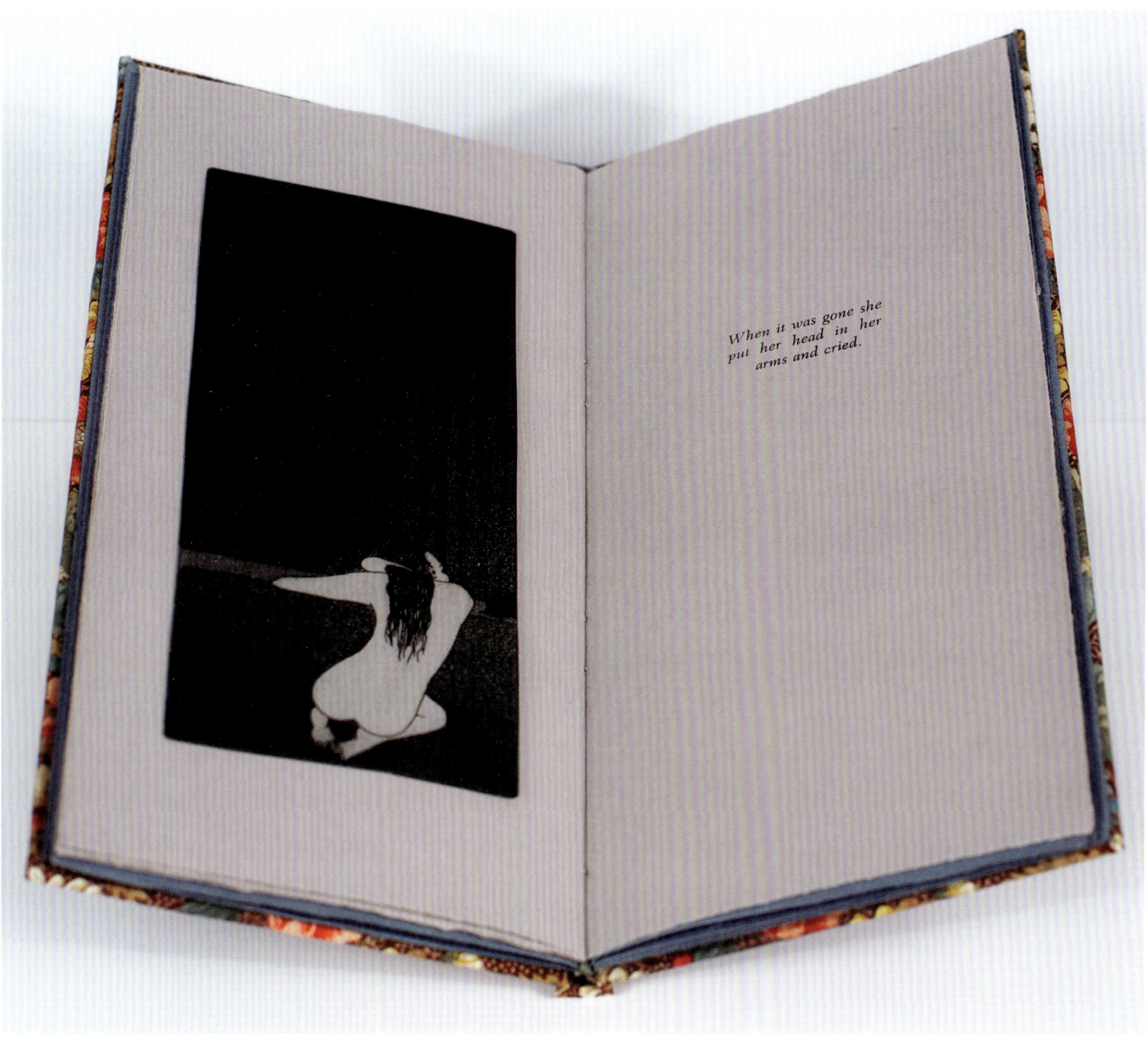

OPPOSITE:
I picked it up off the dirt and tucked it under my jacket..., from *The Spinster*

ABOVE:
When it was gone, she put her head in her arms and cried., from *The Spinster*

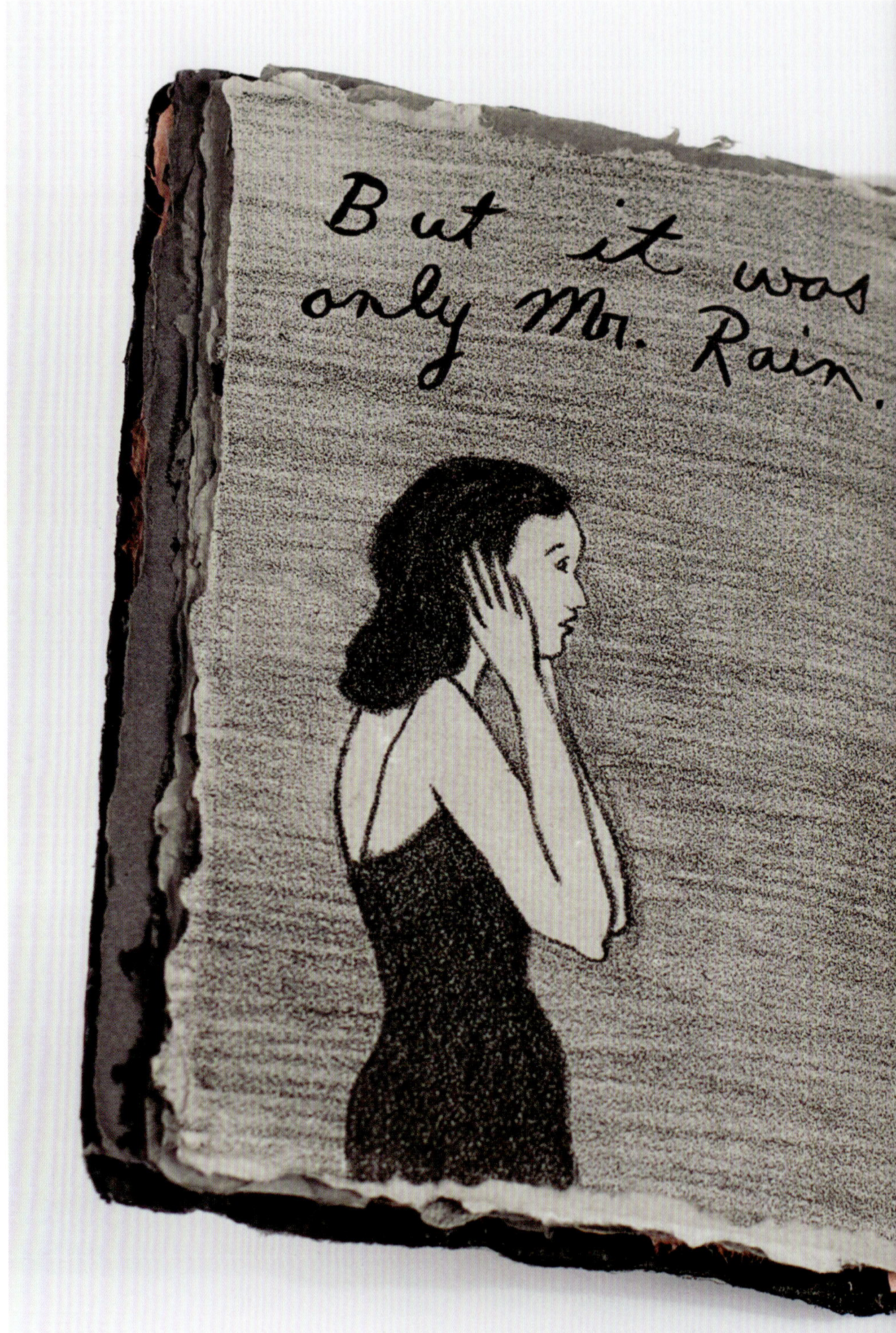
But it was
only Mr. Rain.

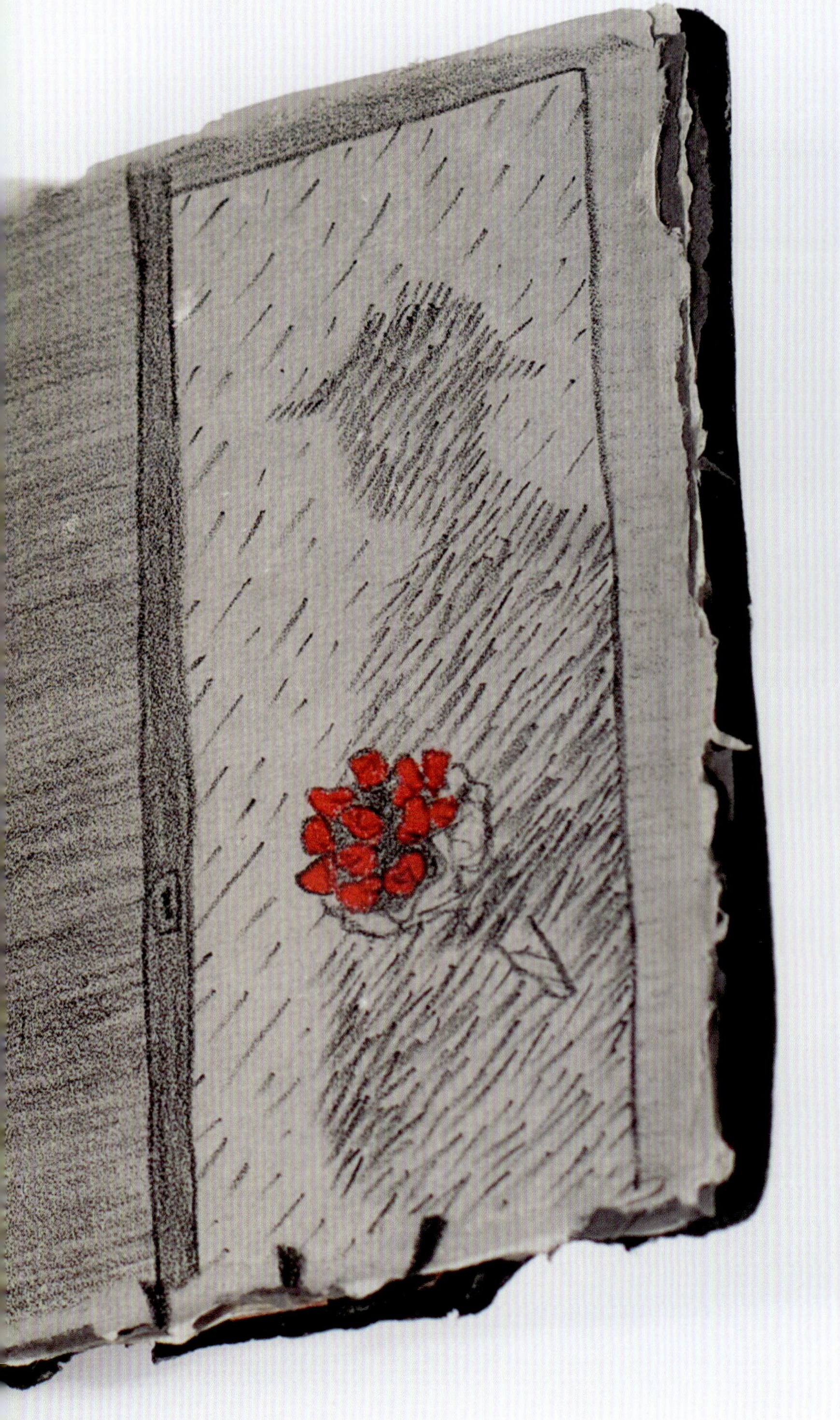

But it was only Mr. Rain., from *Spring*

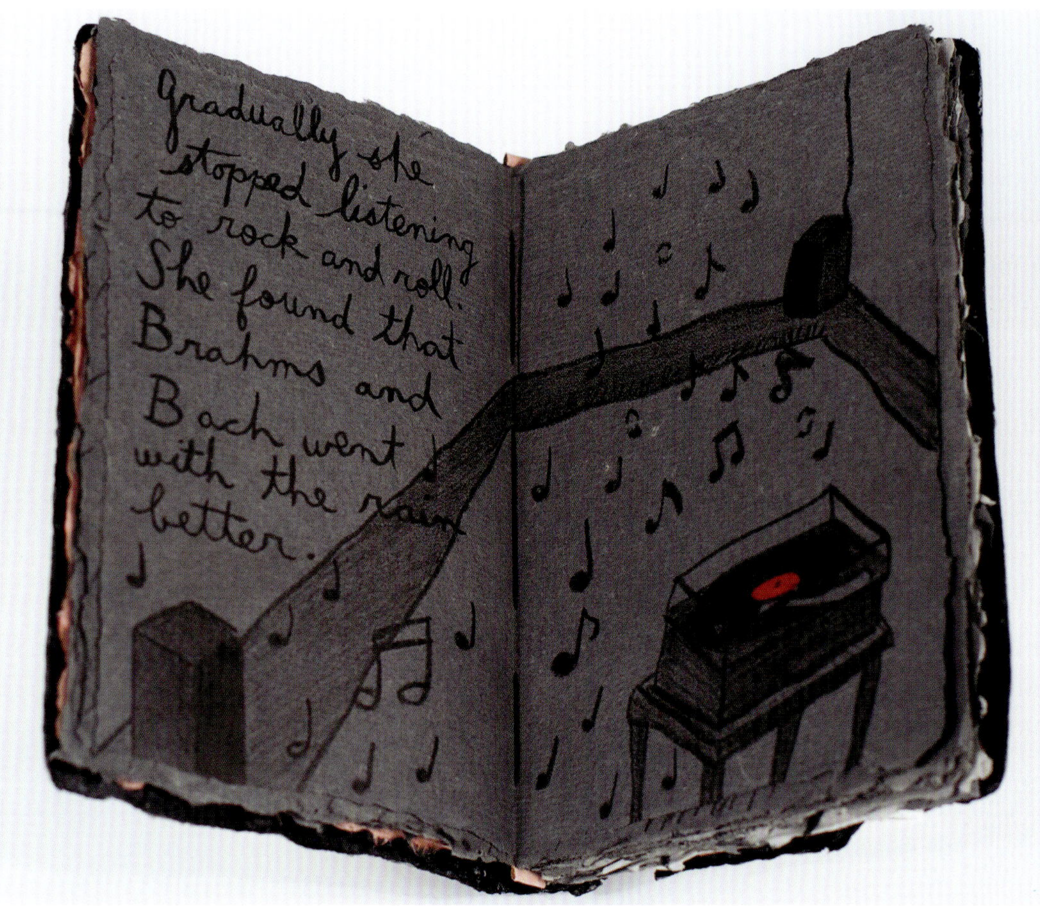
Gradually she
stopped listening
to rock and roll.
She found that
Brahms and
Bach went
with the rain
better.

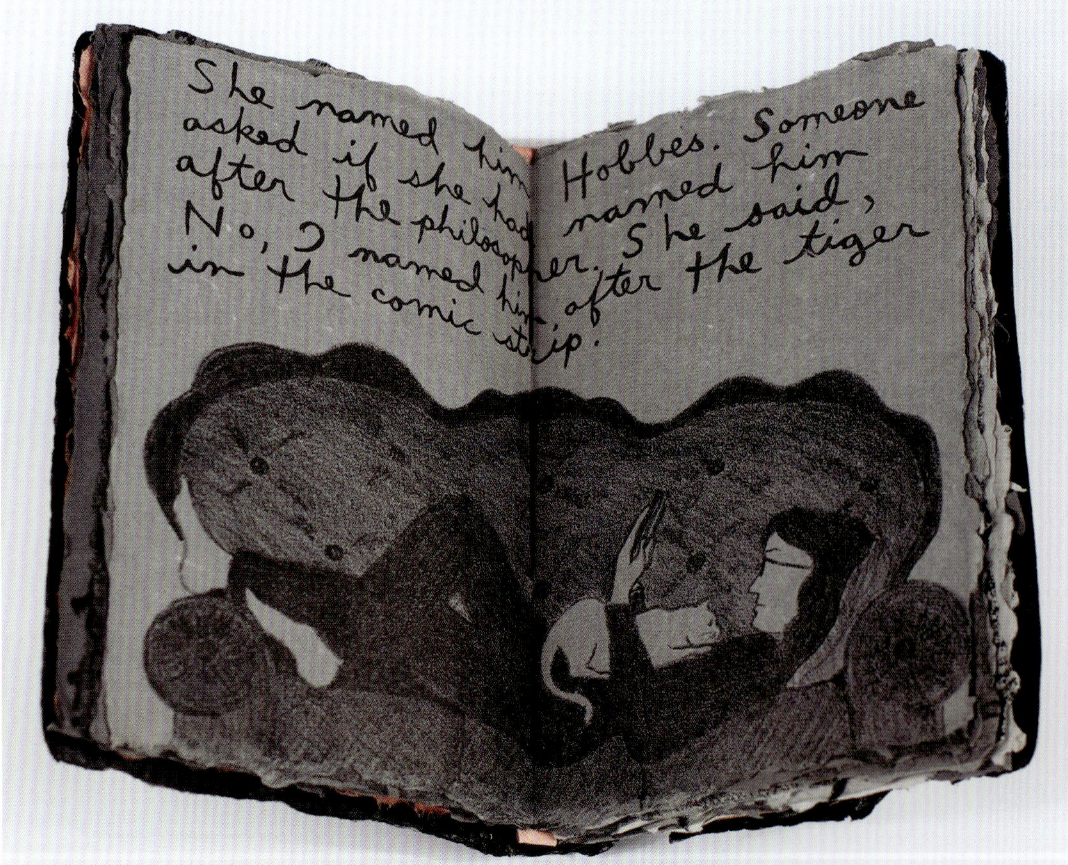
She named him Hobbes. Someone
asked if she had named him
after the philosopher. She said,
No, I named him after the tiger
in the comic strip.

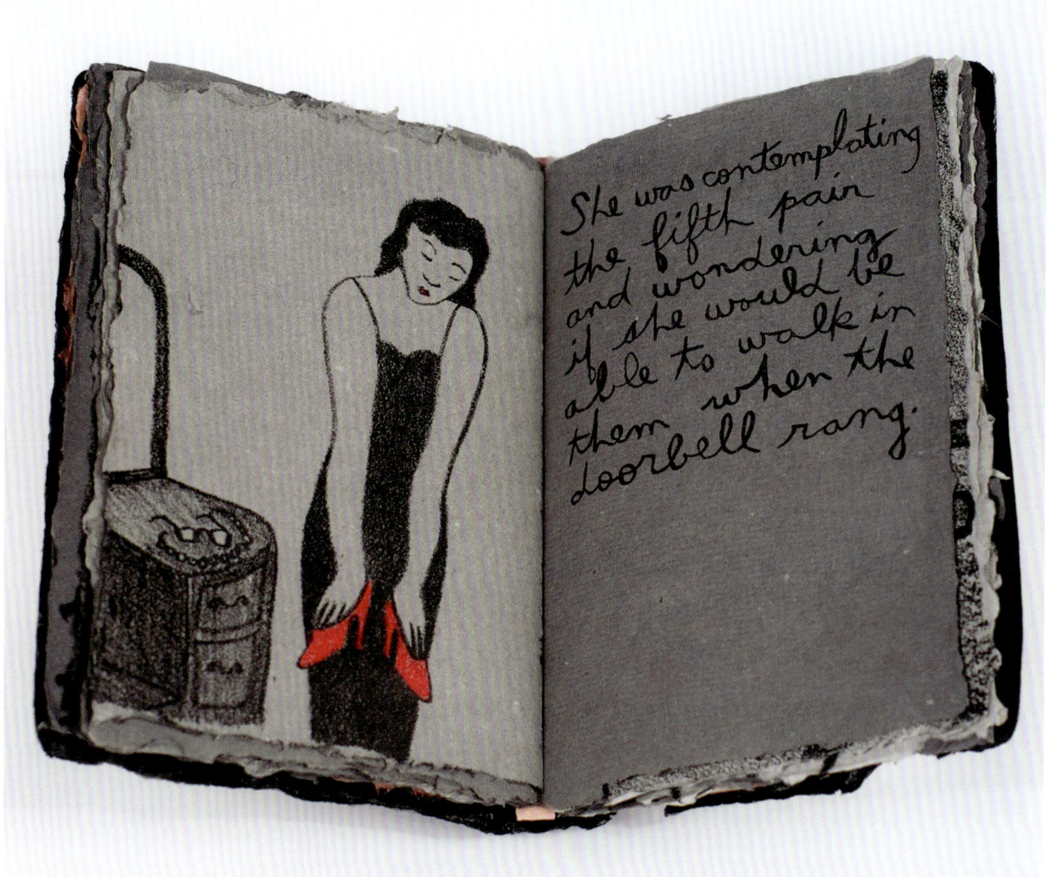

OPPOSITE, TOP:
Gradually she stopped listening to rock and roll. She found that Brahms and Bach went with the rain better., from *Spring*

OPPOSITE, BOTTOM:
She named him Hobbes. Someone asked if she had named him after the philosopher. She said, No, I named him after the tiger in the comic strip., from *Spring*

ABOVE:
She was contemplating the fifth pair and wondering if she would be able to walk in them when the doorbell rang., from *Spring*

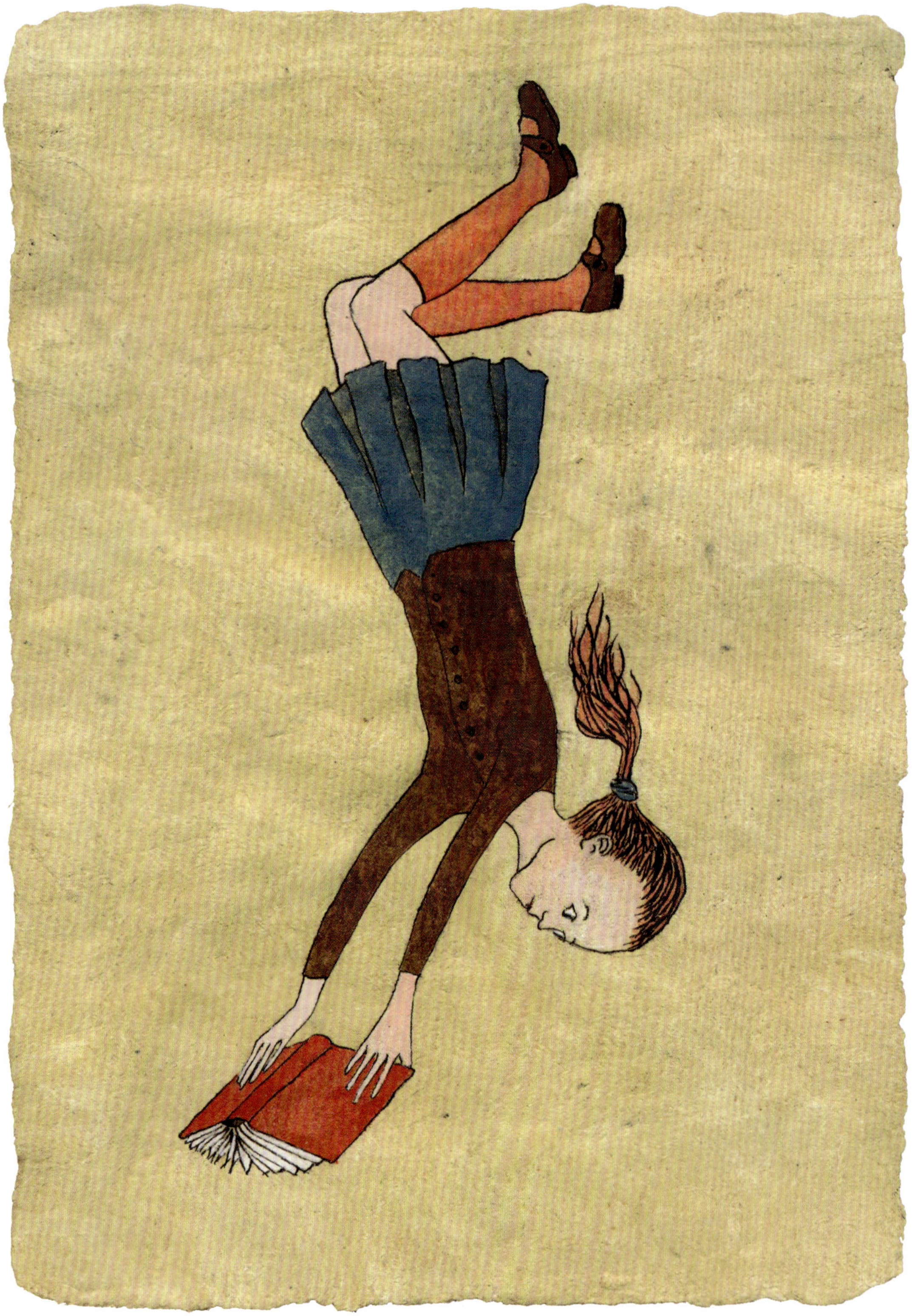

Falling, 2004
Ink and gouache on handmade paper
8 x 5 1/2 in.
Collection of Mary Jean Thomson, Riverwoods, Illinois

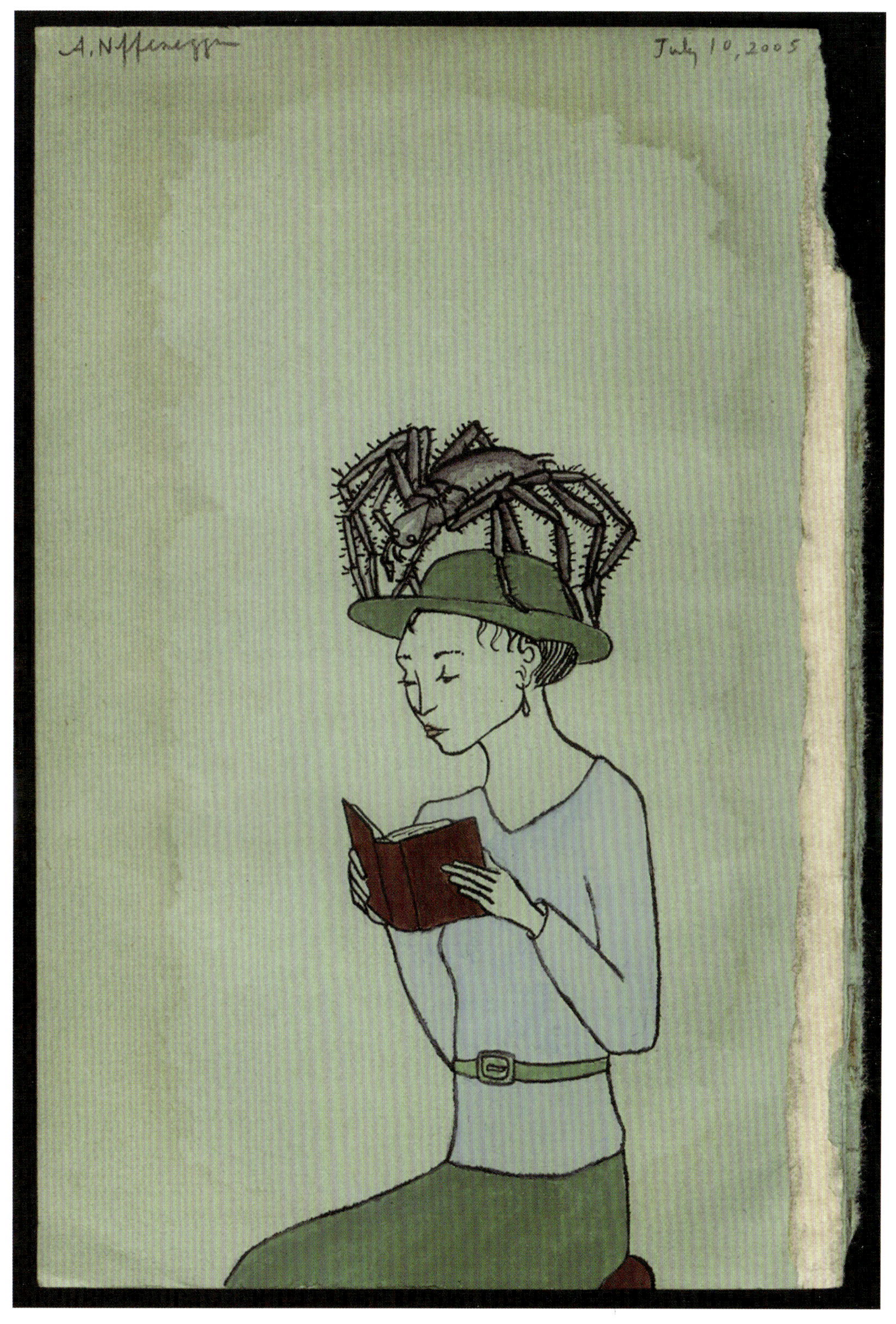

Reader, Spider, 2005
Ink and gouache on found paper
6 3/4 x 4 1/2 in.
Collection of Larry and Laura Gerber, Highland Park, Illinois

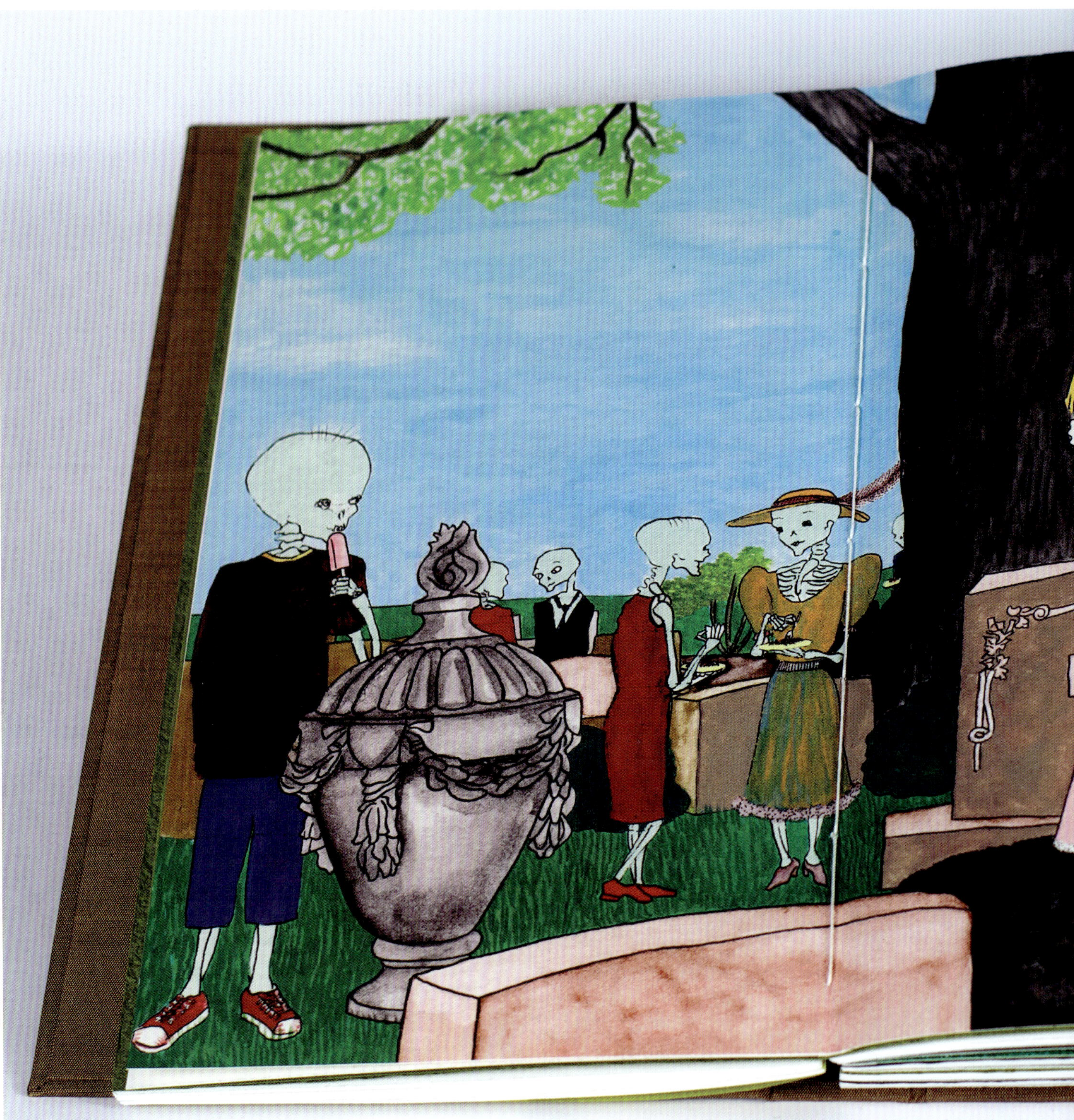

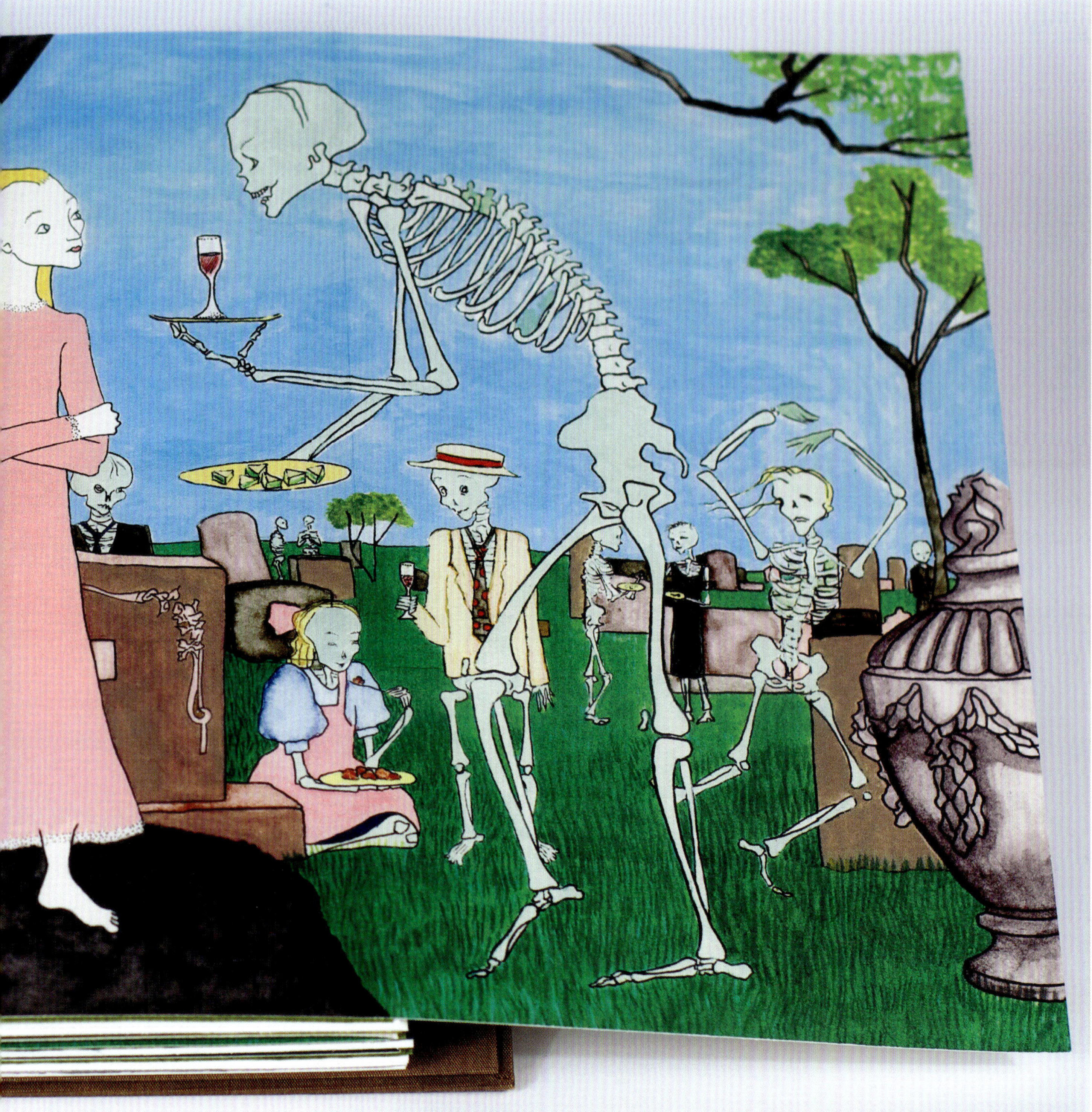

Ides of Spring Party, from *Poisonous Plants at Table and Prudence: The Cautionary Tale of a Picky Eater*

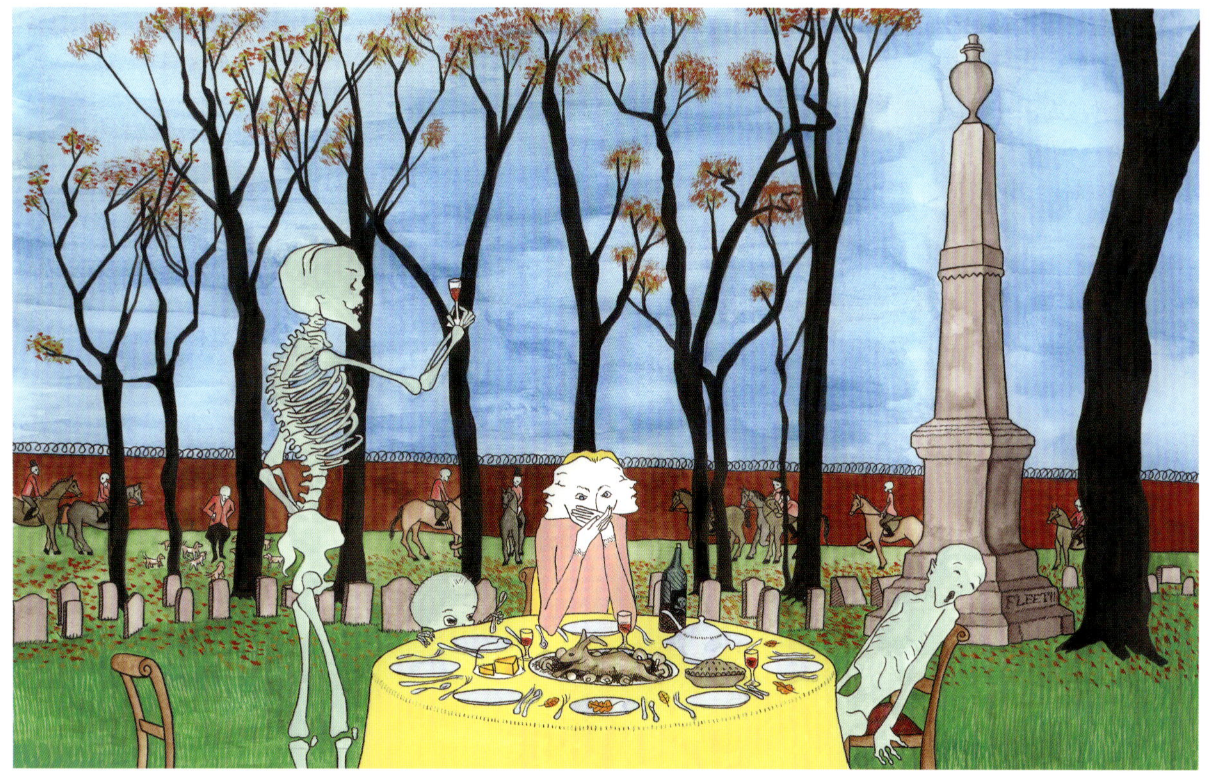

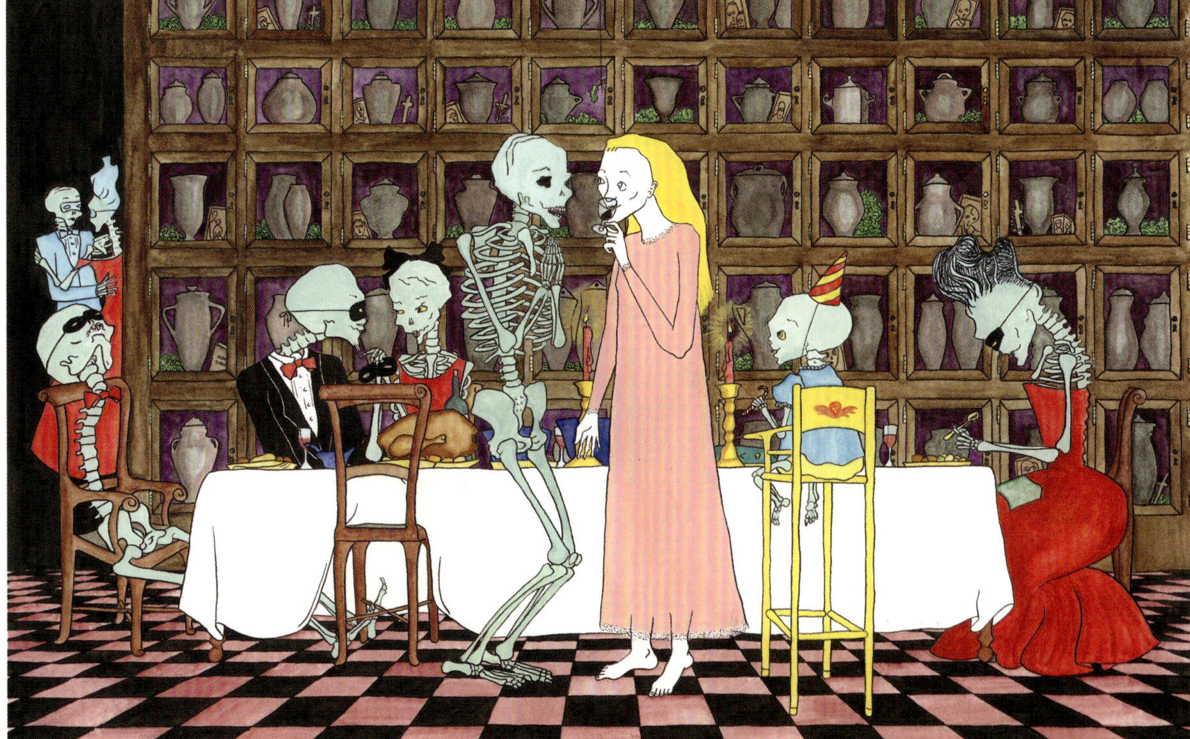

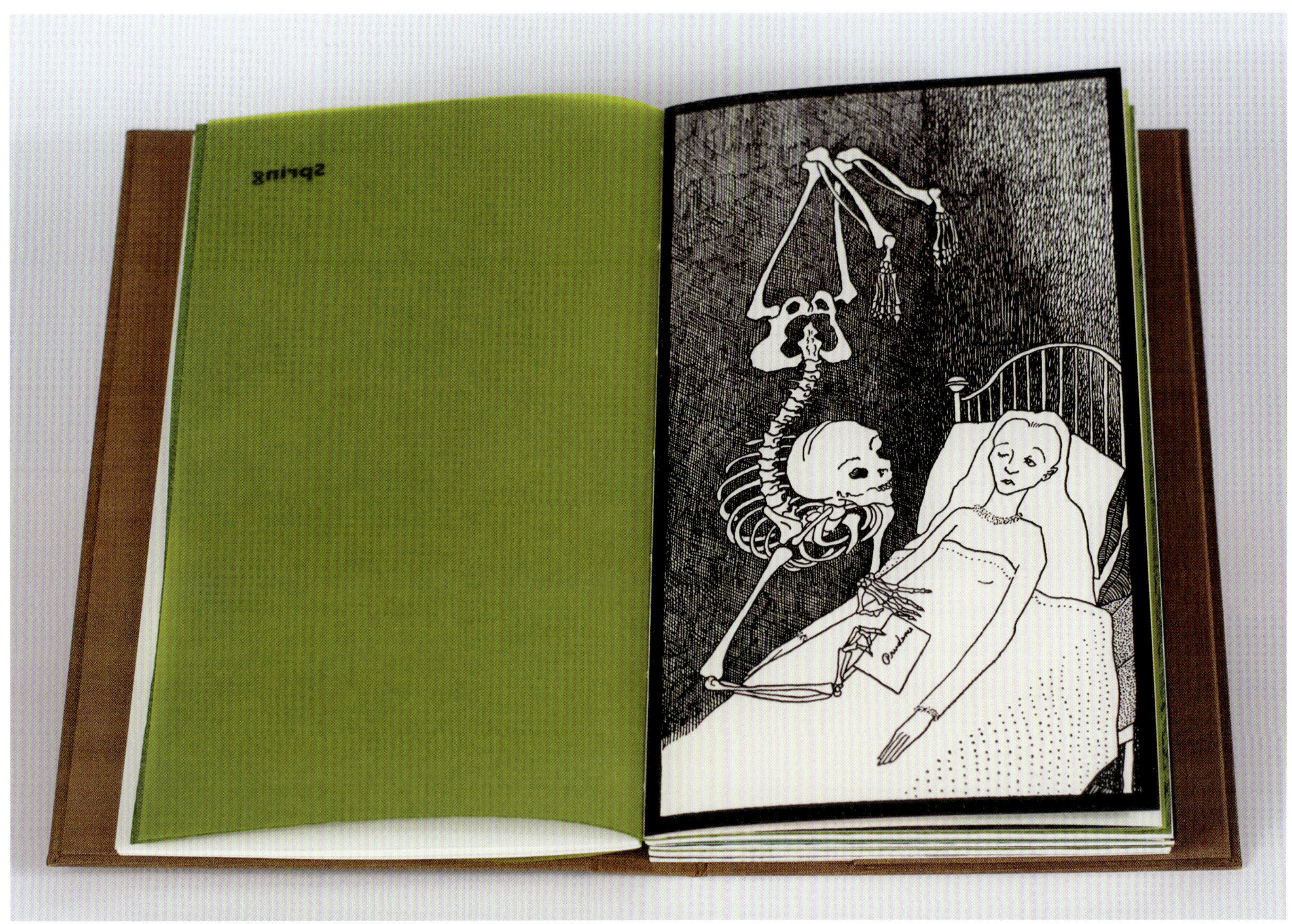

OPPOSITE, TOP:
Autumn Hunt Luncheon, from *Poisonous Plants at Table and Prudence:
The Cautionary Tale of a Picky Eater*

OPPOSITE, BOTTOM:
Twelfth Night Costume Ball, from *Poisonous Plants at Table and Prudence:
The Cautionary Tale of a Picky Eater*

ABOVE:
Spring, from *Poisonous Plants at Table and Prudence:
The Cautionary Tale of a Picky Eater*

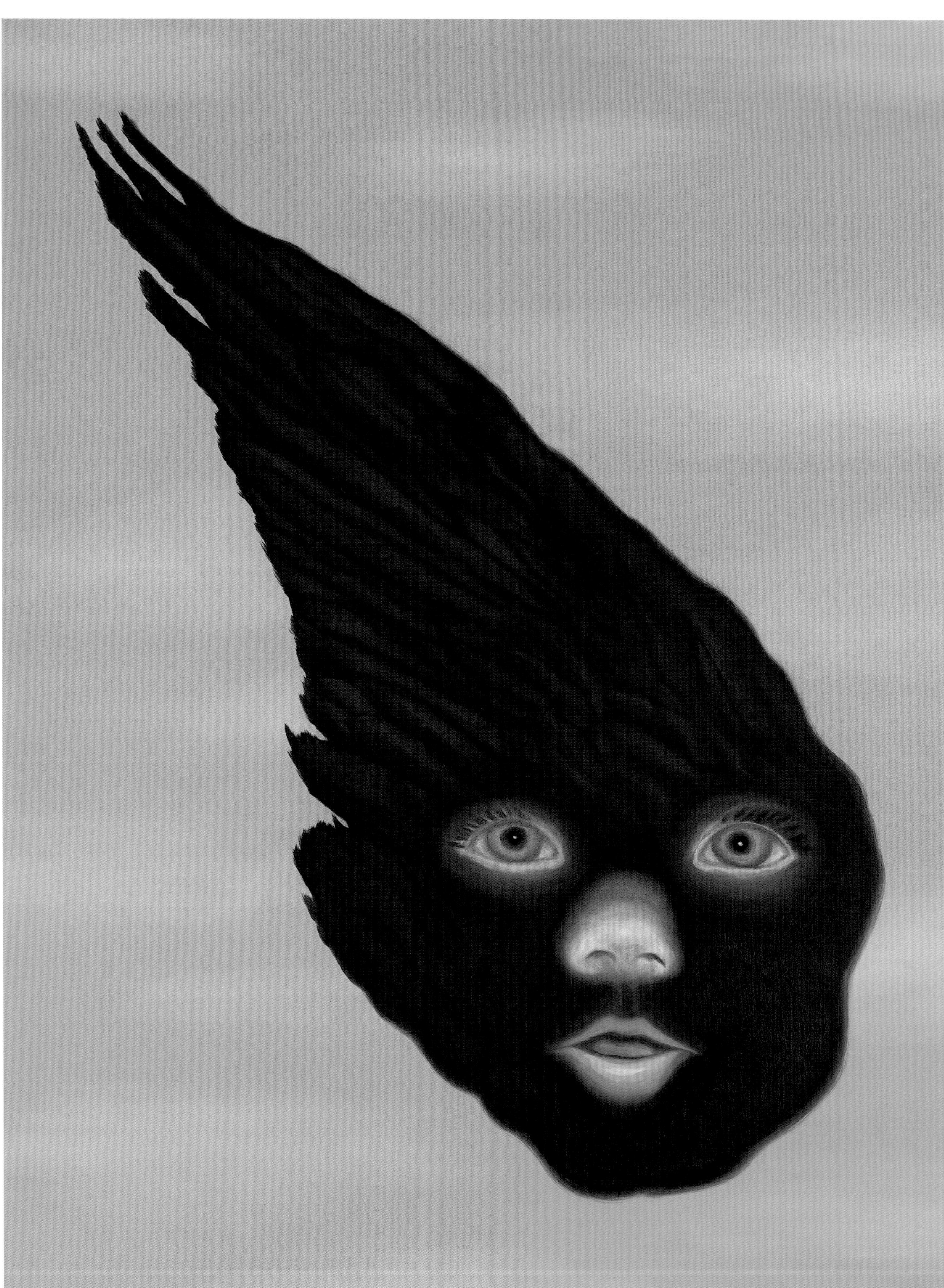

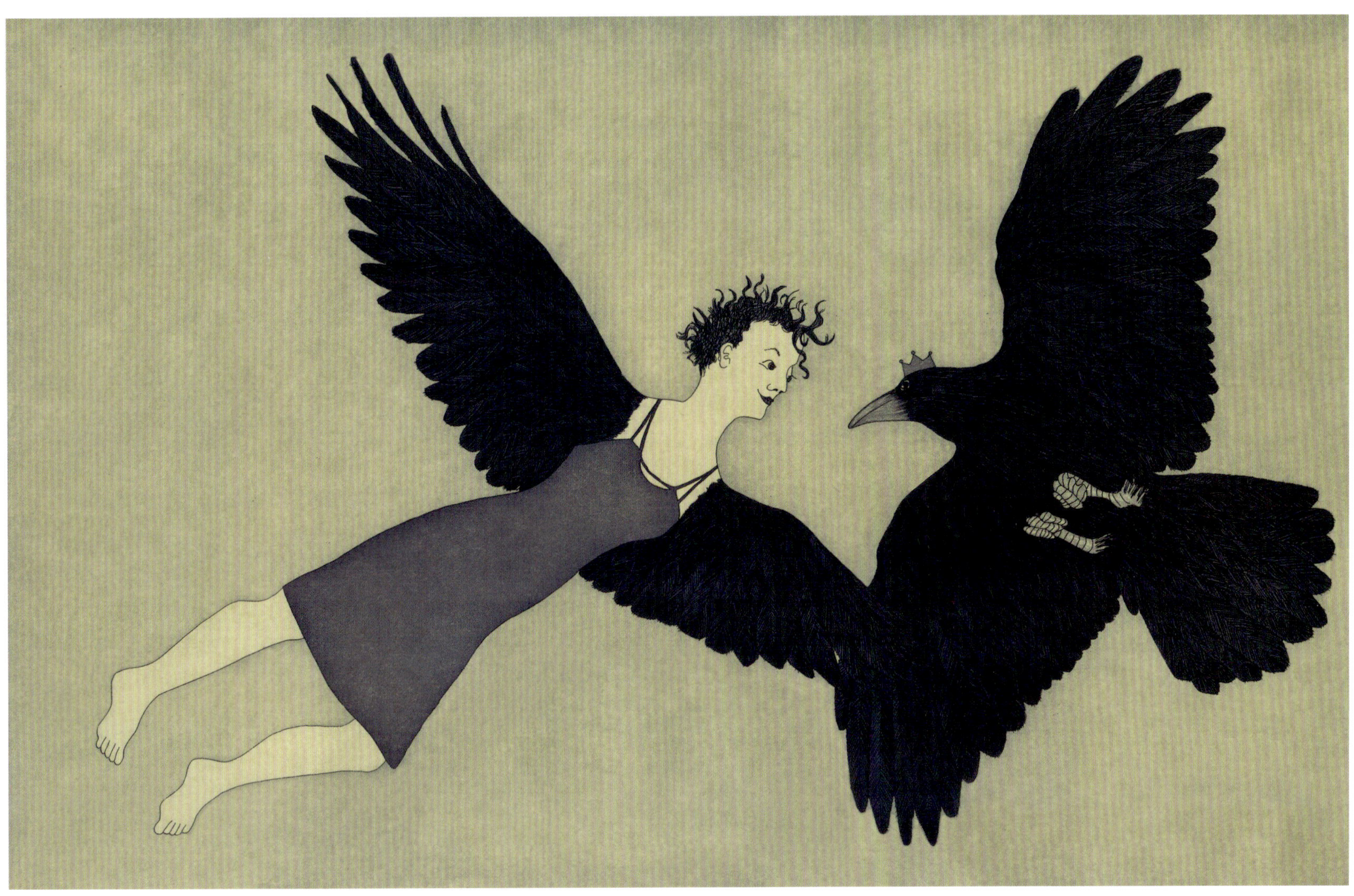

OPPOSITE:
Raven Girl, 2012
Oil on wooden panel
23 3/4 x 17 3/4 in.
Collection of Audrey Niffenegger, Chicago, Illinois

ABOVE:
And They Lived Happily Together Ever After,
from *Raven Girl*

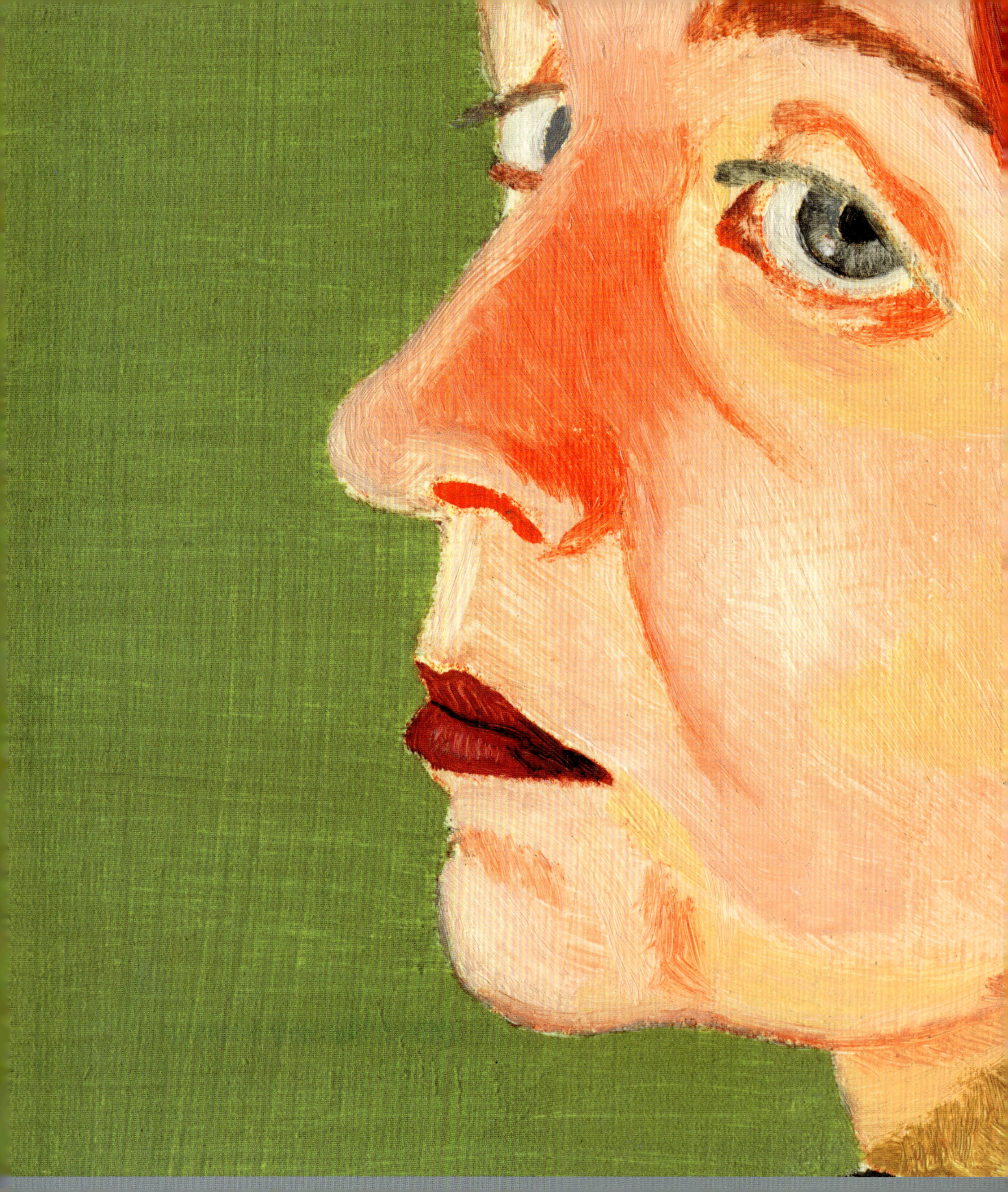

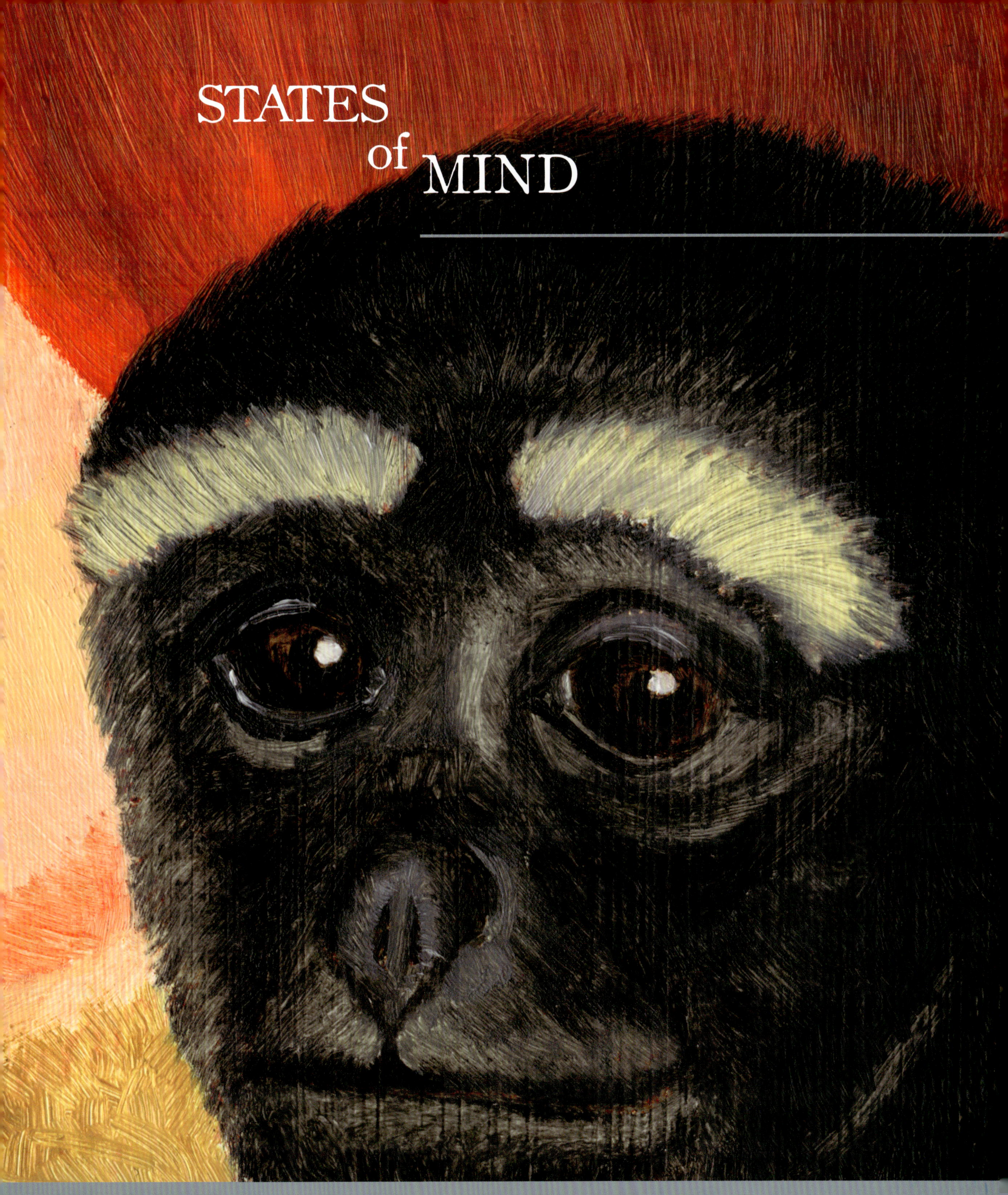
STATES
of
MIND

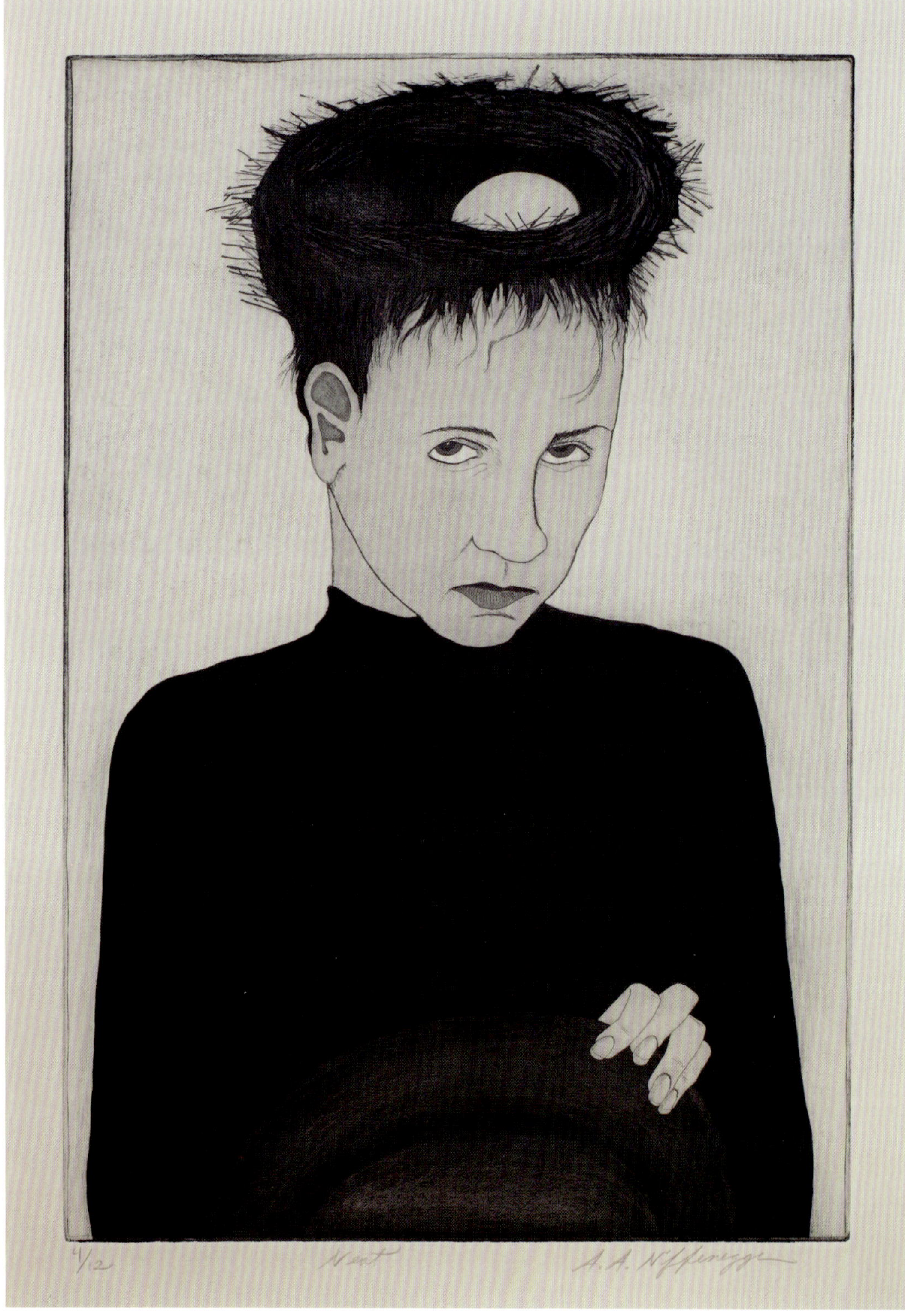

Nest, 1985
Aquatint on Fusuma Grey paper
18 x 12 in.
Edition 4/12
Collection of Audrey Niffenegger, Chicago, Illinois

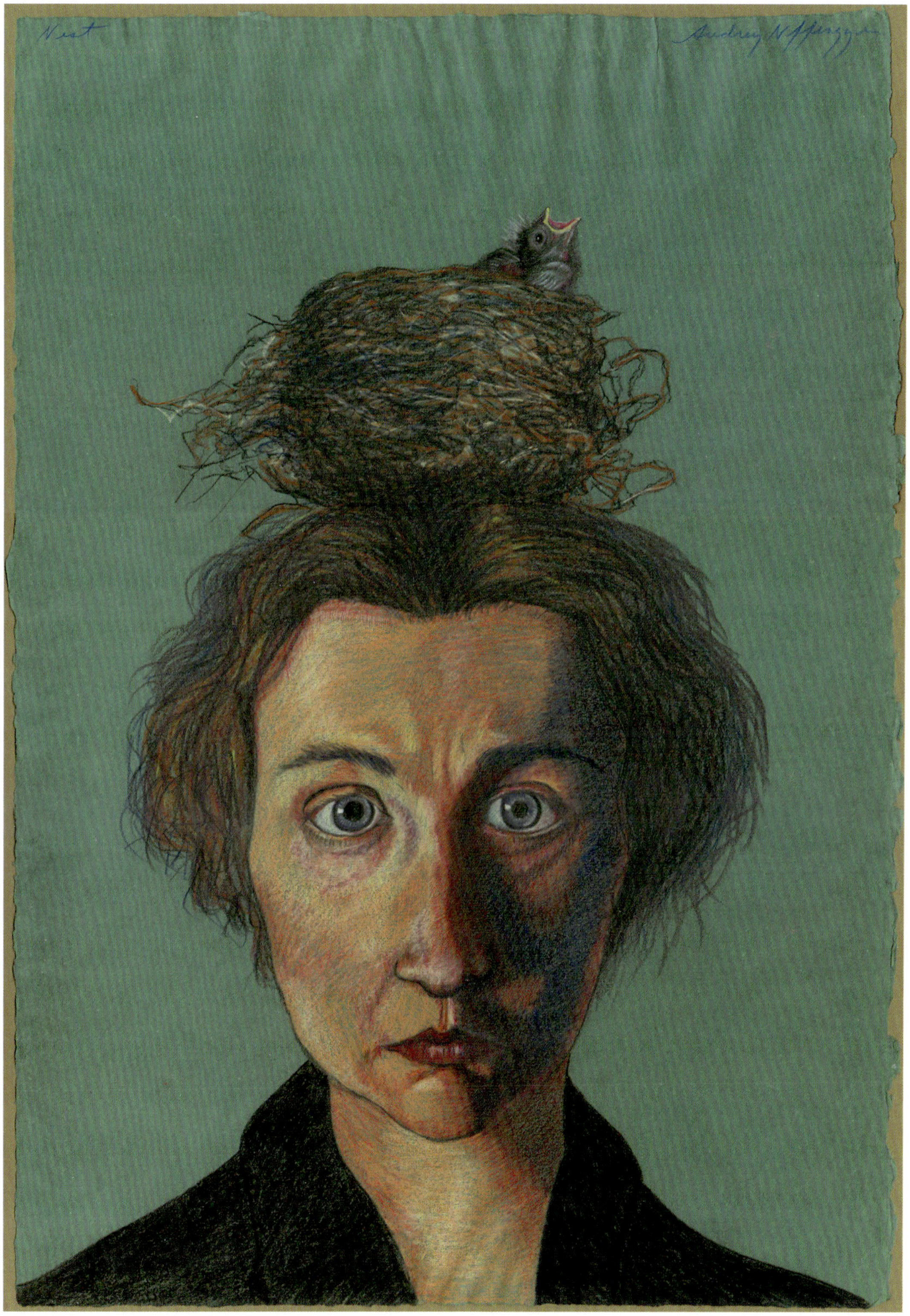

Nest, 2000
Colored pencil and charcoal on paper
17 7/8 x 12 1/4 in.
Collection of Mary Jean Thomson, Riverwoods, Illinois

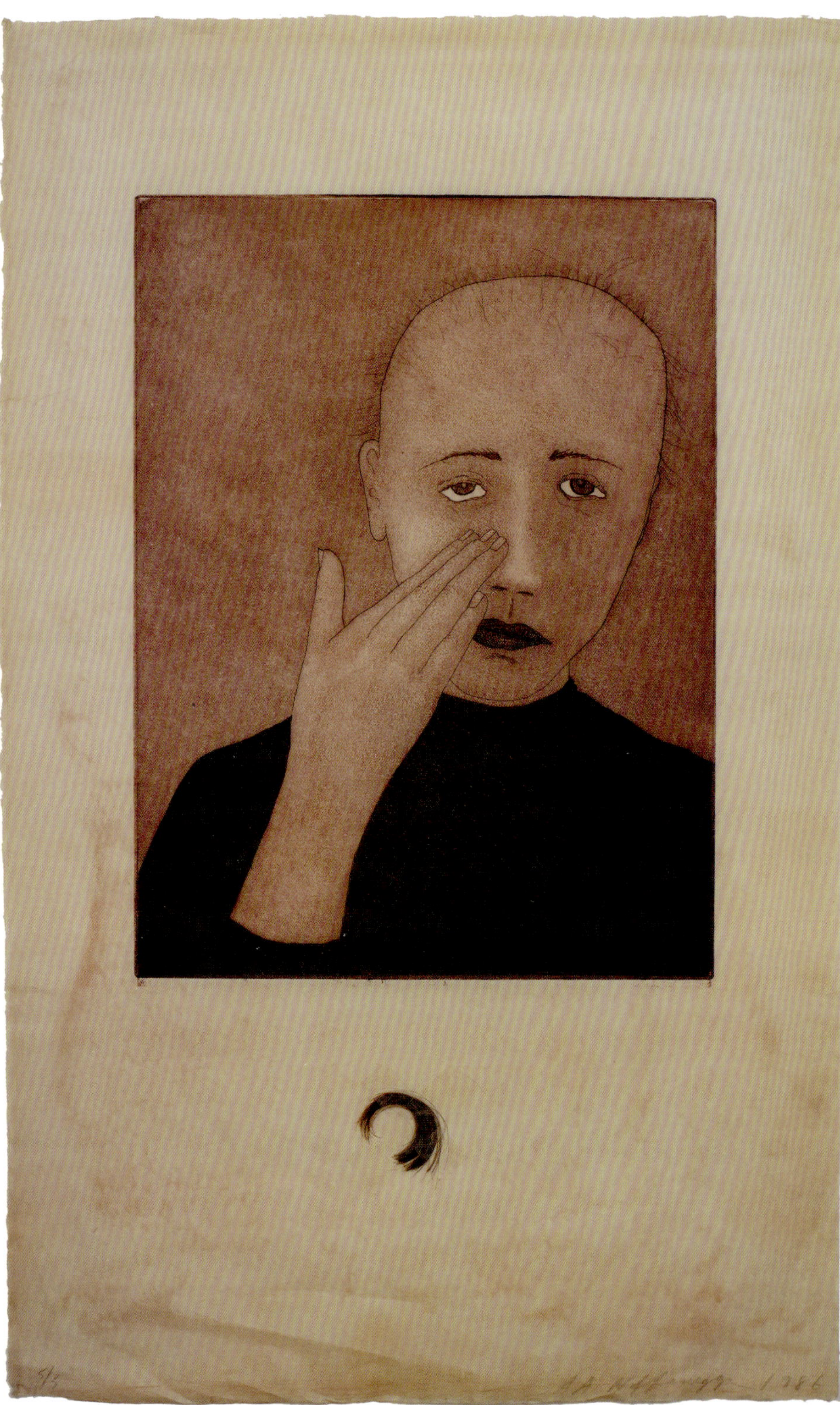

Hairpiece, 1986
Aquatint and hair on persimmon paper
21 1/2 x 13 in.
Edition 5/5
Collection of Audrey Niffenegger, Chicago, Illinois

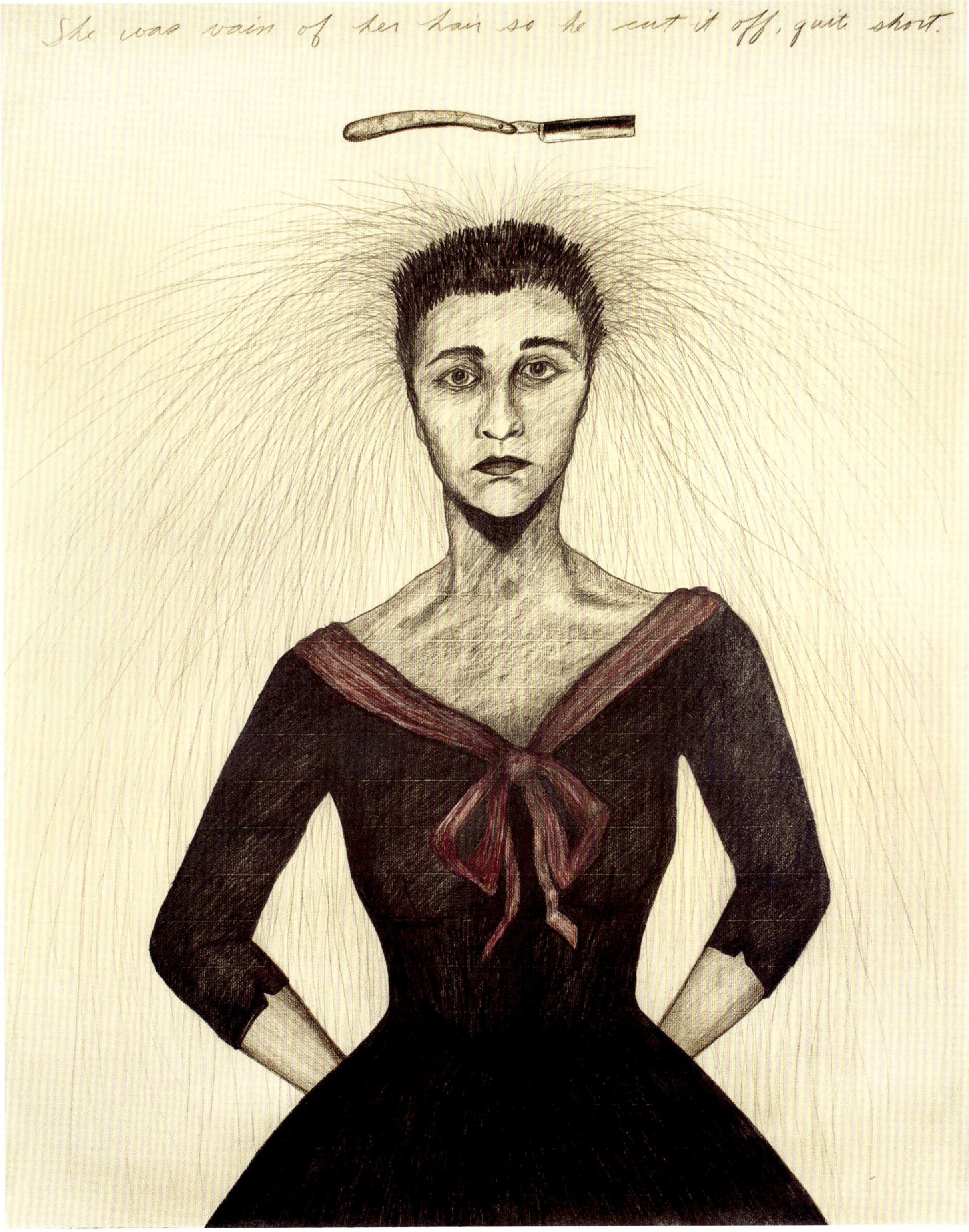

She Was Vain of Her Hair, 1986
Graphite and colored pencil on Bugra paper
37 x 29 in.
Collection of Mary Jean Thomson, Riverwoods, Illinois

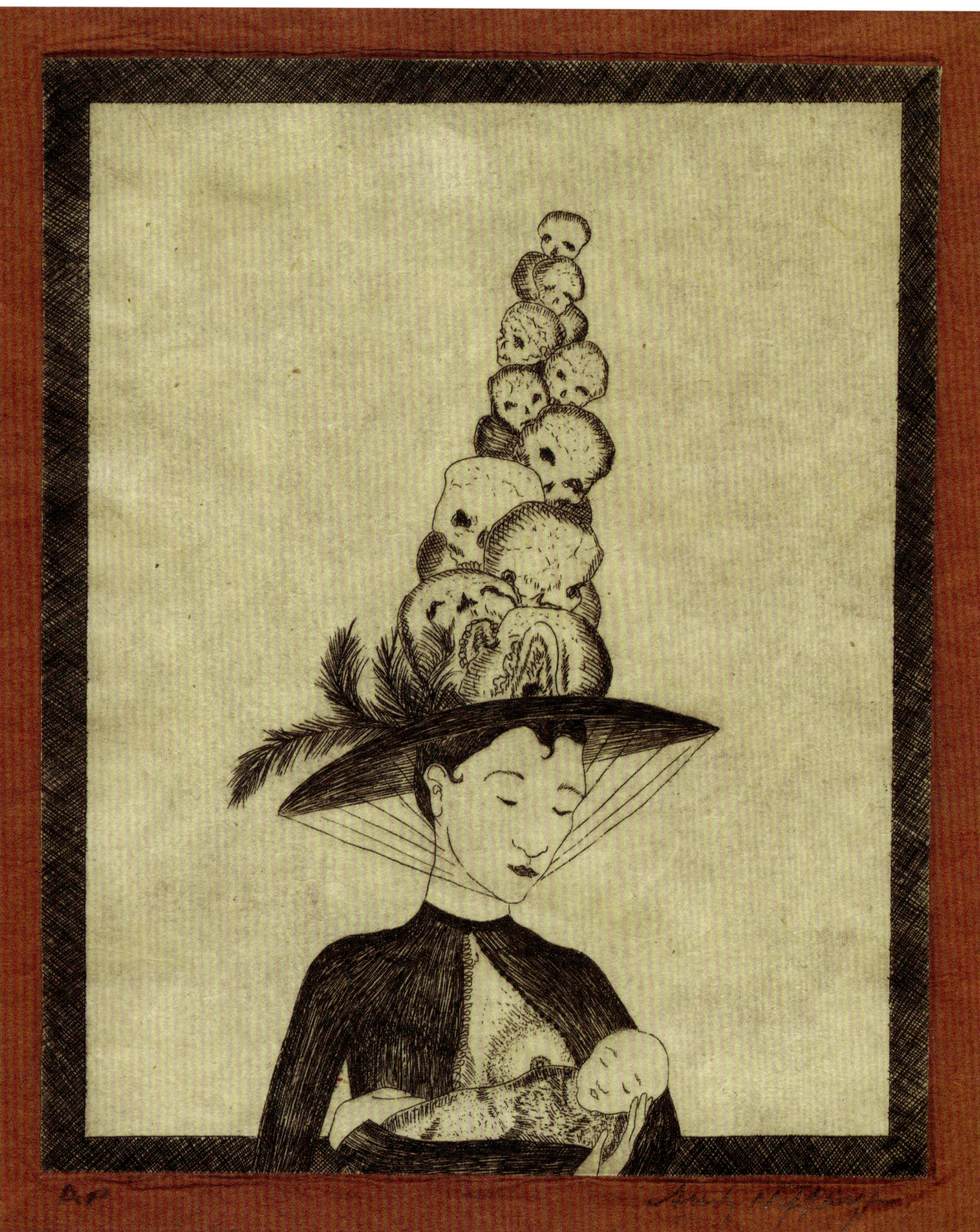

Skull Hat, 1998
Etching, chine collé on Japanese paper; Printed by Anchor Graphics, Chicago
4 3/4 x 4 in.
Edition of 10; artist's proof
Collection of Audrey Niffenegger, Chicago, Illinois

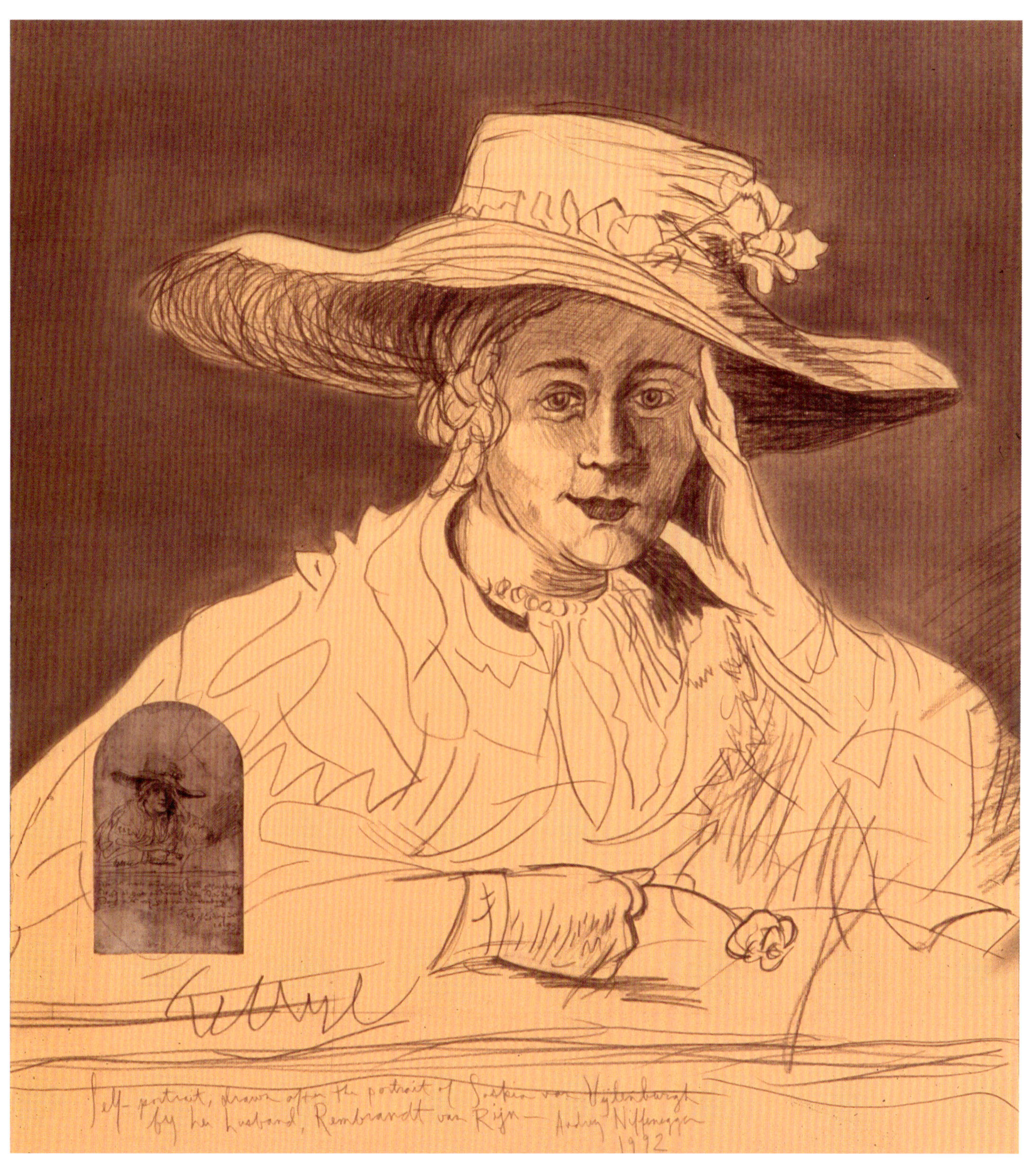

Self-Portrait as Rembrandt's Wife, Saskia, 1992
Graphite with Xerox and ink on Bugra paper
34 x 28 1/2 in.
Collection of Chapman & Cutler LLP, Chicago, Illinois

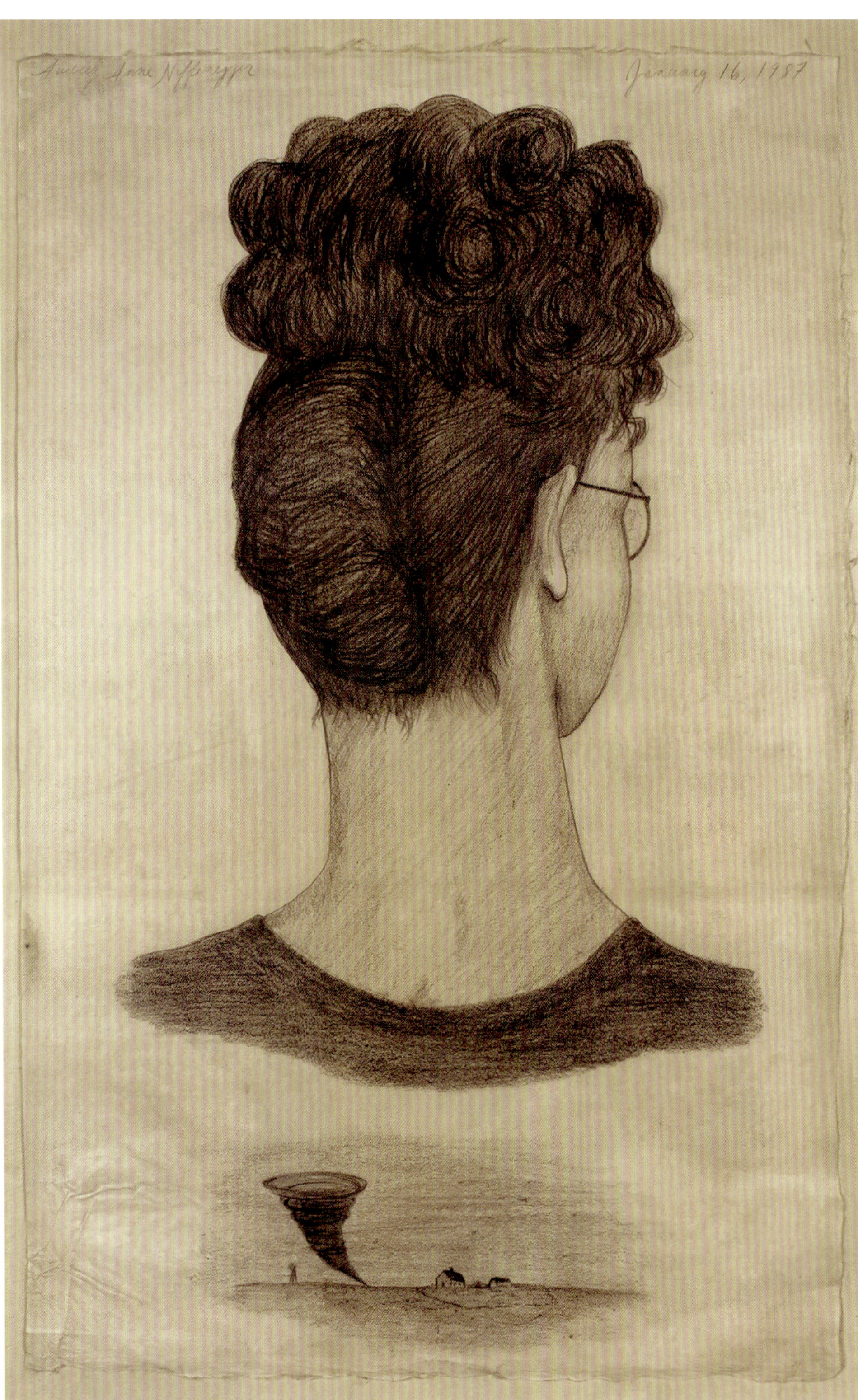

Tornado Head, 1987
Graphite on persimmon paper
22 1/2 x 12 3/4 in.
Collection of Carol Rosofsky, Chicago, Illinois

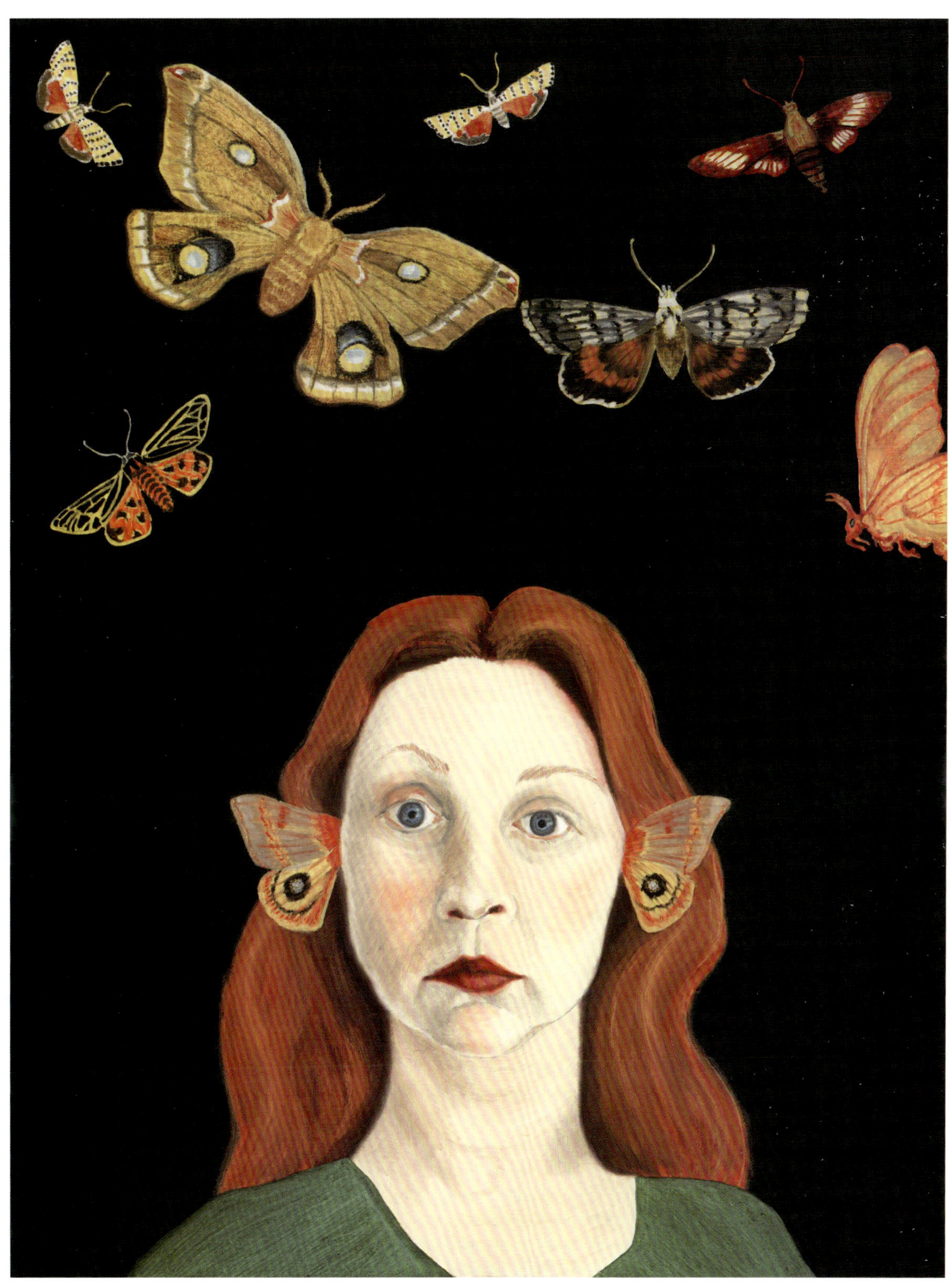

Moths of the New World, 2005
Oil on wooden panel
12 x 9 in.
Collection of Mary Jean Thomson, Riverwoods, Illinois

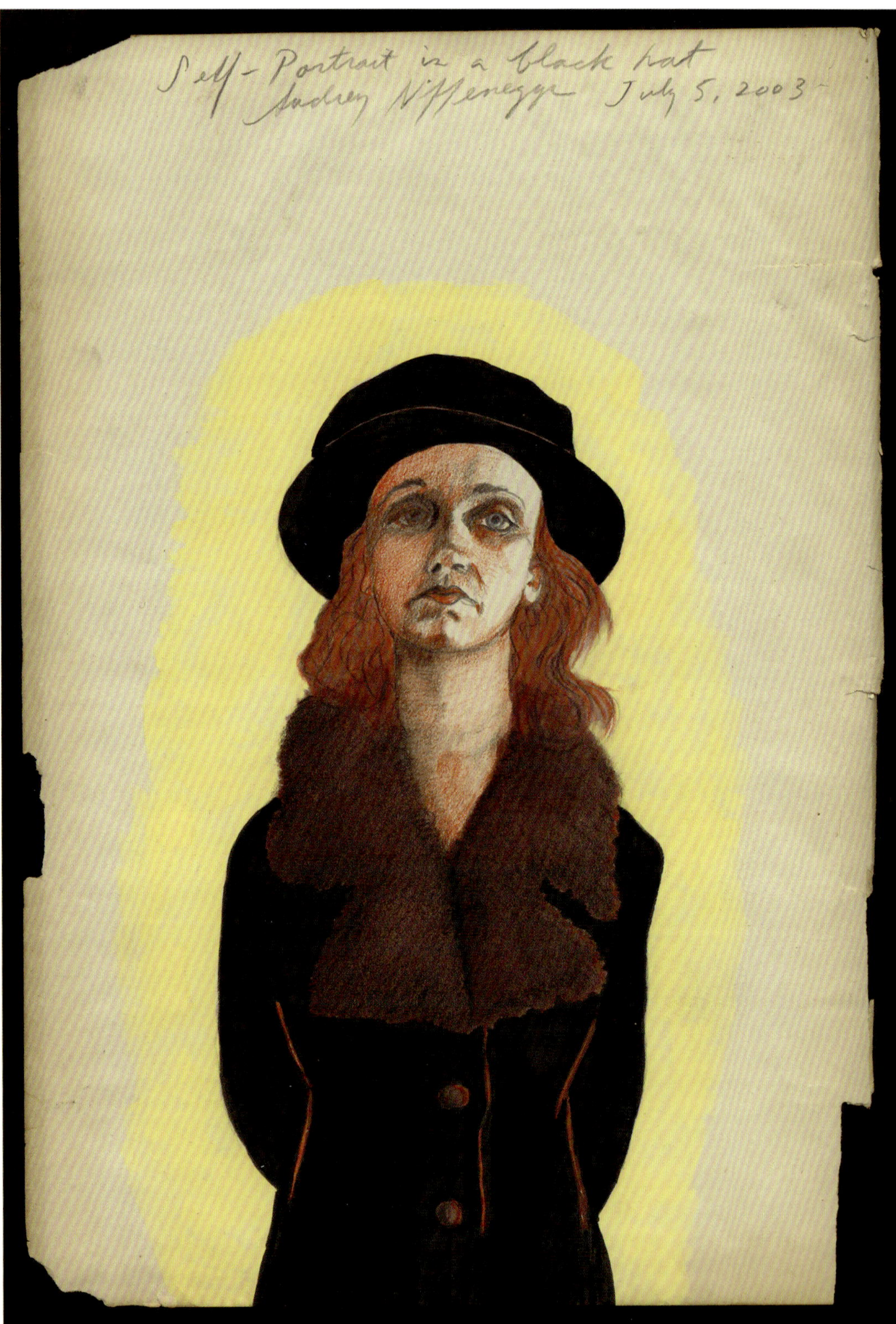

Self-Portrait in Black Hat, 2003
Ink, gouache, and colored pencil on found paper
9 7/8 x 6 3/4 in.
Collection of Mary Jean Thomson, Riverwoods, Illinois

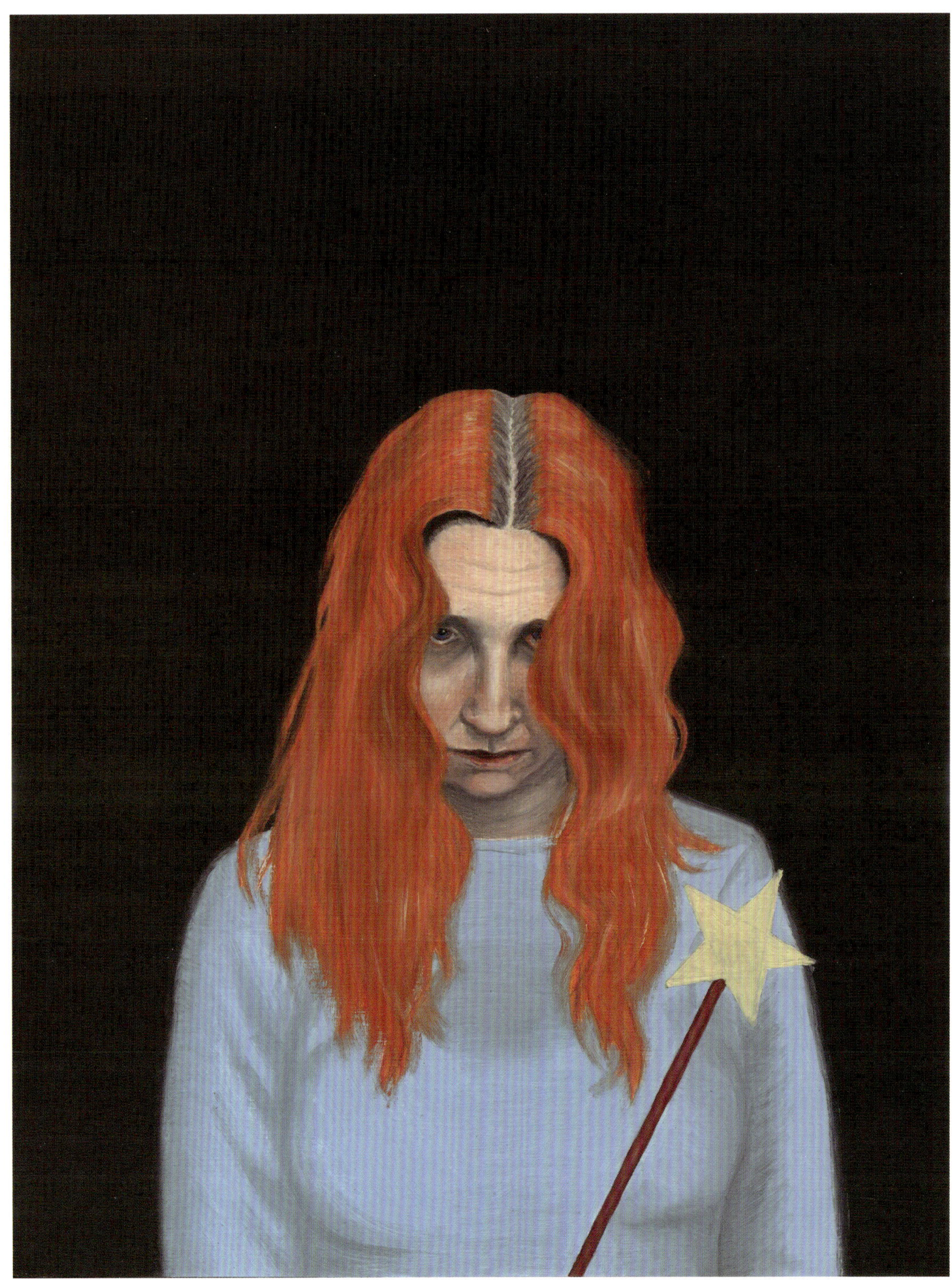

Bad Fairy, 2005
Oil on wooden panel
12 x 8 3/4 in.
Collection of Larry and Laura Gerber, Highland Park, Illinois

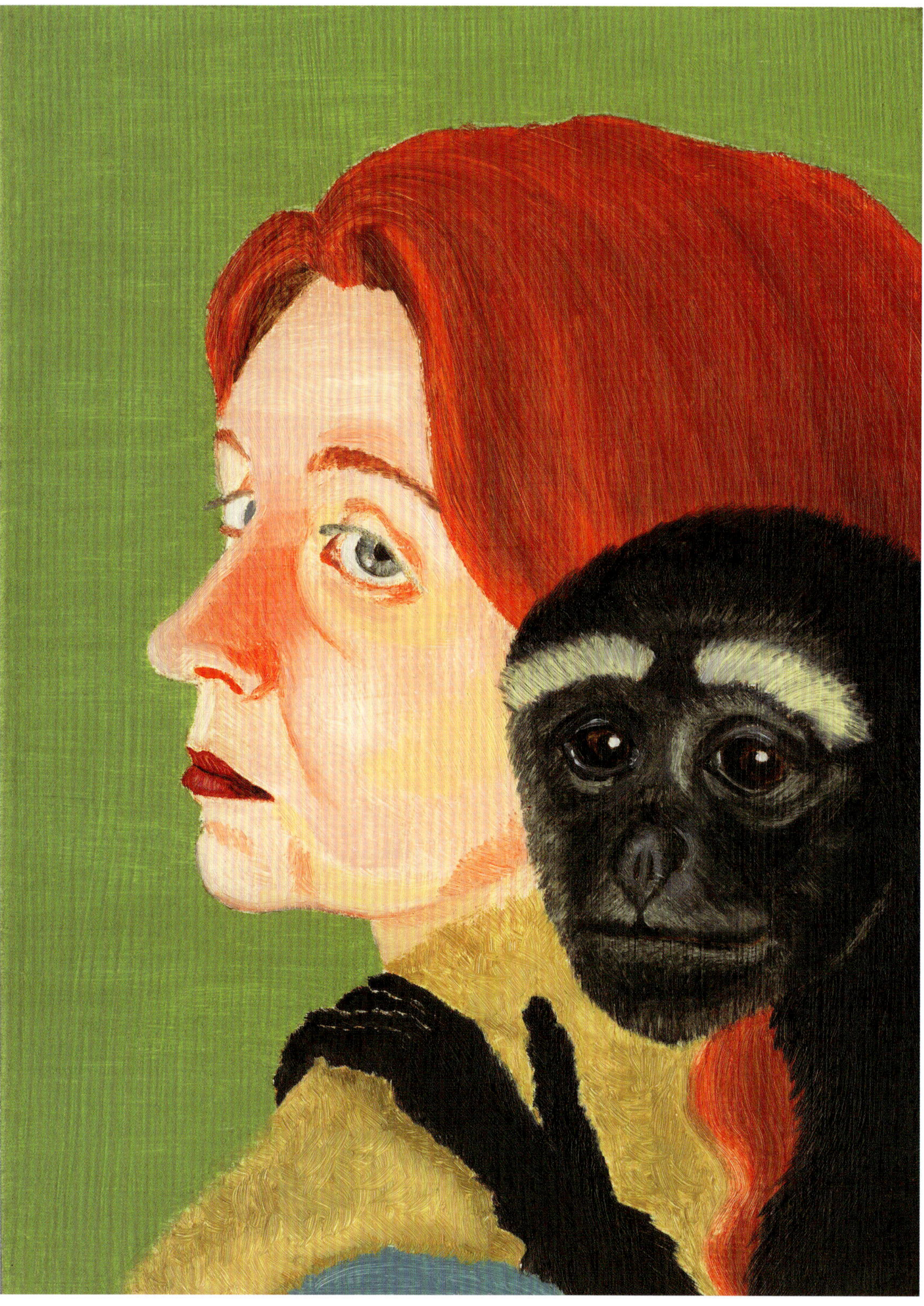

Lady with Monkey, 2005
Oil on wooden panel
7 x 5 in.
Collection of Larry and Laura Gerber, Highland Park, Illinois

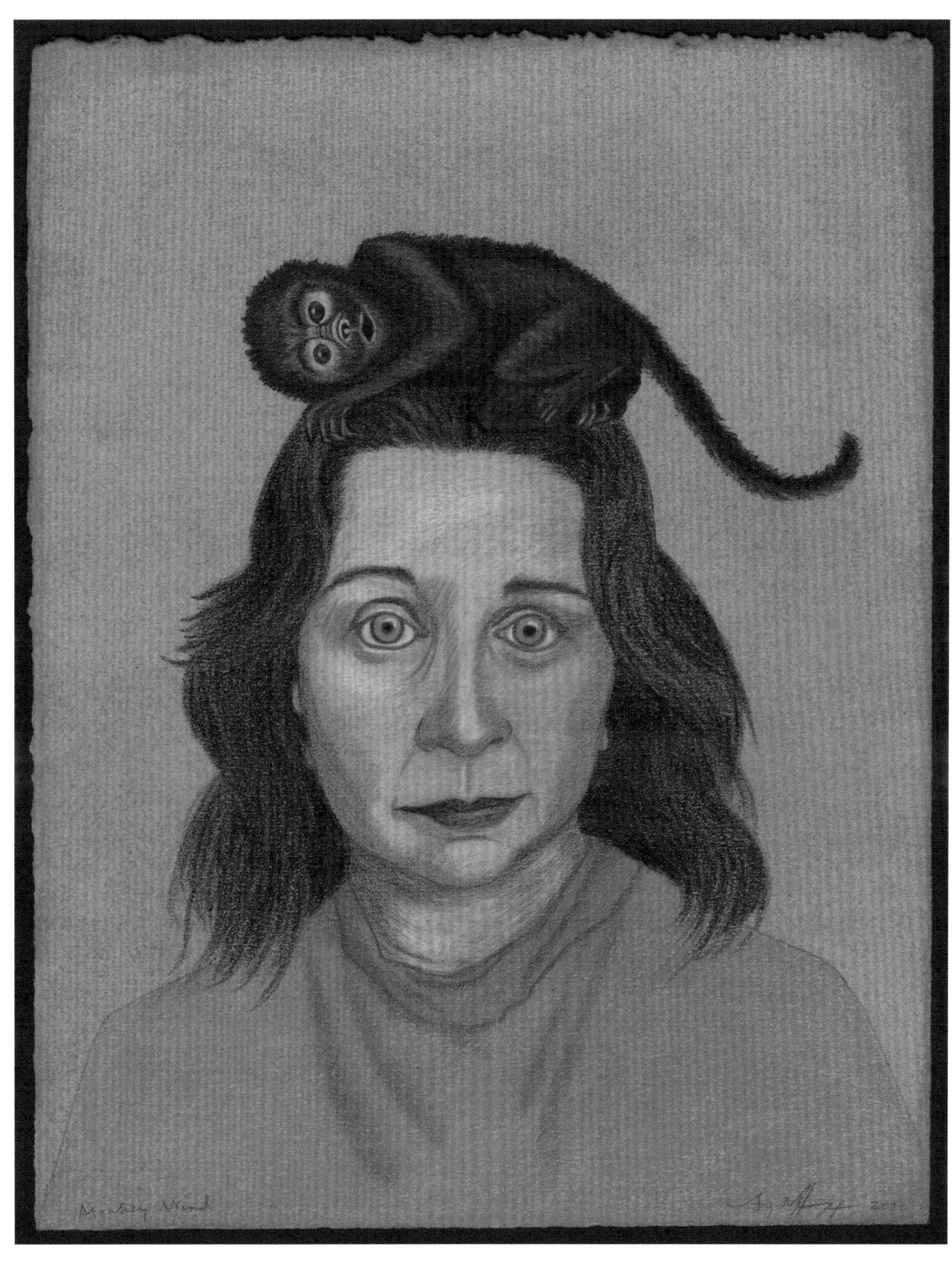

Monkey Mind, 2010
Colored pencil on hand-dyed paper
12 x 9 in.
Collection of Jim Tonsgard, Chicago, Illinois

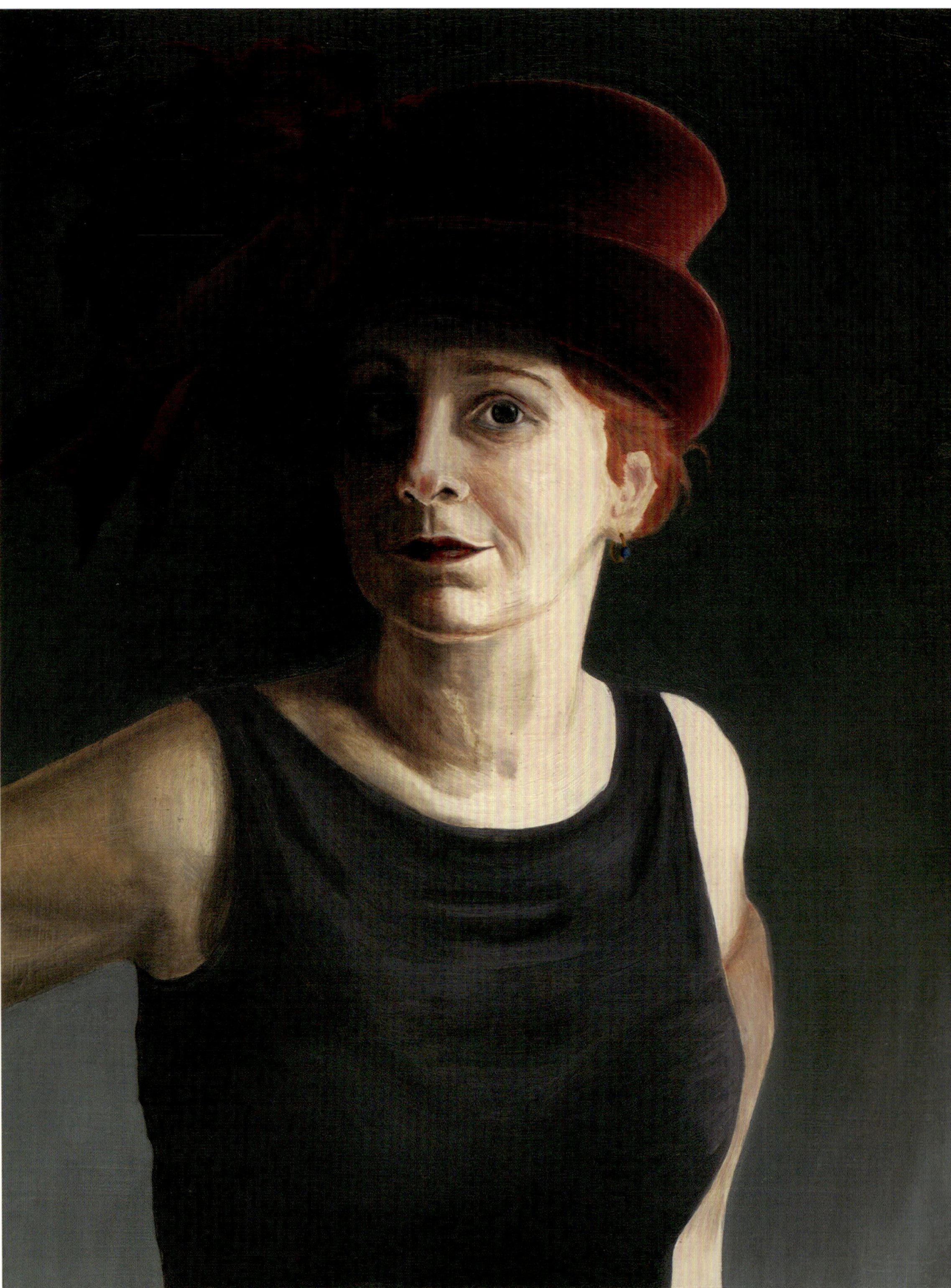

Self-Portrait with Philip Treacy Hat, 2007
Oil on wooden panel
15 3/4 x 11 3/4 in.
Collection of Mary Jean Thomson, Riverwoods, Illinois

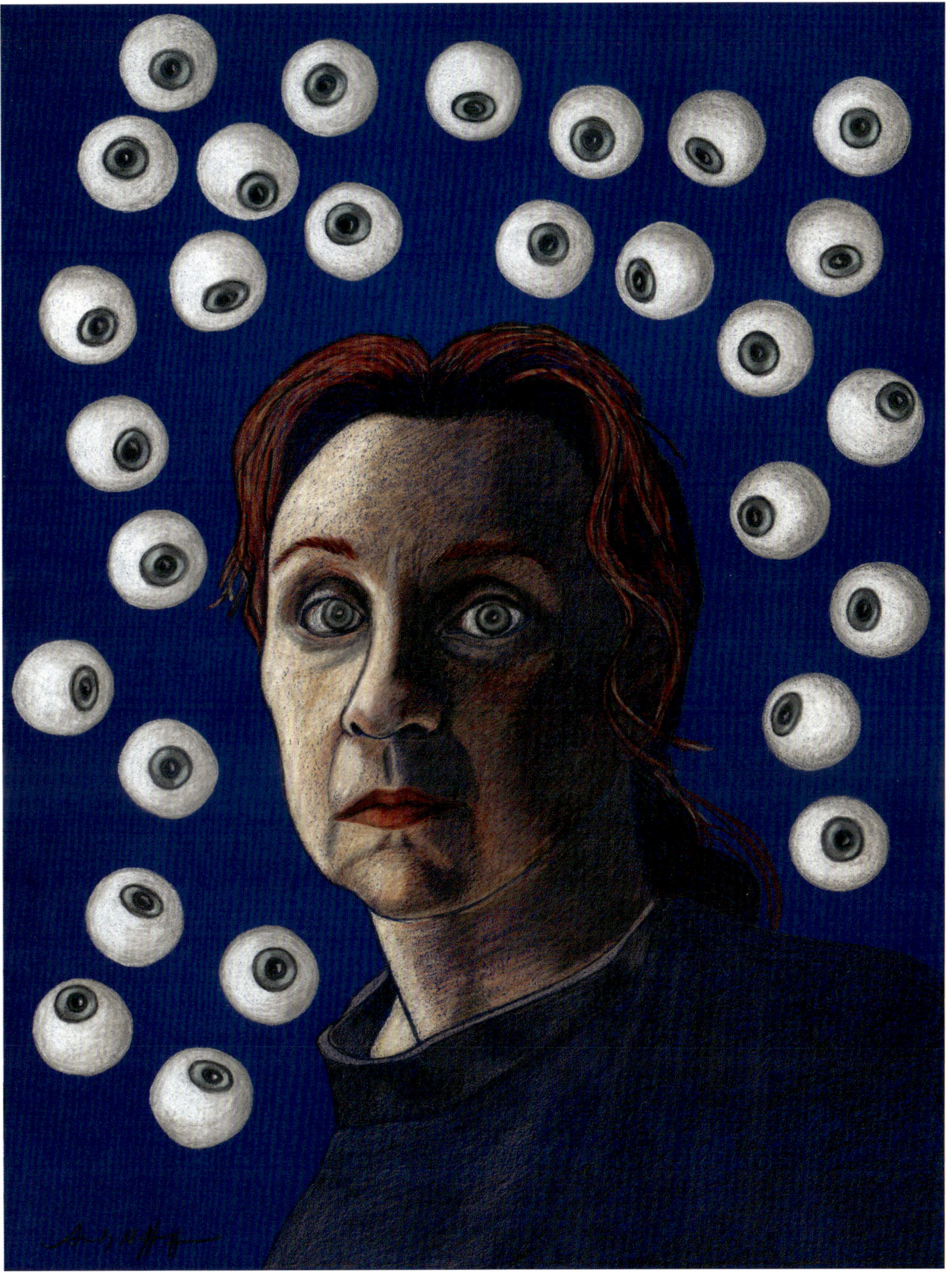

Observation, 2010
Colored pencil on paper
15 x 11 in.
Collection of Larry and Laura Gerber, Highland Park, Illinois

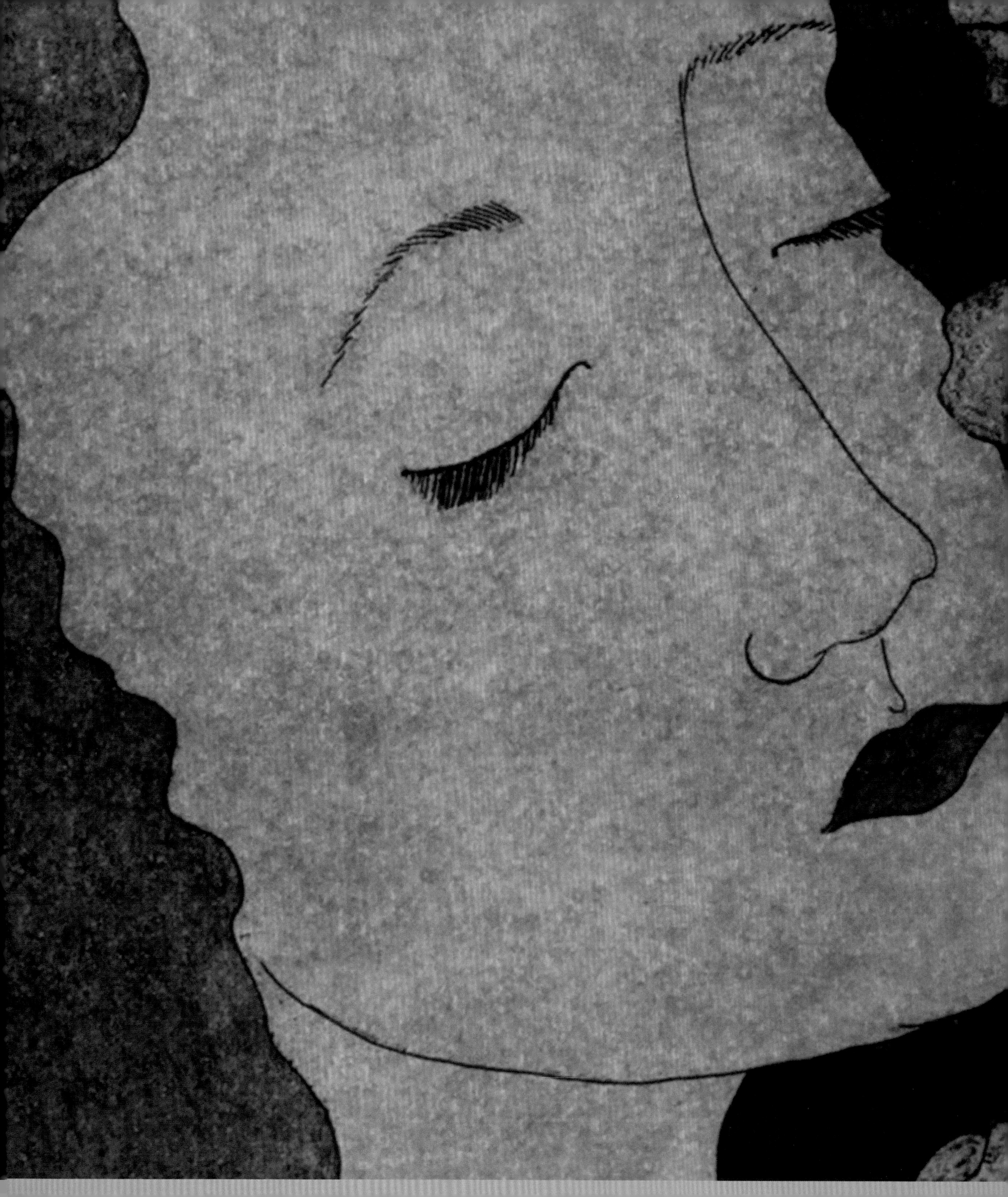

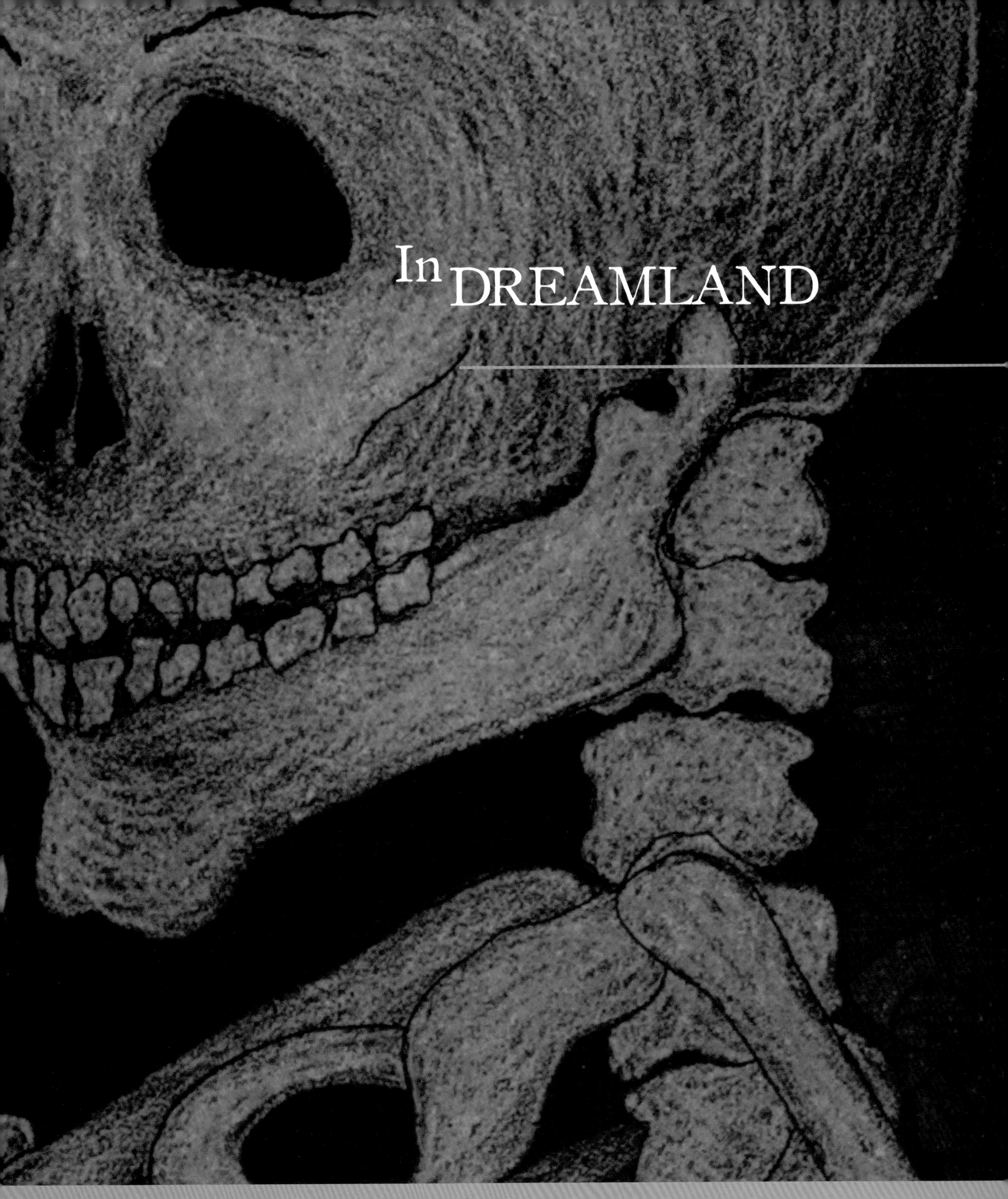
In DREAMLAND

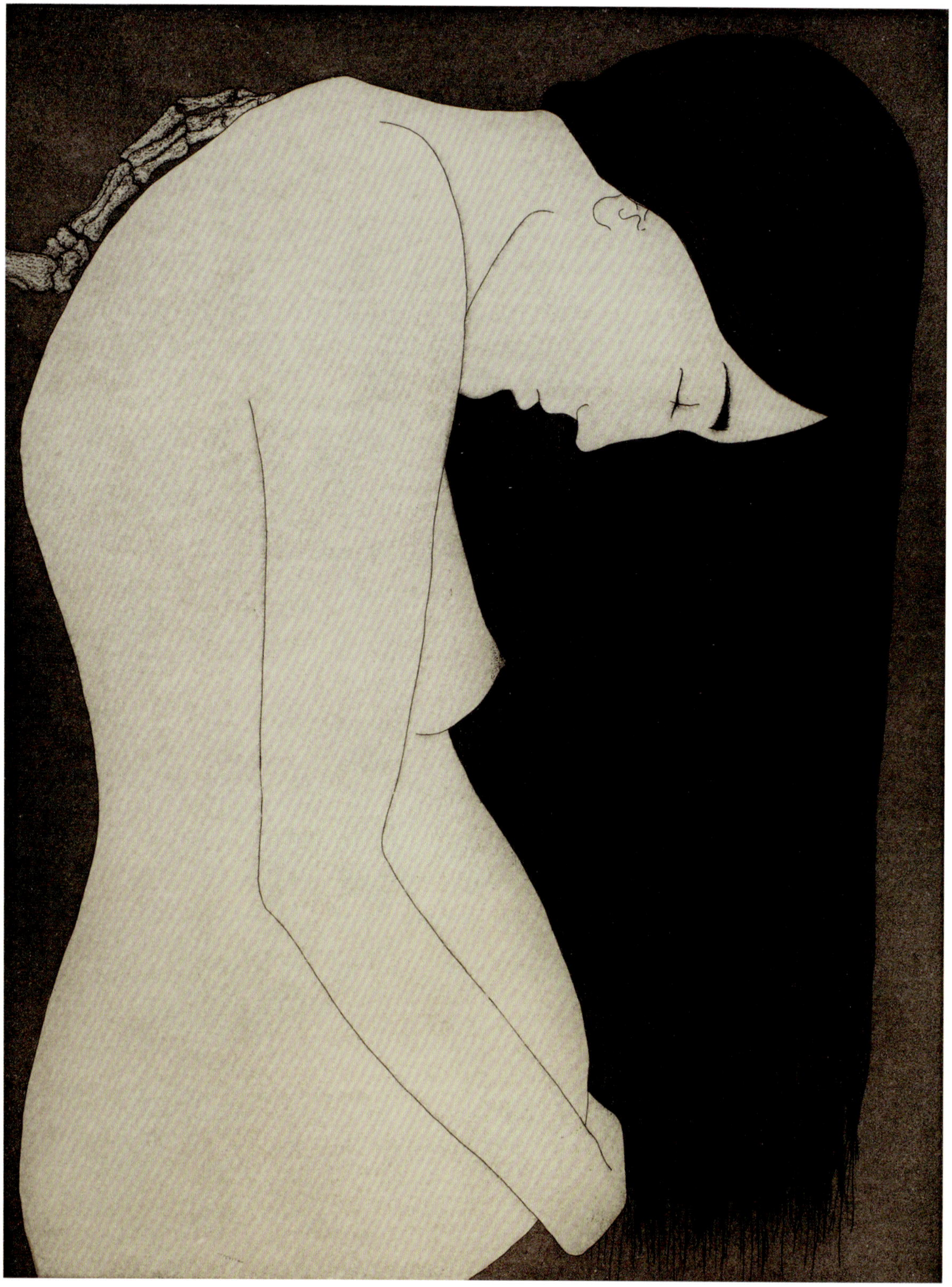

Death Comforts the Mother, from portfolio *Vanitas*, 1989
Poem "Before the Birth of One of her Children," by Anne Bradstreet
Etching with aquatint on Stonehenge Natural paper
30 x 22 1/4 in.
Edition 1/20
Collection of Audrey Niffenegger, Chicago, Illinois

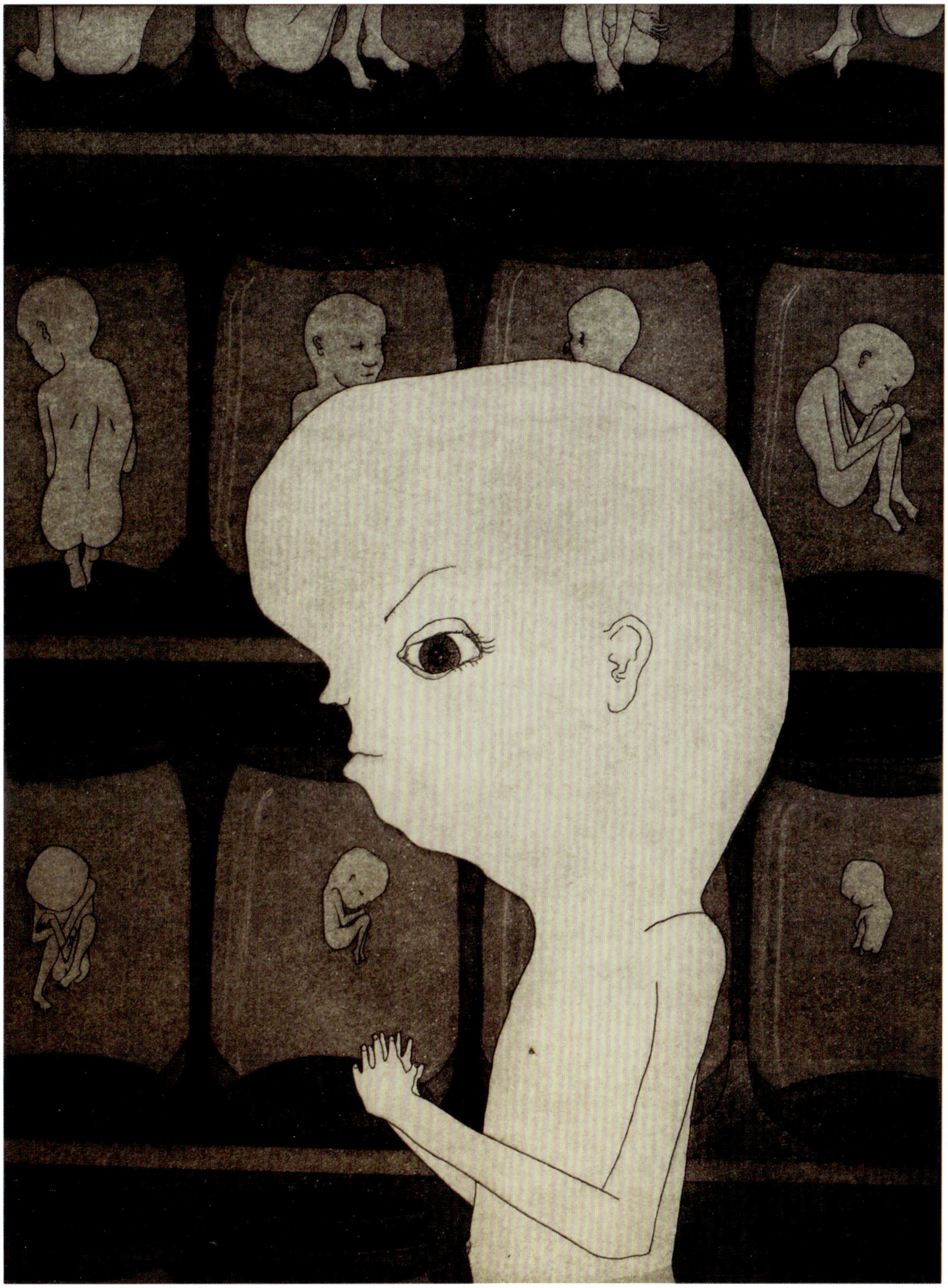

The Embryos, from portfolio *Vanitas*, 1989
Poem "A Cradle Song," by Thomas Dekker
Etching with aquatint on Stonehenge Natural paper
30 x 22 1/2 in.
Edition 1/20
Collection of Audrey Niffenegger, Chicago, Illinois

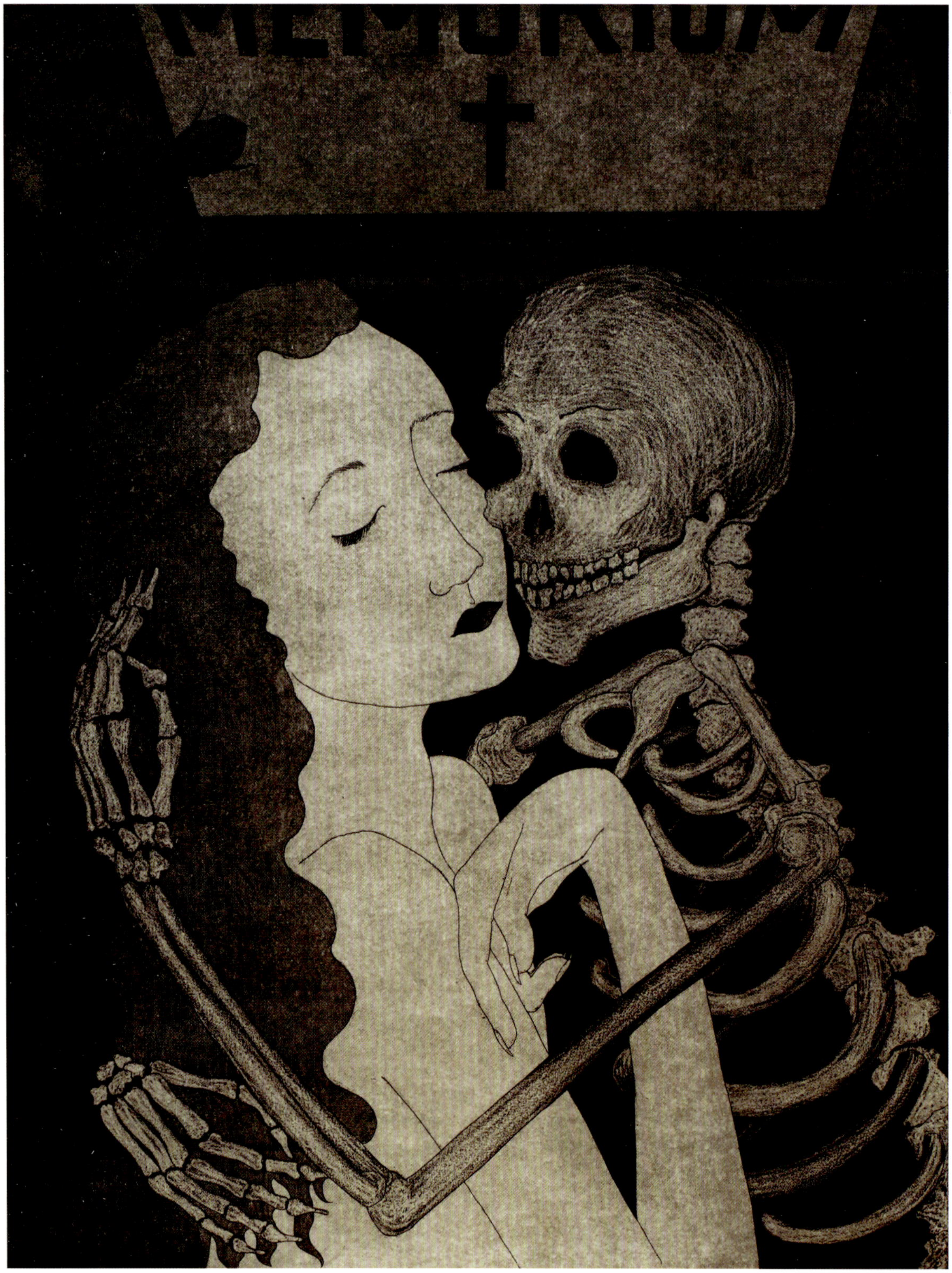

Lovers' Embrace, from portfolio *Vanitas*, 1989
Poem "Dismissal" by Thomas Campion
Etching with aquatint on Stonehenge Natural paper
30 x 22 1/4 in.
Edition 1/20
Collection of Audrey Niffenegger, Chicago, Illinois

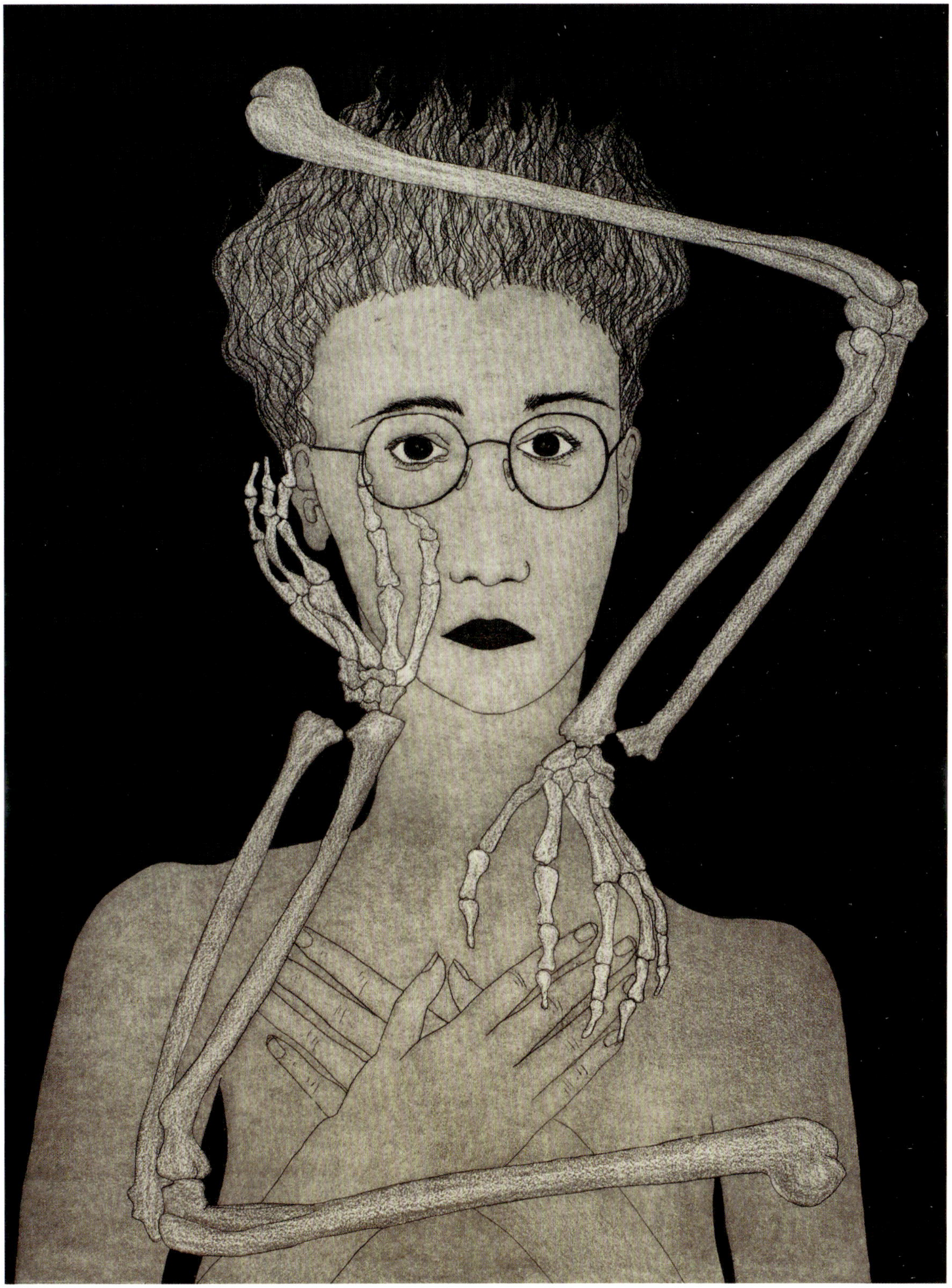

Self-Portrait with Arms, from portfolio *Vanitas*, 1989
Poem "The Apparition" by John Donne
Etching with aquatint on Stonehenge Natural paper
30 x 22 1/4 in.
Edition 1/20
Collection of Audrey Niffenegger, Chicago, Illinois

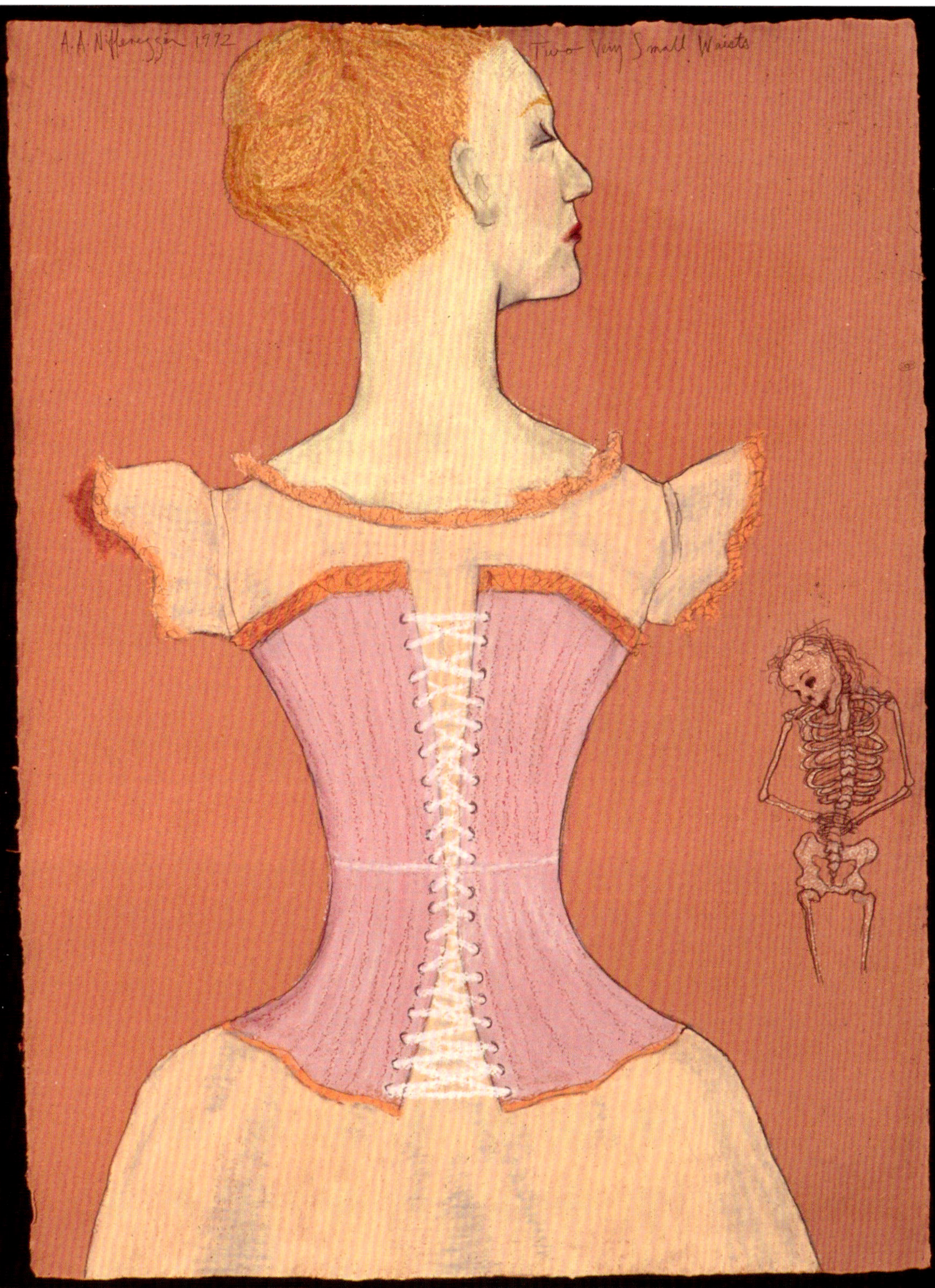

Two Very Small Waists, 1992
Gouache and ink on paper
30 x 21 3/4 in.
Collection of Mary Jean Thomson, Riverwoods, Illinois

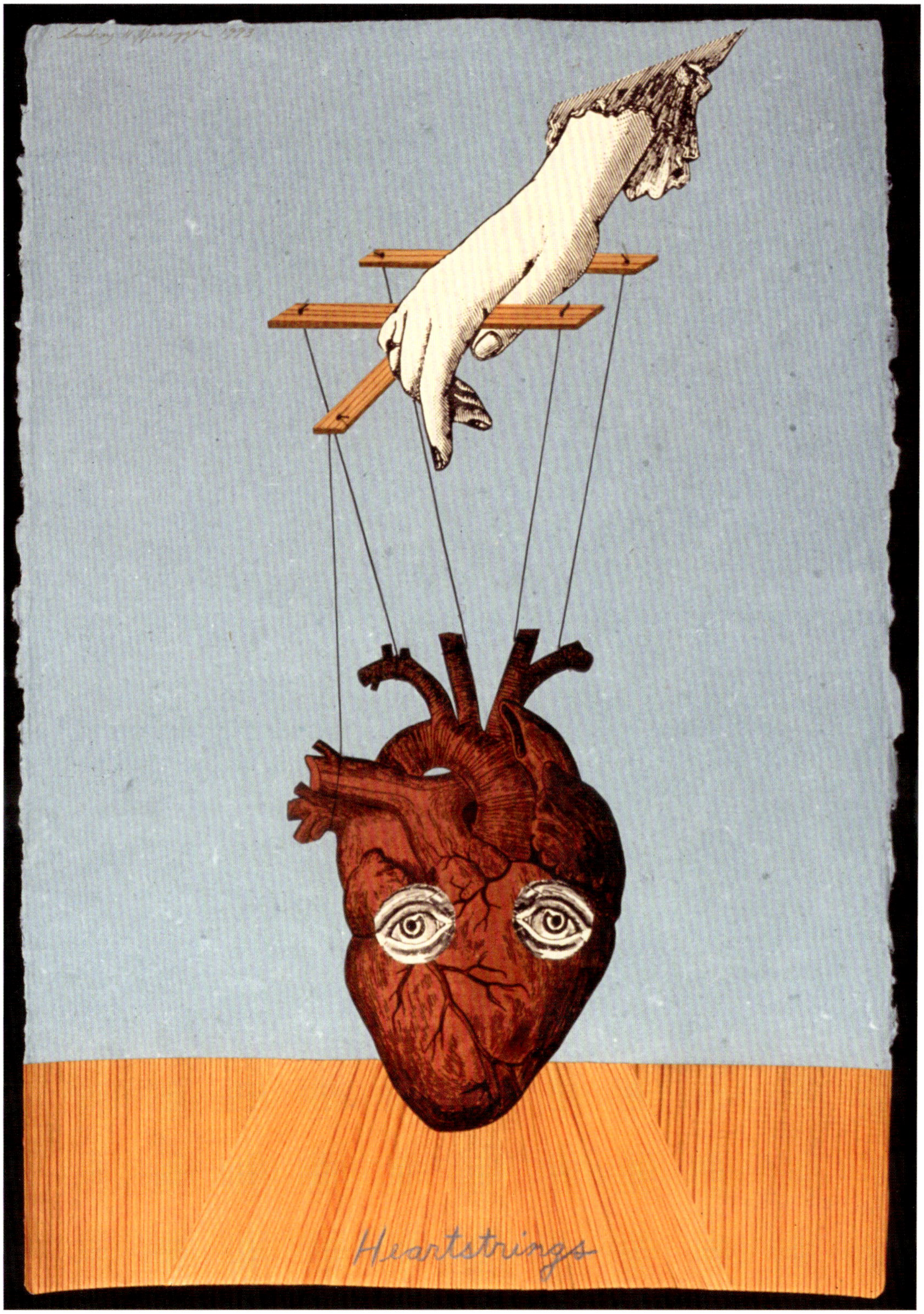

Heartstrings, 1993
Collage on handmade paper
18 x 12 in.
Collection of Jerry Ginsburg, Glenview, Illinois

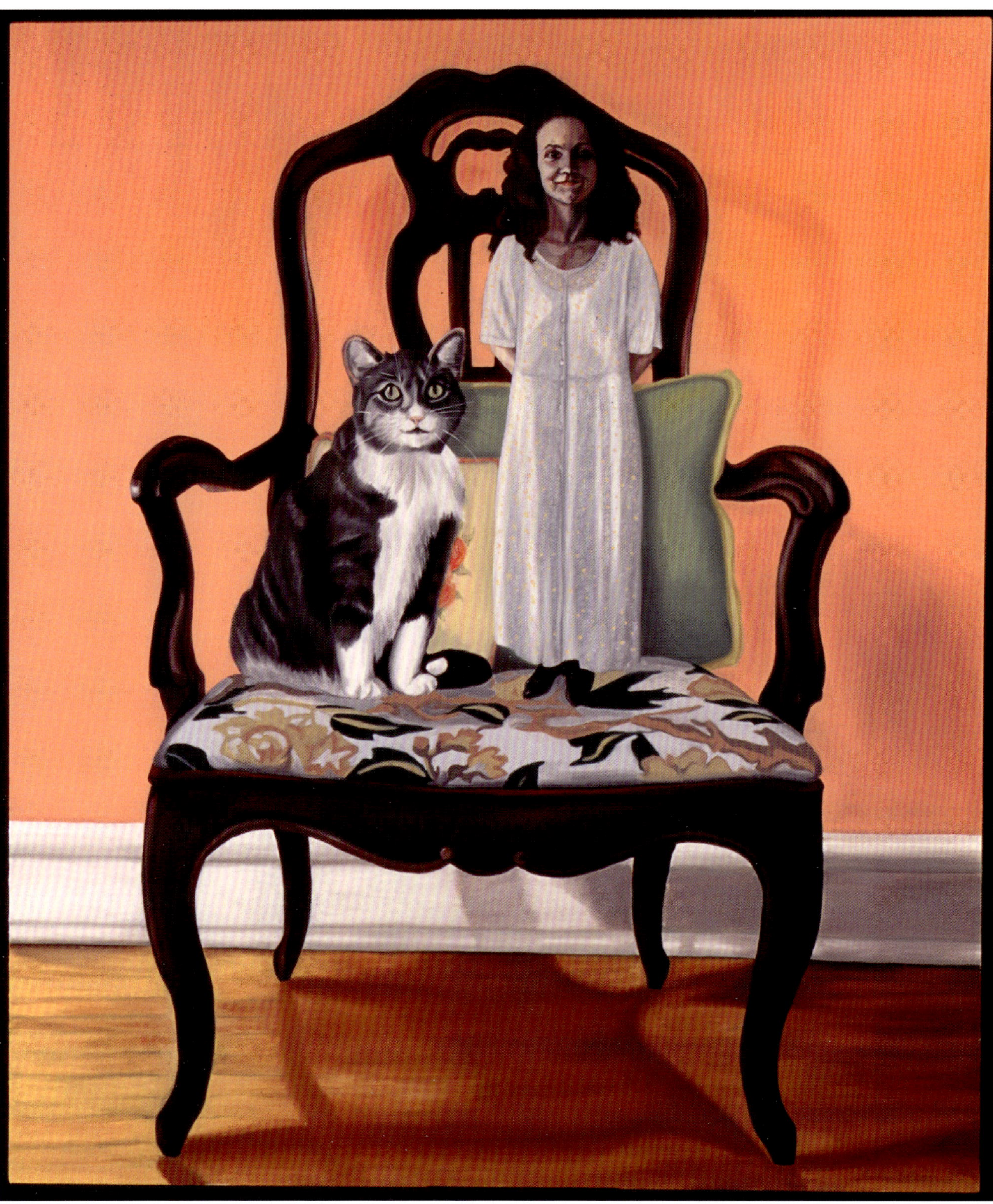

Pam and Zuzu, 1995
Oil on canvas
52 x 40 in.
Collection of Audrey Niffenegger, Chicago, Illinois

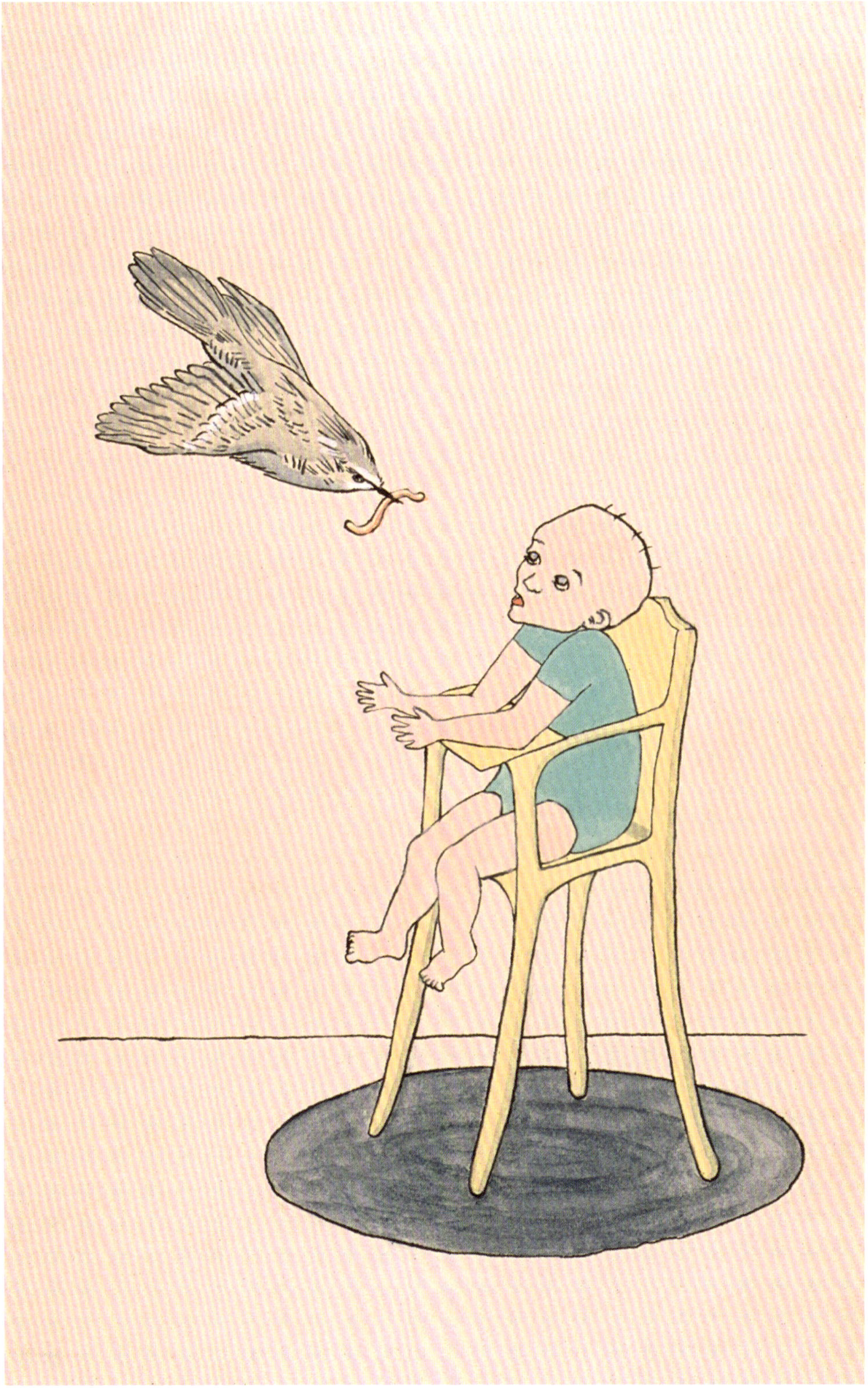

Mother and Child, 2003
Ink and gouache on found paper
10 x 6 1/2 in.
Collection of Janet and Sidney Cohen, Highland Park, Illinois

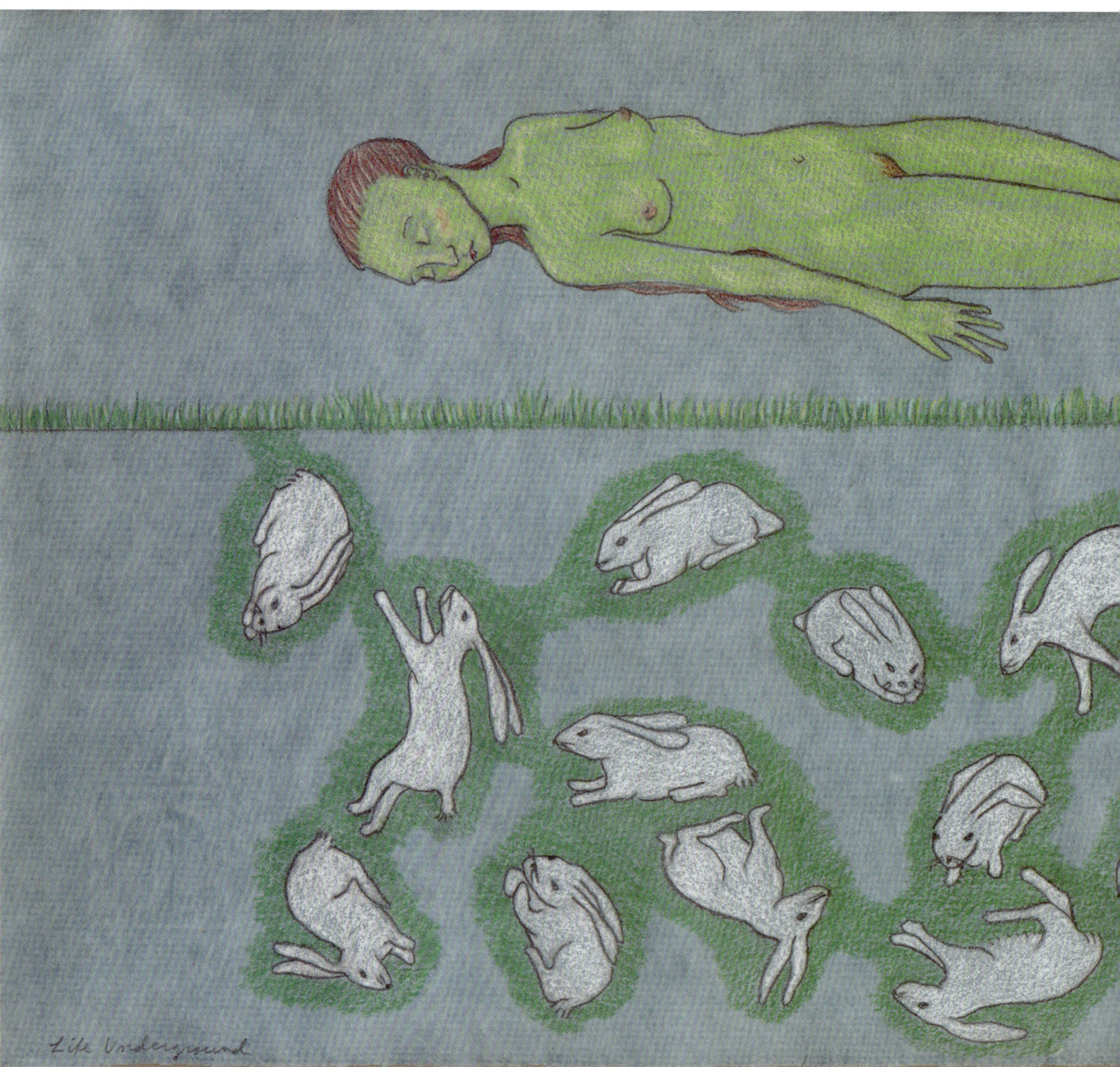
Life Underground

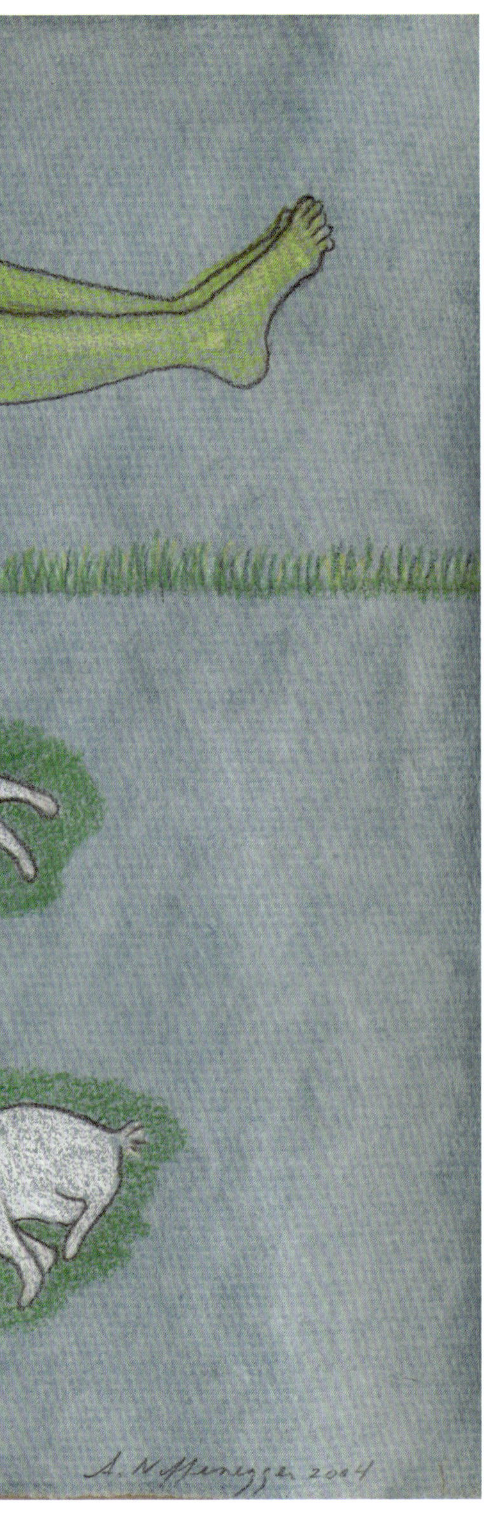

Life Under Ground, 2004
Colored pencil and graphite on paper
8 x 12 in.
Collection of Mary Jean Thomson, Riverwoods, Illinois

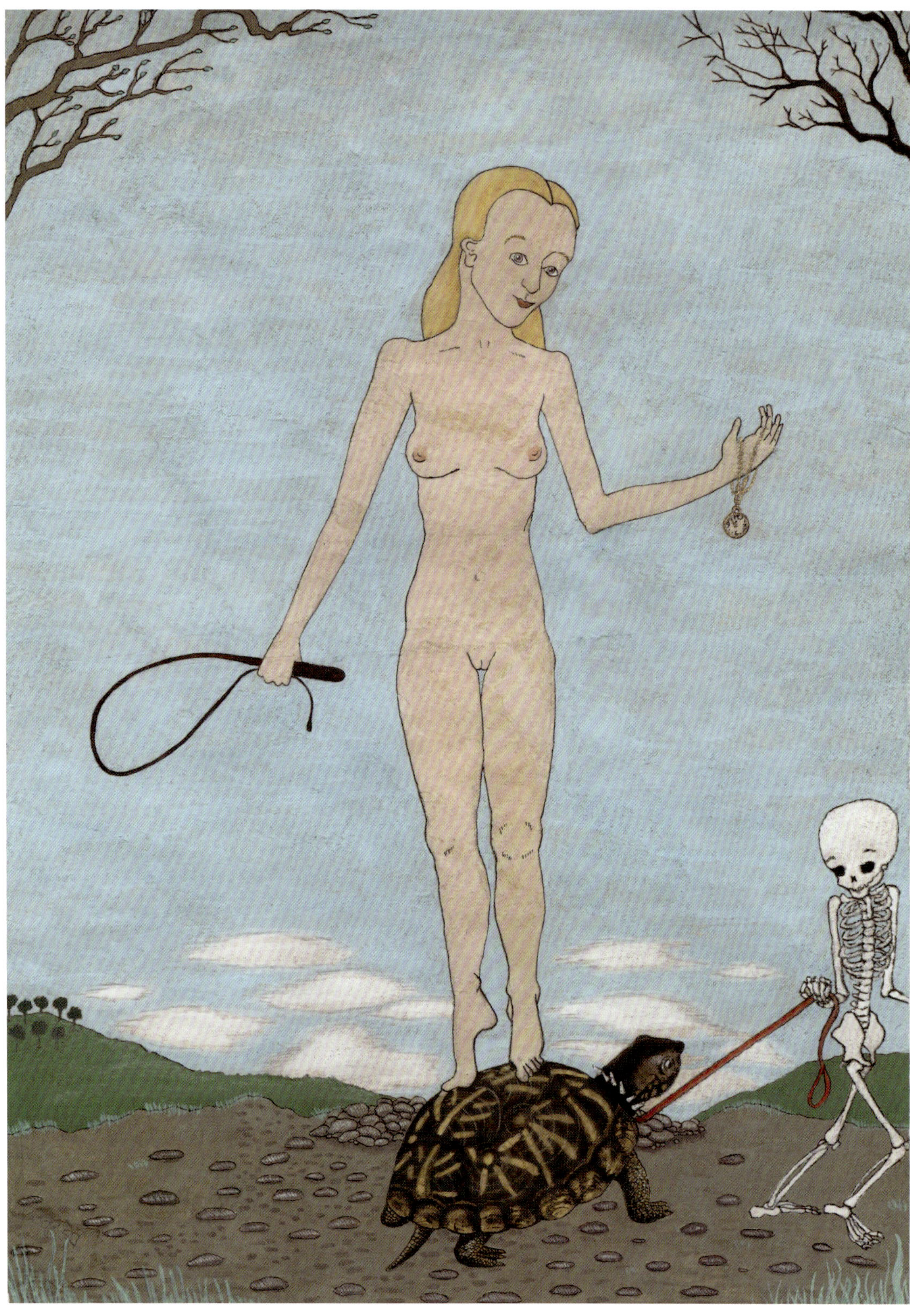

Allegory of Time, 2005
Gouache and ink on amate paper
18 x 12 in.
Collection of Larry and Laura Gerber, Highland Park, Illinois

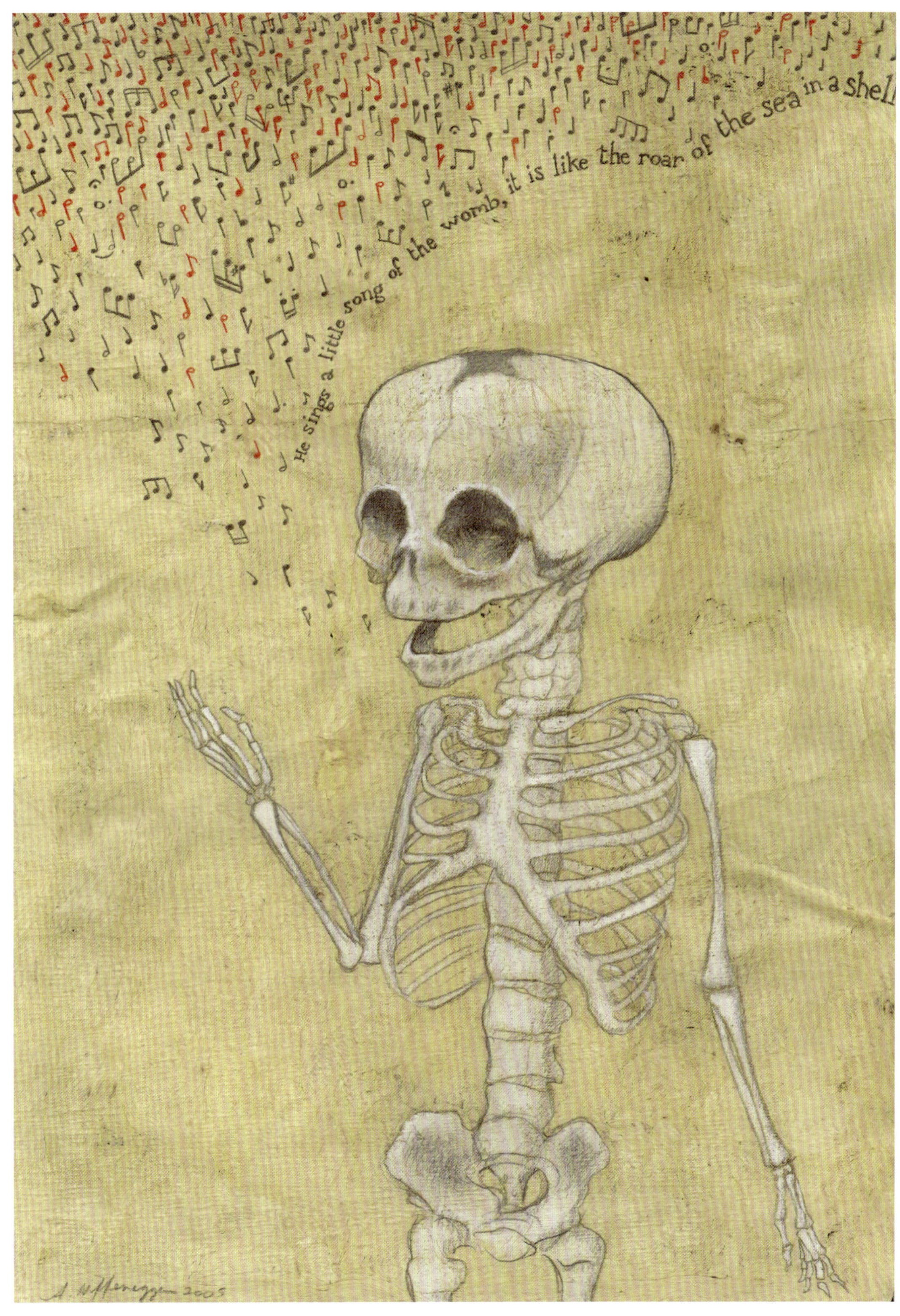

Song of the Womb, 2005
Graphite and colored pencil on handmade paper
17 1/2 x 12 in.
Collection of Larry and Laura Gerber, Highland Park, Illinois

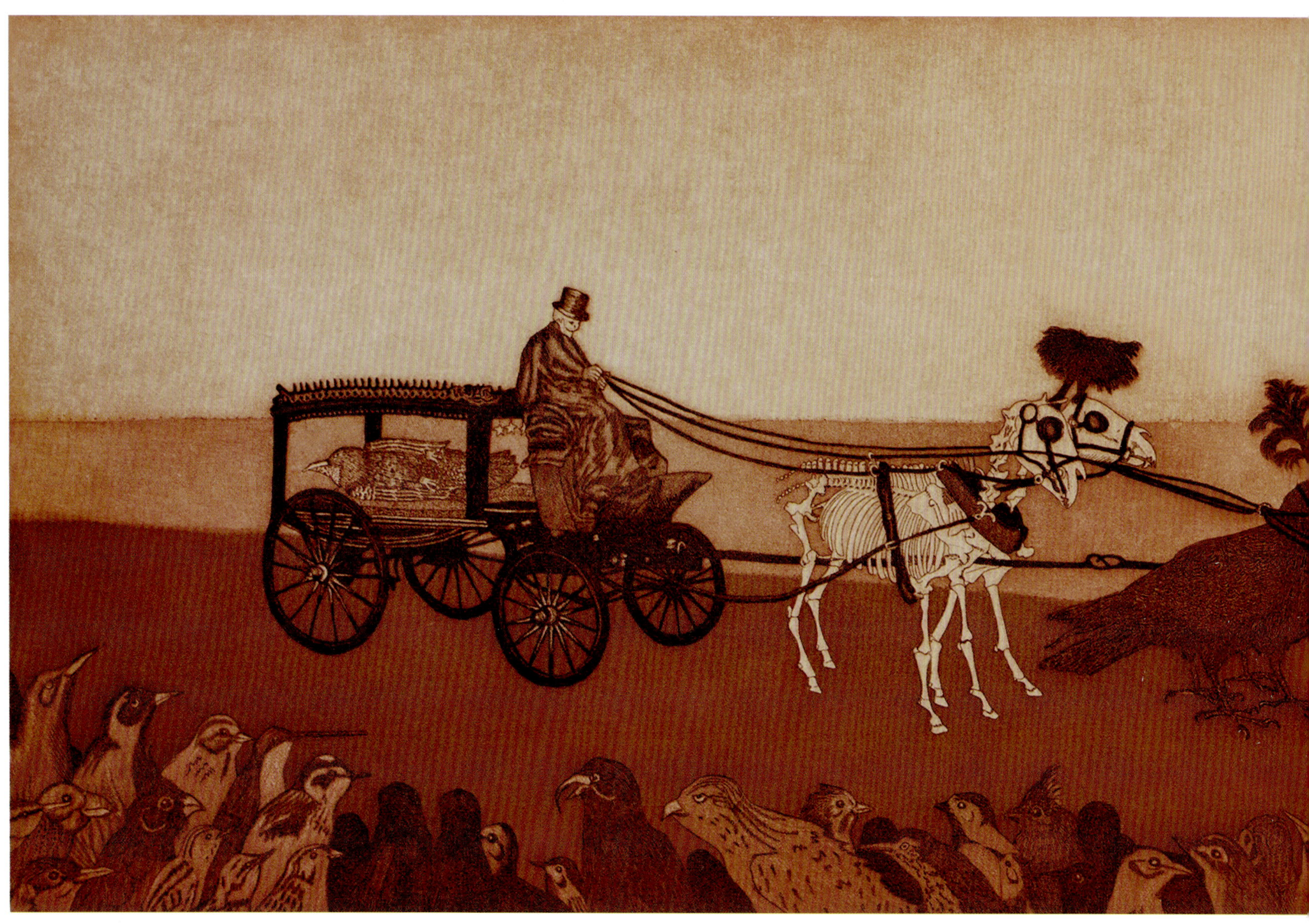

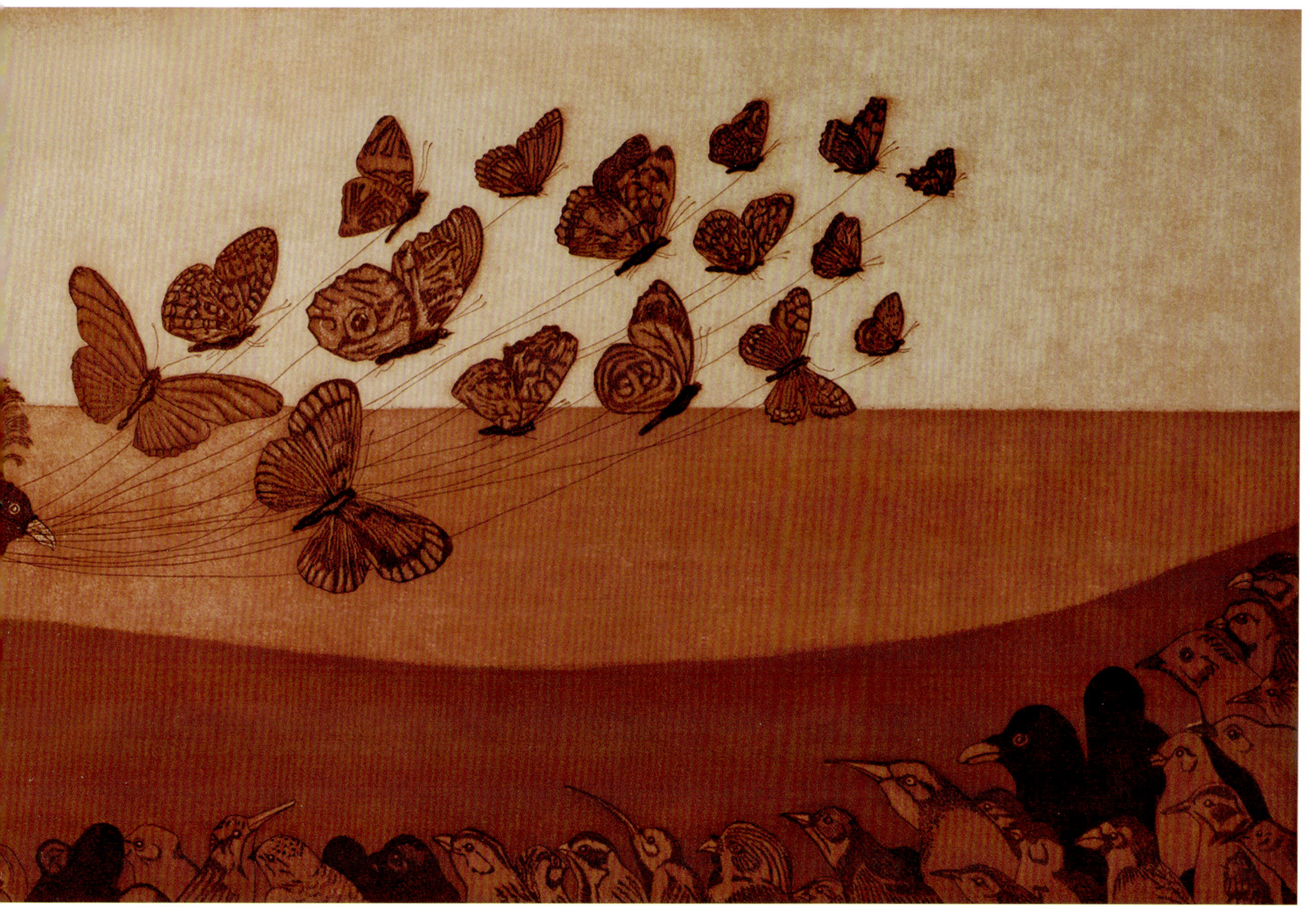

The Starling's Funeral, 2008
Aquatint on Sakamoto paper
12 x 35 1/2 in.
Edition of 15; artist's proof
Collection of Audrey Niffenegger, Chicago, Illinois

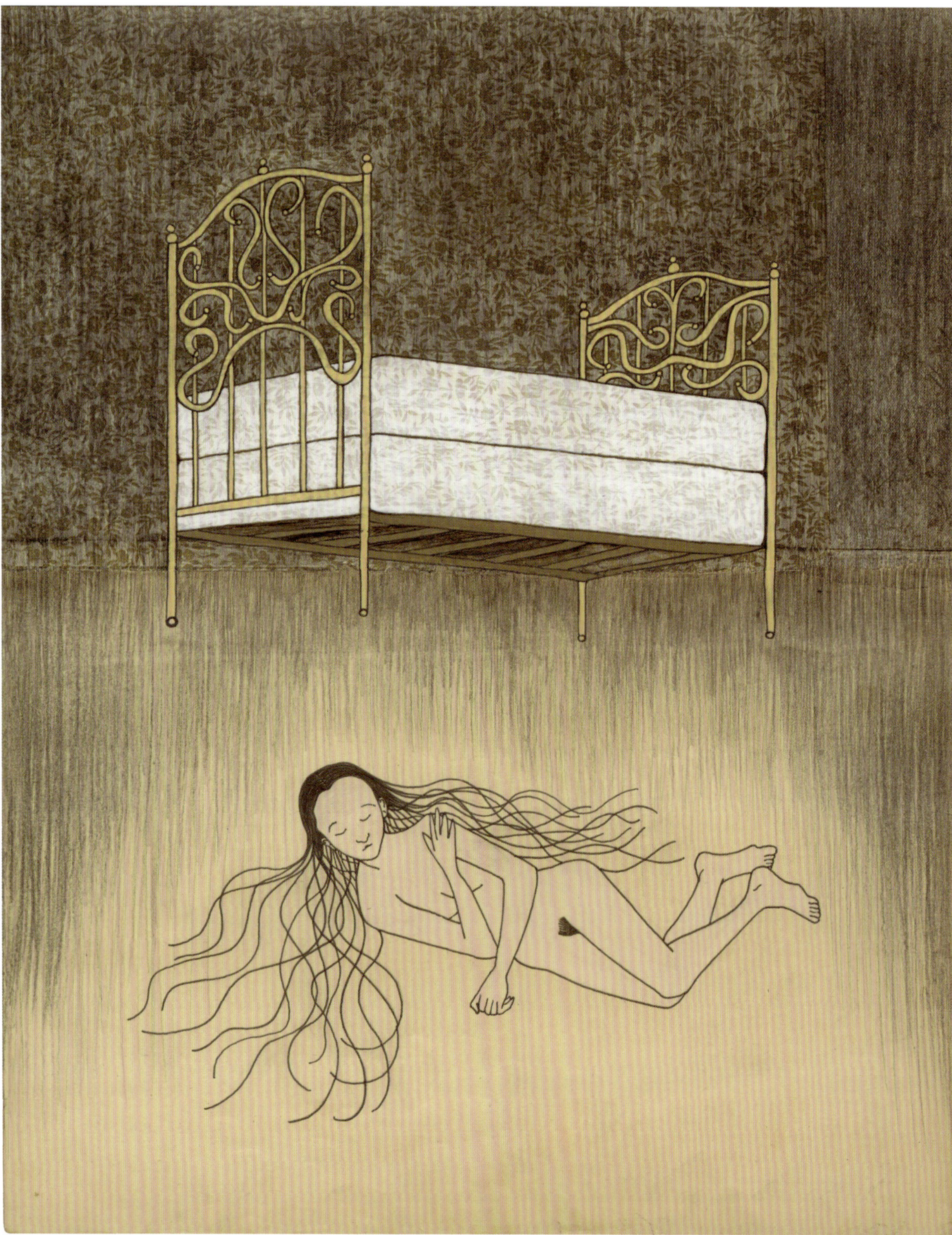

Falling Asleep, 2010
Ink, gouache, and colored pencil on found paper
12 3/4 x 10 in.
Collection of Pauline Silberman, Chicago, Illinois

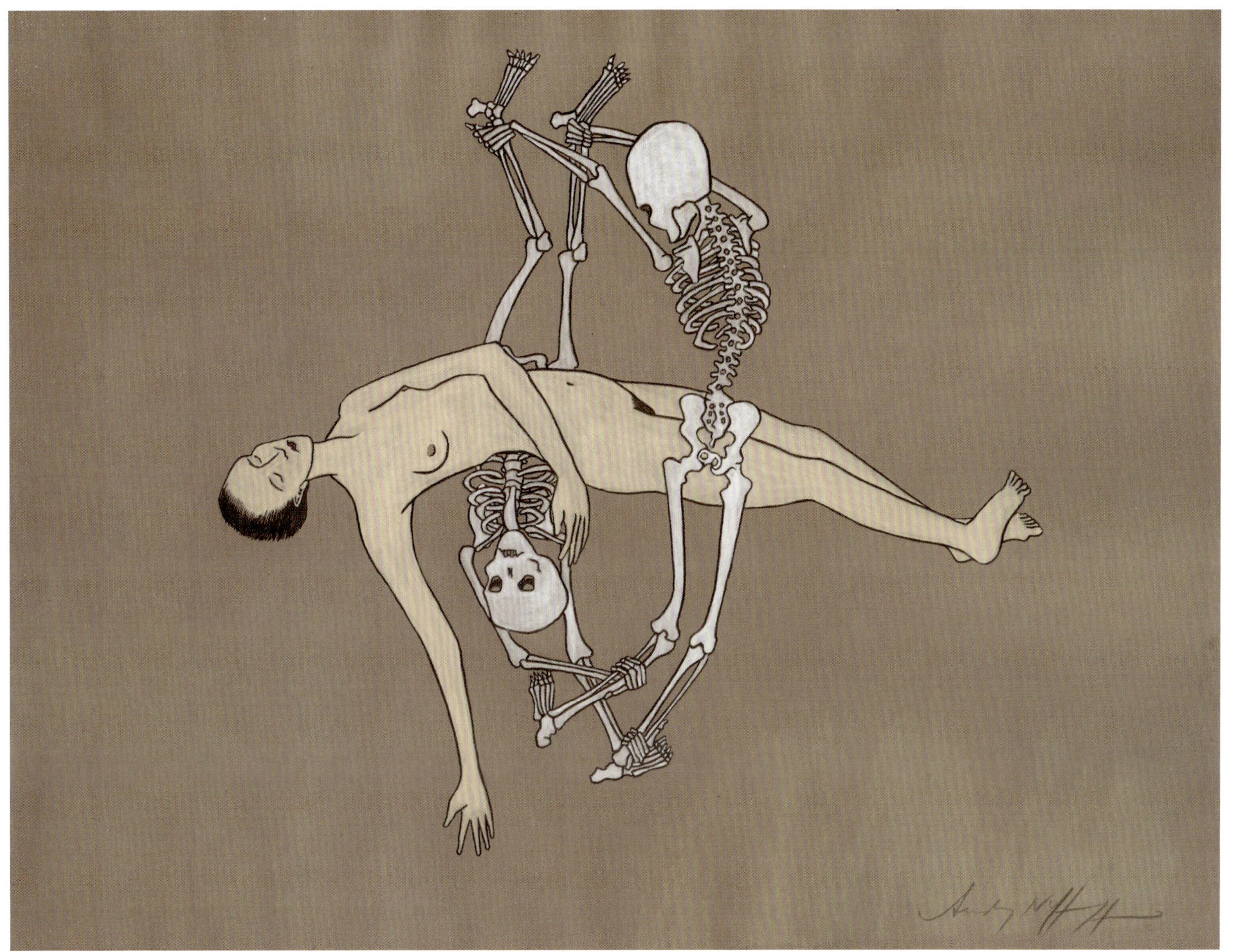

Isa's Dream, 2010
Ink and gouache on paper
9 3/4 x 12 3/4 in.
Collection of Dr. Andrew Griffin, Chicago, Illinois

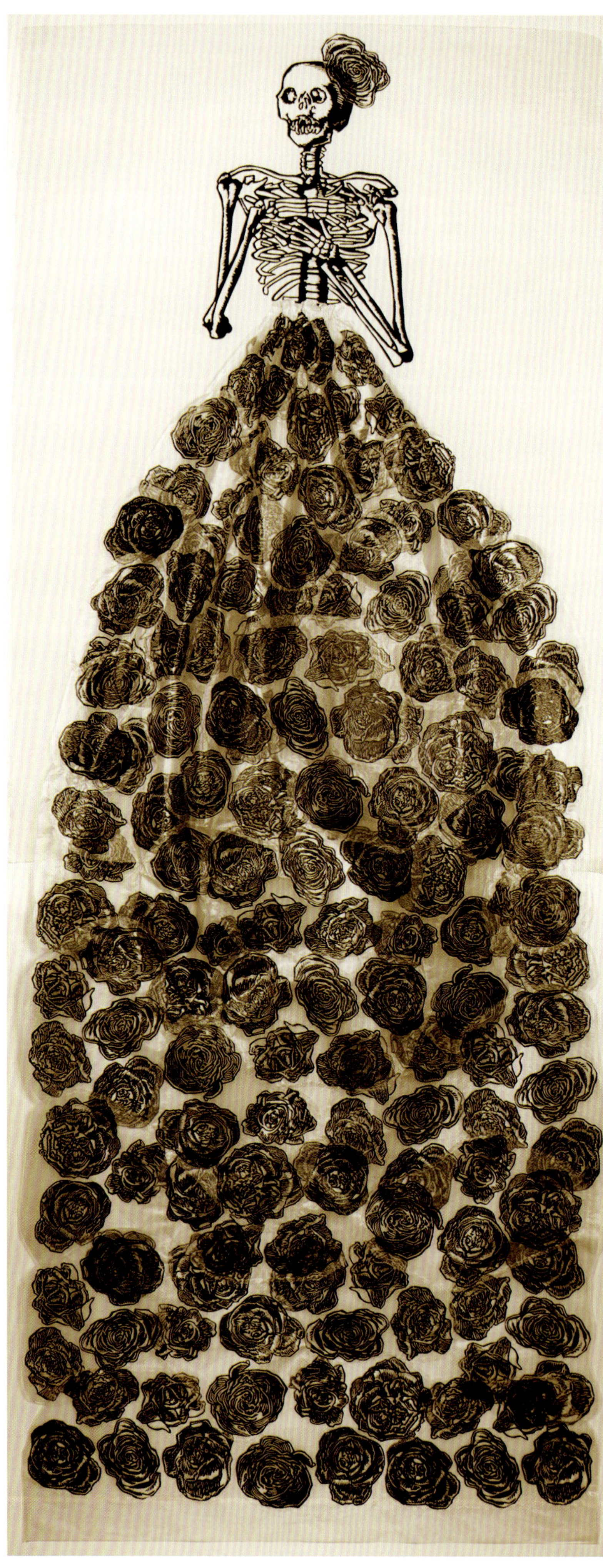

Black Roses *(In Memory of Isabella Blow)*, 2007
Linocut, Gampi tissue, and thread on Japanese paper
67 x 25 1/2 in.
Edition 3/6
Collection of Audrey Niffenegger, Chicago, Illinois

EXHIBITION CHECKLIST

AWAKE IN THE DREAM WORLD: THE ART OF AUDREY NIFFENEGGER

I. ADVENTURES IN BOOKLAND

The Adventuress, 1983–85
Artist's book consisting of sixty-six aquatints on Japanese paper, hand-marbled end papers, and letterpress-printed text. Ultra-suede binding.
11 1/2 x 9 1/2 x 1 5/8 (book); 7 7/8 x 5 7/8 in. (aquatints)
Edition 8/10
Collection of the National Museum of Women in the Arts, Washington, D.C.

The Three Incestuous Sisters, 1985–98
Artist's book consisting of eighty aquatints, watercolor on paper, and letterpress-printed text. Calf leather book binding; intaglio printed and colored with aniline dyes.
12 7/8 x 16 x 2 1/4 (book); 9 x 12 in. (aquatints)
Edition 10/10
Collection of Audrey Niffenegger, Chicago, Illinois

The Spinster, 1986
Artist's book consisting of four aquatints on paper and letterpress-printed text.
11 x 5 3/8 in. (book); 7 3/4 x 3 1/2 in. (aquatints)
Edition 8/12
Collection of Audrey Niffenegger, Chicago, Illinois

Spring, 1994
Artist's book consisting of twenty-four lithographs on handmade cotton and abaca paper, carbon and antique silver pigment, colored pencils, and acrylic paint.
6 x 4 in. (book); 6 x 8 in. (lithographs)
Edition 61/100
Collection of Audrey Niffenegger, Chicago, Illinois
Collaboration with Marilyn Sward

Falling, 2004
Ink and gouache on handmade paper
8 x 5 1/2 in.
Collection of Mary Jean Thomson, Riverwoods, Illinois

Reader, Spider, 2005
Ink and gouache on found paper
6 3/4 x 4 1/2 in.
Collection of Larry and Laura Gerber, Highland Park, Illinois

The Time Traveler's Wife, 2005
Dust jacket for MacAdam/Cage hardcover limited edition, San Francisco, California, 2005
Offset lithography
9 1/2 x 22 in.
Collection of Audrey Niffenegger, Chicago, Illinois

Poisonous Plants at Table and Prudence: The Cautionary Tale of a Picky Eater, 2006
Artist's book with four Giclée color prints; black-and-white letterpress prints and letterpress-printed text on
Twinrocker handmade paper and Thiebierge & Comar Chromatica; and Kozo Momi paper. Designed and conceived
by Trisha Hammer. Published by Sherwin Beach Press, Chicago. Incorporates selections from *Poisonous Plants in
Field and Garden* by the Reverend Professor G. Henslow, originally published in 1901, with *Poisonous Plants at Table*,
selected menus and recommendations by Dr. E. Coffin, irregular practitioner.
9 1/4 x 5 1/4 in.
Edition 68/75
Collection of the National Museum of Women in the Arts, Washington, D.C.

Her Fearful Symmetry, 2009
Dust jacket for Scribner hardcover limited edition, New York and London, 2009
Offset lithography
9 1/2 x 6 1/4 x 1 3/8 in.
Collection of Audrey Niffenegger, Chicago, Illinois

Her Fearful Symmetry, 2009
Book cover for Waterstones limited edition, Jonathan Cape, London, 2009
Offset lithography
9 1/2 x 6 3/8 x 1 1/2 in.
Collection of Audrey Niffenegger, Chicago, Illinois

Book cover for ***Persuasion*** by Jane Austen, for Penguin, New York, 2011
Offset lithography
8 1/2 x 5 5/8 in.
Collection of Audrey Niffenegger, Chicago, Illinois

Book cover for ***Persuasion*** by Jane Austen, for Penguin softcover edition, New York, 2011
Ink and gouache on Bristol board
9 x 19 1/2 in.
Collection of Audrey Niffenegger, Chicago

Book cover for ***Sense and Sensibility*** by Jane Austin, for Penguin, New York, 2011
Offset lithography
8 1/2 x 5 3/4 in.
Collection of Audrey Niffenegger, Chicago

Book cover for ***Sense and Sensibility*** by Jane Austin, for Penguin, New York, 2011
Ink and gouache on Bristol board
9 x 19 1/2 in.
Collection of Audrey Niffenegger, Chicago

Raven Girl, 2012
Original artwork for the book published by Abrams, New York, 2013
Aquatint on Japanese Sakamoto paper
8 3/4 x 11 3/4 in.
Edition of 20; artist's proof
Collection of Audrey Niffenegger, Chicago, Illinois

Raven Girl, 2012
Oil on wooden panel
23 3/4 x 17 3/4 in.
Collection of Audrey Niffenegger, Chicago, Illinois

II. STATES OF MIND

Nest, 1985
Aquatint on Fusuma Grey paper
18 x 12 in.
Edition 4/12
Collection of Audrey Niffenegger, Chicago, Illinois

Self-Portrait with Imaginary Dog, 1985
Graphite and colored pencil on grey Bugra paper
40 x 32 1/4 in.
Collection of Mary Jean Thomson, Riverwoods, Illinois

Hairpiece, 1986
Aquatint and hair on persimmon paper
21 1/2 x 13 in.
Edition 5/5
Collection of Audrey Niffenegger, Chicago, Illinois

Self-Portrait with Death Head, 1986
Graphite and colored pencil on persimmon paper
25 1/4 x 15 1/2 in.
Collection of Larry and Laura Gerber, Highland Park, Illinois

She Was Vain of Her Hair, 1986
Graphite and colored pencil on Bugra paper
37 x 29 in.
Collection of Mary Jean Thomson, Riverwoods, Illinois

Toss, 1986
Graphite on Bugra paper
41 x 40 in.
Collection of Larry and Laura Gerber, Highland Park, Illinois

Tornado Head, 1987
Graphite on persimmon paper
22 1/2 x 12 3/4 in.
Collection of Carol Rosofsky, Chicago, Illinois

Unreasonableness of Angels, 1987
Graphite on Fusuma Cream paper
38 x 24 in.
Collection of Larry and Laura Gerber, Highland Park, Illinois

Self-Portrait as Rembrandt's Wife, Saskia, 1992
Graphite with Xerox and ink on Bugra paper
34 x 28 1/2 in.
Collection of Chapman & Cutler LLP, Chicago, Illinois

Jailbird, 1993
Graphite and colored pencil on Bugra paper
44 3/4 x 32 in.
Collection of Joyce Leavitt, Chicago, Illinois

Self-Portrait as Medusa, 1993
Graphite, watercolor, and collage
25 1/2 x 19 1/2 in.
Collection of Richard Harris, Chicago, Illinois

Heart on Head, 1993
Collage, gouache, and pastel on Twinrocker handmade paper
12 3/4 x 9 3/4 in.
Collection of Mary Jean Thomson, Riverwoods, Illinois

Skull Hat, 1998
Etching, chine collé on Japanese paper; Printed by Anchor Graphics, Chicago
4 3/4 x 4 in.
Edition of 10; artist's proof
Collection of Audrey Niffenegger, Chicago, Illinois

Nest, 2000
Colored pencil and charcoal on paper
17 7/8 x 12 1/4 in.
Collection of Mary Jean Thomson, Riverwoods, Illinois

Self-Portrait in Black Hat, 2003
Ink, gouache, and colored pencil on found paper
9 7/8 x 6 3/4 in.
Collection of Mary Jean Thomson, Riverwoods, Illinois

Bad Fairy, 2005
Oil on wooden panel
12 x 8 3/4 in.
Collection of Larry and Laura Gerber, Highland Park, Illinois

Flying, 2005
Oil on wooden panel
24 x 13 3/4 in.
Collection of Larry and Laura Gerber, Highland Park, Illinois

Lady with Monkey, 2005
Oil on wooden panel
7 x 5 in.
Collection of Larry and Laura Gerber, Highland Park, Illinois

Moths of the New World, 2005
Oil on wooden panel
12 x 9 in.
Collection of Mary Jean Thomson, Riverwoods, Illinois

Self-Portrait with Philip Treacy Hat, 2007
Oil on wooden panel
15 3/4 x 11 3/4 in.
Collection of Mary Jean Thomson, Riverwoods, Illinois

Observation, 2010
Colored pencil on paper
15 x 11 in.
Collection of Larry and Laura Gerber, Highland Park, Illinois

Monkey Mind, 2010
Colored pencil on hand-dyed paper
12 x 9 in.
Collection of Jim Tonsgard, Chicago, Illinois

III. IN DREAMLAND

Death Comforts the Mother, from portfolio **Vanitas**, 1989
Poem "Before the Birth of One of her Children," by Anne Bradstreet
Etching with aquatint on Stonehenge Natural paper
30 x 22 1/4 in.
Edition 1/20
Collection of Audrey Niffenegger, Chicago, Illinois

The Embryos, from portfolio **Vanitas**, 1989
Poem "A Cradle Song" by Thomas Dekker
Etching with aquatint on Stonehenge Natural paper
30 x 22 1/2 in.
Edition 1/20
Collection of Audrey Niffenegger, Chicago, Illinois

Lovers' Embrace, from portfolio **Vanitas**, 1989
Poem "Dismissal" by Thomas Campion
Etching with aquatint on Stonehenge Natural paper
30 x 22 1/4 in.
Edition 1/20
Collection of Audrey Niffenegger, Chicago, Illinois

Self-Portrait with Arms, from portfolio ***Vanitas***, 1989
Poem "The Apparition" by John Donne
Etching with aquatint on Stonehenge Natural paper
30 x 22 1/4 in.
Edition 1/20
Collection of Audrey Niffenegger, Chicago, Illinois

The World, from portfolio ***Vanitas***, 1989
Poem "On Time" by John Milton
Etching with aquatint on Stonehenge Natural paper
Edition 1/20
30 x 22 1/2 in.
Collection of Audrey Niffenegger, Chicago, Niffenegger

Two Very Small Waists, 1992
Gouache and ink on paper
30 x 21 3/4 in.
Collection of Mary Jean Thomson, Riverwoods, Illinois

Heartstrings, 1993
Collage on handmade paper
18 x 12 in.
Collection of Jerry Ginsburg, Glenview, Illinois

Pam and Zuzu, 1995
Oil on canvas
52 x 40 in.
Collection of Audrey Niffenegger, Chicago, Illinois

19th Century Hair, 2003
Ink on paper
7 x 6 1/2 in.
Collection of Elissa Geier, Glencoe, Illinois

Levitation, 2003
Gouache on found paper
5 1/2 x 6 7/8 in.
Collection of Larry and Laura Gerber, Highland Park, Illinois

Mother and Child, 2003
Ink and gouache on found paper
10 x 6 1/2 in.
Collection of Janet and Sidney Cohen, Highland Park, Illinois

Life Under Ground, 2004
Colored pencil and graphite on paper
8 x 12 in.
Collection of Mary Jean Thomson, Riverwoods, Illinois

Sleeping Girl, 2004
Etching on found paper
5 1/2 x 8 1/2 in.
Collection of Audrey Niffenegger, Chicago, Illinois

Allegory of Time, 2005
Gouache and ink on amate paper
18 x 12 in.
Collection of Larry and Laura Gerber, Highland Park, Illinois

The Letter, 2005
Ink drawing on paper
11 1/2 x 8 in.
Collection of Larry and Laura Gerber, Highland Park, Illinois

Song of the Womb, 2005
Graphite and colored pencil on handmade paper
17 1/2 x 12 in.
Collection of Larry and Laura Gerber, Highland Park, Illinois

Black Roses (In Memory of Isabella Blow), 2007
Linocut, Gampi tissue, and thread on Japanese paper
67 x 25 1/2 in.
Edition 3/6
Collection of Audrey Niffenegger, Chicago, Illinois

Fallen (Red), 2007
Linocut, thread, and gouache on paper
65 x 57 in. (Irregular)
Edition 1/5
Collection of Larry and Laura Gerber, Highland Park, Illinois

The Starling's Funeral, 2008
Aquatint on Sakamoto paper
12 x 35 1/2 in.
Edition of 15; artist's proof
Collection of Audrey Niffenegger, Chicago, Illinois

Falling Asleep, 2010
Ink, gouache, and colored pencil on found paper
12 3/4 x 10 in.
Collection of Pauline Silberman, Chicago, Illinois

Isa's Dream, 2010
Ink and gouache on paper
9 3/4 x 12 3/4 in.
Collection of Dr. Andrew Griffin, Chicago, Illinois

Topsy-Turvy, 2010
Graphite and gouache on paper
44 x 28 1/4 in.
Collection of Larry and Laura Gerber, Highland Park, Illinois

Wallpaper Dream, 2010
Graphite and gouache on found paper
7 3/4 x 10 in.
Collection of Inge Marra, Olympia Fields, Illinois

The Changeling, 2012
Etching with photogravure and aquatint
15 3/4 x 13 7/8 in.
Edition of 20, artist's proof
Published by White Wings Press, Chicago
Collection of Audrey Niffenegger, Chicago, Illinois

CHRONOLOGY

1963   Audrey Niffenegger is born in South Haven, Michigan, on June 13 to Lawrence and Patricia Niffenegger. Her sisters Beth and Jonelle are born in 1966 and 1969.

1965   The Niffenegger family moves to Evanston, Illinois, a Chicago suburb.

1968–1976   She attends St. Joan of Arc, a parochial school.

1977–1981   She attends Evanston Township High School, where she studies with William Wimmer, who introduces her to etching and is also her drawing teacher.

1979   Niffenegger takes a job working as a picture framer. For the next ten years she will work at various frame shops, handling all sorts of art and discovering the work of artists such as Lee Godie and Jiri Anderle. At one of her framing jobs she meets the artist William Frederick, who will later become a friend and studio partner.

1981–1985   Niffenegger attends the School of the Art Institute of Chicago, earning a BFA. Most of her courses are in printmaking, photography, and drawing. She studies lithography with Mark Pascale, bookbinding with Joan Flasch, drawing with Marion Kryczka, and takes a course on Symbolist art with Sue Taylor. She tries her hand at performance art and writes short stories in which all the characters die.

1983–1985   She works on *The Adventuress,* her first editioned artist's book and the first Magravane's Press publication.

1985   She graduates from SAIC and is awarded the George D. and Isabella A. Brown Traveling Fellowship, which she uses to go to Europe for the first time. She meets Bert Menco who will become an important artistic influence, boyfriend, and lifelong friend. They travel together in Holland and go to Paris where they eat snails and get mugged in front of the Centre Pompidou.

1985–1998   She works on *The Three Incestuous Sisters.*

1987   Niffenegger has her first exhibition at Printworks Gallery. This is the first of eleven solo shows to date and begins an important relationship with her dealers, Sidney Block and Robert Hiebert, which continues to the present day.

She begins teaching printmaking at the Evanston Art Center. The group of printmakers who converge at the EAC in the '80s and '90s are still making prints together in 2012, now at the North Shore Art League. They include Paula Campbell, Elizabeth Ockwell, Diane Thodos, Bert Menco, John Rush, and Janet Lefley.

Bookworks by Audrey Niffenegger, a solo show at the Evanston Art Center, Evanston, IL.

1989   Together with book artists Pamela Barrie and Teresa Pankratz, Niffenegger forms Green Window Printers. This is a letterpress and intaglio studio in the Ravenswood neighborhood in Chicago. When Pankratz leaves the studio her place is taken by Mary Kennedy. Barrie and Niffenegger will continue as studio partners until 2002.

1989–1991   She studies at Northwestern University, earning an MFA from the Department of Art Theory and Practice. Her professors include Phillip Chen, James Valerio, Ed Paschke, James Yood, and William Conger.

1990   *The Vanitas*, a solo show, at Printworks Gallery, Chicago.

1992   *An Abridged History of Magic*, a solo show, at Printworks Gallery, Chicago.

1993   Niffenegger begins teaching at Columbia College Chicago. She starts as an adjunct printmaking professor in the Art and Design Department.

She begins sharing a painting studio with William Frederick. In 1997 they merge this studio with Green Windows and take a new space together in Lincoln Square, Chicago.

1994   Together with a group of artists including Marilyn Sward, Bill Drendel, and Suzanne Cohan-Lange, Niffenegger founds the Columbia College Chicago Center for Book and Paper Arts. They are soon joined by Barbara Lazarus Metz, Melissa Jay Craig, Mary Kennedy, Barbara Korbel, Andrea Peterson and many other paper and book artists. Niffenegger becomes Assistant Director of the Center in 1995. Marilyn Sward is the Director.

Autobiography and Superstition, a solo show, at the Chicago Cultural Center, Chicago.
A Feast for the Mnemonist, a solo show, at Printworks Gallery, Chicago.

1995   *Teratology*, a solo show, at Lyons-Wier+Ginsburg, Chicago.

1996   Audrey Niffenegger has her first residency at Ragdale, an artists' community in Lake Forest, IL. She will return many times over the years, eventually serving on the Foundation's Board of Trustees. Ragdale will inspire Meadowlark House in *The Time Traveler's Wife*.

1997   She begins writing *The Time Traveler's Wife*.

1998   Niffenegger becomes an assistant professor in the Book and Paper Arts MFA program in the Columbia College Interdisciplinary Arts department.

The Three Incestuous Sisters is shown for the first time at Printworks Gallery, Chicago.

2000   *Night Revelry at the Establishment of Madame Deyrolle*, a solo show, at Printworks Gallery in Chicago.

2002   Niffenegger completes *The Time Traveler's Wife* in January and begins searching for an agent. After being rejected more than thirty times she writes to Joseph Regal, who emails her, "Don't do anything, I'm reading." He becomes her agent in October and sells the manuscript to MacAdam/Cage in December.

Green Window Printers dissolves and Niffenegger moves her print and painting studios into her home.

2003   *The Time Traveler's Wife* is published by MacAdam/Cage in September. The book receives a kind endorsement from Scott Turow. *The Time Traveler's Wife* is chosen for the Today Show's book club. It becomes an international bestseller.

Because of the success of the book, Niffenegger begins a long and extensive book tour. Much of her work over the next few years is made in far-flung hotel rooms.

She begins work on her second novel, *Her Fearful Symmetry*. It is set in London, in Highgate Cemetery. She meets Jean Pateman, Chairman of the Friends of Highgate Cemetery, who will become a friend and a character, Jessica, in the book. Niffenegger spends a great deal of the next seven years researching in London and becomes a tour guide for the cemetery.

Ferocious Bonbons, a solo show, at Printworks Gallery in Chicago.

2004   Niffenegger receives tenure and becomes an associate professor at Columbia College Chicago.

The Time Traveler's Wife is published by Jonathan Cape in the U.K.

2005   *The Three Incestuous Sisters* is published in a trade edition by Harry N. Abrams.

Mister Death's Ephemeral Pageant, a solo show, at Printworks Gallery in Chicago.

2006   *The Adventuress* is published in a trade edition by Harry N. Abrams.

Sherwin Beach Press publishes *Field Guide to Poisonous Plants*. This is a collaboration with Trisha Hammer. Niffenegger contributes the short story "Prudence: A Cautionary Tale of a Picky Eater," which she also illustrates.

2007   *Elegy for Isabella Blow*, a solo show, at Printworks Gallery in Chicago.

Niffenegger goes to the artists' community Yaddo for the first time, where she works on her second novel.

2008   *The Night Bookmobile*, a graphic short story, is serialized in the *Guardian*.

2009   *Her Fearful Symmetry* is published in September by Scribner and by Jonathan Cape in the U.K.

Audrey is granted a residency at Yaddo, where she meets the composer Andrew Norman. In 2012 they begin to collaborate with John Caird on an opera based on *The Three Incestuous Sisters*.

The Time Traveler's Wife is made into a movie.

2010   *The Night Bookmobile* is published by Harry N. Abrams and Jonathan Cape in trade editions.

Seeing in the Dark, a solo show, at Printworks Gallery in Chicago.

Niffenegger joins Columbia College's Fiction Writing Department.

2012   Jean Pateman dies at the age of ninety.

Niffenegger spends the year working on *Raven Girl*.

She is made a full Professor at Columbia College.

2013   *Raven Girl* is published by Harry N. Abrams and Jonathan Cape. The ballet, which was choreographed by Wayne McGregor, premieres in May at the Royal Opera House Ballet, Covent Garden, London.

Awake in the Dream World: The Art of Audrey Niffenegger opens at the National Museum of Women in the Arts in June.

She continues to work on her third novel, *The Chinchilla Girl in Exile*.